"This book is a gem! Sean McGever addresses an issue of continuing vital importance based on broad-ranging research and engaged in an evenhanded manner with pastoral sensitivity. He models the all-too-uncommon stance in our times of humbly 'owning' the traditions within which each of us is shaped—while calling our communities toward ever-greater faithfulness to the God whose mercy is over all God's works."

Randy L. Maddox, William Kellon Quick Emeritus Professor of Wesley and Methodist Studies at Duke Divinity School

"Among the tragic inheritances of the English Dissenters in America are the oppressive inequities they built and perpetuated around race and ethnicity, the dispossession of Indigenous peoples, and the condoning and expansion of enslavement. If Whitefield, Wesley, and Edwards were not 'founding fathers' of the United States, they were spiritual founders of America's evangelical tradition. These figures' involvement in, support for, or silence about the sin of slavery need to be confronted and owned without attempts to make excuses for them. McGever's work is part of the critical work of reassessing claims about our origins as a 'Christian nation.'"

Kenneth P. Minkema, Jonathan Edwards Center at Yale University

"This book is unusually well researched (showing that Wesley, Edwards, and Whitefield actively or passively supported slavery even after Quaker Bible believers had published solid arguments showing the system's evil). It is patiently argued (bending over backward to explain charitably why these landmark evangelicals acted as they did). It is also painstakingly self-reflective (asking, *If we condemn earlier Christians for unthinking support of their society's evil, what evils might we be supporting unthinkingly today?*). The result is unusual clarity about the past and, even more, a compelling imperative for examining our own lives today."

Mark Noll, author of *America's Book: The Rise and Decline of a Bible Civilization, 1794–1911*

"In this revealing book, Sean McGever sensitively delves into the complicated history of the relationship between evangelical Christianity and slavery by examining the lives and words of its three renowned founders: John Wesley, George Whitefield, and Jonathan Edwards Sr. A trumpet call for American Christians to honestly examine history, it is a must-read for all evangelicals who wish to confront the legacy of slavery and racism in our society today."

Manisha Sinha, Draper Chair in American History at the University of Connecticut and author of *The Slave's Cause: A History of Abolition*

"This carefully researched book invites evangelicals as well as all Protestants to consider the tragic positions that Jonathan Edwards, George Whitefield, and John Wesley held on slavery. While Wesley eventually condemned slavery, it was due to the influence of the Quakers and after both Edwards and Whitefield had died. Sean McGever is to be commended for his convicting treatment that not only challenges readers that all heroes of the church are redeemed sinners but also shows how we have perception gaps and may be missing issues that will look obvious to future Christians. This book deserves a wide circulation to foster the needed conversations for our current day."

Tom Schwanda, author of *The Emergence of Evangelical Spirituality: The Age of Edwards, Newton, and Whitefield*

"Sean McGever offers a comprehensive account of the extent to which these celebrated religious figures practiced or accepted the enslavement of Africans. While not excusing them as 'men of their time,' McGever reminds us that, instead of feeling self-righteous, we should consider the moral perception gaps that we may have today."

George Marsden, professor emeritus of history at the University of Notre Dame and author of *An Infinite Fountain of Light: Jonathan Edwards for the Twenty-First Century*

"Sean McGever's *Ownership* offers a timely discussion of a most perplexing issue: early evangelicals' involvement with slavery. McGever's thought-provoking analysis is thoroughly historical, and yet it also considers how Christians today can apply such difficult lessons from the past."

Thomas S. Kidd, research professor of church history at Midwestern Baptist Theological Seminary

OWNERSHIP

THE EVANGELICAL LEGACY OF SLAVERY IN EDWARDS, WESLEY, AND WHITEFIELD

SEAN McGEVER

Foreword by VINCENT E. BACOTE

An imprint of InterVarsity Press
Downers Grove, Illinois

InterVarsity Press
P.O. Box 1400 | Downers Grove, IL 60515-1426
ivpress.com | email@ivpress.com

Cover design: David Fassett
Interior design: Jeanna Wiggins
Image: John Wesley preaching to Native Americans, engraving, public domain

ISBN 978-1-5140-0415-9 (print) | ISBN 978-1-5140-0416-6 (digital)

Printed in the United States of America ♾

Library of Congress Cataloging-in-Publication Data
A catalog record for this book is available from the Library of Congress.

31 30 29 28 27 26 25 24 | 12 11 10 9 8 7 6 5 4 3 2 1

CONTENTS

FOREWORD

VINCENT E. BACOTE

I NEVER HEARD A BAD WORD about my paternal grandparents from my dad or any of his many siblings. With my own siblings, I have sometimes jokingly stated that "I don't think they walked on the ground" and also referred to them as "our sainted grandparents." It is also no surprise that while I never heard any negative words from my dad or his siblings, I eventually heard that there may have been a rumor or two about something less than saintly about my grandparents. In other words, they had complications like other human beings.

But it is not only my grandparents that get "the saintly treatment." This also happens with the way many of us learn about figures and traditions. We discover there are figures who are good and figures who are bad. Often, the angels and the devils are set before us in a world neatly divided into the team with heroes and the team with villains. In the many stories we encounter as we learn about our world, this is a fairly standard approach. It happens with the way we learn about the unfolding of the history of the church, whether it is a denomination, movement, the development of doctrine, the story of prominent figures—and on it goes.

This approach seems to work fairly well as long as we look at the surface and remain at a familiar but also comfortable distance. The truth of the matter is that we are being set up for at the least disappointment and at the most devastation. What I have called "the standard approach" has the unfortunate hazard of leading us to believe that the angels and heroes are like messianic figures. No one (or at least no one I have encountered) refers to these figures as messiahs, but the way they are presented to us suggests that while they are not quite on the level of Jesus, they are very close to his level, at least when it comes to the tradition or topic in question. Problems emerge, however, when we go beneath the surface. I experienced this personally when I was considering my dissertation figure, Abraham Kuyper. In a way, I fell in love with this hero because of this theology of culture and politics, and this made me excited. The problem emerged when I learned he was a racist—it was like getting hit by a bus. I did not know what to do because I had great appreciation for part of his work and I also found racism in it. This was a major crisis.

My experience is not unique. Many who become enamored of a tradition or figure may find themselves in a kind of honeymoon phase where the tradition or figure provides tremendous benefit; sometimes the person or tradition may seem to provide the key that "puts it all together" for certain matters of the faith. In other cases, there may be a figure without whom a tradition or movement would not exist—they have been truly great and foundational. But what do we do when we find ourselves swept up in a kind of historical and theological bliss only to discover that "it's complicated" is now part of the story?

Enter Sean McGever, who helps us find our way when we encounter complications with three figures of great prominence and significance for the modern evangelical movement: Jonathan Edwards, John Wesley, and George Whitefield. All three were men of deep faith and considerable influence. And all of them, for most or all of their lives, regarded slavery as "just the way things are." Edwards and Whitefield owned enslaved people, and we can only speculate whether the same would be true of Wesley if most of his life had been spent in the British colonies that became the United States. Only Wesley reached a point of opposing not only the treatment of enslaved people but also the institution itself. McGever carefully helps us to see and understand not only what these great men believed but also the social, cultural, and political context that formed them and in which they went about their influential ministries.

McGever helps us to understand Edwards, Wesley, and Whitefield and also prompts us to look at ourselves. One of the great challenges is the temptation to make snap judgments when we encounter people from "back then" who either did not discuss or address things of importance to us or who said or did things we find shocking or reprehensible. Because "we know better and see more clearly" we can suggest that had we lived in those times and places we would never had said or done the bad things we have discovered. McGever both models and invites us into an approach where we have to take time with the complicated realities of Edwards, Whitefield, and Wesley and also take the time to turn to ourselves with honesty. This is the kind of approach that is helpful when the easier and more reflexive response is either to downplay or dismiss the complications or banish figures because of their transgressions. While these are understandable in the face of the shock we may feel when facing difficult truths, McGever bids us to move our finger from the button that says "ignore" or "cancel" and to sit with complicated legacies.

McGever helps us to have a better understanding of these great figures and invites us to not only look at ourselves but also the traditions that are our ecclesial and theological homes. While his primary audience is white evangelicals, he provides what Christians of all traditions need: an honest and caring guide who will take us on a journey that shows deep knowledge of the path, skill amid challenges that may seem scary or daunting, and tremendous help that can equip us to better understand the complications we can't escape with any tradition or figure.

Sometimes our encounter with the complications of figures and traditions threatens to overwhelm us. At times we may feel sad, distressed, betrayed, or angry, and maybe even find ourselves tempted to feel hopeless. Walking with McGever through this encounter with Edwards, Wesley, and Whitefield on slavery will help readers move toward honest, courageous, and ultimately hopeful faith. Take up and read, and pass this book on to others.

WHY SLAVERY?

SLAVERY HAS NOTHING TO DO WITH ME

ON SEPTEMBER 30, 2020, I spoke at Old South Presbyterian Church in Newburyport, Massachusetts, at a memorial for a man who never knew me. But I knew him.

George Whitefield died on that day, 250 years before, and his body is buried in a crypt below the church. Tom Schwanda, a theologian from Wheaton College, Mark Noll, a historian from Notre Dame, and I spoke at a (virtual) worship service to commemorate Whitefield's life, legacy, and ministry. The event organizers had invited me to speak on one of Whitefield's favorite topics: the new birth.

The event went well. I gave my talk, then returned to my other commitments. A month later, I received an unexpected package in the mail. It included a generous thank-you note from the church and a gift. I opened the small package with curiosity and was surprised to find a coin. The church had minted a commemorative coin for the occasion of the 250th anniversary of Whitefield's death.

One side of the coin was embossed with the words *Rev. George Whitefield* over a portrait of Whitefield's characteristic round face and crossed left eye. He is wearing his minister's wig, robe, and preaching bands—the classic image of Whitefield.

On the other side of the coin, the outer ring stated, *America's Spiritual Founding Father*. This declaration about Whitefield is common among secular and Christian historians of early America, and as we will see, its truth is both inspiring and chilling. But it was what was written in the middle of that side of the coin in small font that caught my attention. It was from a letter Whitefield wrote on July 12, 1749:

> I am content to wait till the day of judgment for the clearing up of my character: and after I am dead, I desire no other epitaph than this, "Here lies G. W. What sort of a man he was, the great day will discover."

One of the reasons Whitefield's words caught my attention was that two months before the memorial, on July 2, 2020, the University of Pennsylvania decided to remove a statue of Whitefield that had been standing on the campus for over a hundred years. In 2006 and 2016 the University denied having any connections to slavery. A team of researchers, led by VanJessica Gladney, presented Whitefield's enslavement of Black people and his successful efforts to legalize slavery in Georgia. The University of Pennsylvania revisited "what sort of a man" Whitefield was and came to their own conclusion. Whitefield may have been waiting for God's judgment, but the University of Pennsylvania made their judgment much sooner.[1]

Few Christians, if any, doubt Whitefield's genuine faith in Jesus Christ. Yet many admirers have come to doubt aspects of "America's Spiritual Founding Father's" character—myself included. Still, 250 years ago, at Whitefield's official memorial, one of his closest friends, John Wesley, didn't publicize the doubts that the University of Pennsylvania and I have about his character.

The organizers at Old South Presbyterian Church addressed Whitefield's checkered legacy in their 250th memorial of his death. They titled the several-months-long series of events "The Great Awakening Meets a Just Awakening." This memorial was quite different from the one John Wesley spoke at shortly after Whitefield's death. As we'll see, this funeral was a pivotal moment in evangelical history regarding slavery. Old South Presbyterian Church designed their events to acknowledge the "gap between the inclusive gospel message that Whitefield preached and his devastating failure to embrace the full personhood of African Americans." I was proud to be part of a series of events to admire the strengths of Whitefield while also acknowledging the harm he brought to the people he enslaved, the people of the state of Georgia, and so many others. The man who proclaimed the gospel of liberty from slavery to sin held Jeremy, Abraham, Abigail, Fanny, and forty-five other people as slaves to him—and upon his death gave all of them to his top financial donor.

I meet admirers of Whitefield who don't know about his slaveholding or about his political and doctrinal support for its legality. I am quick to educate them on these details. Yet education is not enough. James Baldwin writes, "History, as nearly no one seems to know, is not merely something to be read. And it does not refer merely, or even principally, to the past. On the contrary, the great force of history comes from the fact that we carry it within us, are unconsciously controlled by it in many ways, and history is literally present in all that we do."[2]

The work of historical retrieval is, in a way, the easy part. The hard part is choosing how I will navigate, and *own*, what happens in my country, in my state, in my city, in my neighborhood, and in my home—*today*.

HOW COULD CHRISTIANS SUPPORT SLAVERY?

It's no secret that one of the most glaring embarrassments of Christianity is its complicity with slavery. Most Christian leaders did not question the institution of slavery for nearly eighteen hundred years. When questions were asked, it was just the beginning of a whole host of other questions, some of which remain today. When we look at the first eighteen hundred years of Christianity, most of us want to throw our hands in the air and scream, "How did they miss it?" We can't imagine Christians today purchasing another person, controlling—frequently by force—their actions, profiting from their labor, and owning their children. How did they miss it? Keep reading; I will show you.

But first—and I write this very cautiously—I urge you to avoid thinking that you are any smarter, holier, or better than the Christians of the first eighteen centuries. Why? Because assuming that you are innately better than any other human is at the core of the issue of slavery itself.

Rather than asking, "how did *they* miss it back then," I have a harder question for you to ask yourself: "What am *I* missing right now?" This book highlights the stories of three men from the eighteenth century. You will discover what they missed, what they learned, and the legacy they left—much of which endures today. But before we go back in the past, one of the purposes of this enterprise is to challenge you, as it does me, with a question about the present: "What am *I* missing right now?" The final chapter will bring us back to this question and highlight lessons these three men learned along the way in hopes of shedding light on our path today.

This book will examine how Christians in the eighteenth century began to understand slavery differently than their own predecessors. Today, things progress differently than in the eighteenth century. A major difference is acceleration. In today's connected age, the issues confronted in the eighteenth century regarding slavery would progress much faster. Accelerating change also accelerates errors, but at this point in our society the speed and expectation of change is permanently faster than it was two centuries ago. This means that we are expected to make changes faster than our ancestors did—and we'd better be correct because it is more difficult to hide today.

For example, sending a letter to Jonathan Edwards and receiving a reply would have taken weeks in his era. The email you receive today, however, might expect a response in a day or two. You might be expected to reply to a text message in a few minutes, and a social media post might draw a response out of you in a few seconds. The expectation of lightning-quick responses in our modern world underscores the importance and benefits of learning from the past. We rarely have the leisure and space to figure out things for ourselves—and maybe that's a good thing, but only if we know how to choose our response wisely.

You had no choice over when, where, or who you were when you were born. But here you are. One invaluable resource to navigate the life you've been given is the ability to learn from your predecessors. I have dug deep to find the successes and failures—the convictions to hold on to and the sacred cows to let loose—of a century of Christians who, we must assume, wanted to do the right thing while also navigating their own corrupted natures and environment. The issue of slavery engages deep personal, economic, societal, political, and religious implications—not unlike some of the issues we still face today. In today's accelerated world, we are too busy *not* to stop and learn from the past. It is more urgent than ever.

WHY DISCUSS SLAVERY NOW?

In my research for this book, I spent time in Savannah, Georgia—a city and a state that play an important part in the story of evangelicals and slavery. When I was there, I already knew what the history books stated. I went to Savannah because I wanted to know what people thought about the history of slavery *now*.

I am White, and I was a stranger to all the people I encountered; these things certainly affected my conversations. I found that the people of Savannah don't want to talk about slavery—at all. No one I encountered wanted to talk about slavery. White people told me in succinct and well-practiced phrases that they knew their predecessors had engaged in a terrible thing—and then moved on quickly to other topics. They tended to highlight good things that are happening in their community now.

The Black people I encountered didn't want to talk about slavery either. I spent several hours in conversation with the director of the African American Cultural Center in Savannah. He helped me understand that discussions about slavery today belittle the dignity of their ancestors. Black people gained their emancipation long ago. The discussion of slavery itself adds a weight to their shoulders even as they continue to face daily challenges due to the color of their skin.

There was a pointed difference in my conversations with White and Black people in Savannah. White folks are embarrassed by the conversation about slavery. Black folks are worn out by it. When I became curious about early evangelical history regarding slavery, I began discussing it with my friends of color back home. They were genuinely interested in the details and encouraged me to keep doing the research and to write the book you are reading now. They also said they were tired of explaining things related to race to White people like me. They told me that they were excited for me to do the research and believed it was important that I share it with them, but it was more important that I share my research with other people like me—other White people.

Few Americans are naive enough to think that slavery is irrelevant to our present condition. We recognize that personal and systemic race-based inequalities, beliefs, and experiences persist—these are not issues relegated to the past. While most modern Americans reject the ideology that supported slavery, some American Christians champion the history of American slavery as idyllic.

In 1996, Idaho-based pastors Doug Wilson and Steve Wilkins authored a short book titled *Southern Slavery: As It Was*. In their introduction, they wrote, "Southern slavery is open to criticism because it did not follow the biblical pattern at every point."[3] Regarding Southern slavery, they write, "There has never been a multi-racial society that has existed with such mutual intimacy and harmony in the history of the world."[4] They go on to claim that "slavery produced in the South a genuine affection between the races that we believe we can say has never existed in any nation before the [Civil] War or since."[5] These pastors, promoted by prominent evangelical media outlets, illustrated that slavery is not an issue of the past. In their view, slavery is an ideal social system to aspire to in the present, if done in the way they think aligns with the Bible.

When a 2020 Twitter post revived the opinion of Wilson and Wilkins, Wilson responded on his blog that he stands by the general premises of his initial claim. He added, "The problems [with slavery] became more pronounced as things moved toward the Civil War—e.g., slavery in

Jonathan Edwards's day in New England was not the same sort of thing as slavery in Alabama in 1850."[6] Wilson's focus is on *how* to enslave people in a way that aligns with the Bible, rather than on an outright denunciation of the institution.

John MacArthur has pastored Grace Community Church in Los Angeles since 1969. He leads The Master's University, The Master's Seminary, and the international radio ministry *Grace to You*, and is the author and editor of over one hundred books. MacArthur teaches that Christians should revive a biblical understanding of the institution of slavery and put it into practice today. He explains:

> [It is] strange that we have such an aversion to slavery because historically there have been abuses. . . . For many people, poor people, perhaps people who weren't educated, perhaps people who had no other opportunity, working for a gentle, caring, loving master was the best of all possible worlds. . . . Slavery is not objectionable if you have the right master. It's the perfect scenario.[7]

MacArthur believes that slavery is a part of "the best of all possible worlds" and "the perfect scenario" because, as he writes, "neither the Old nor New Testaments condemns slavery as such. Social strata are recognized and even designed by God for man's good."[8] MacArthur celebrates that "the back of the black slave trade was broken in Europe and America due largely to the powerful, Spirit-led preaching of such men as John Wesley and George Whitefield."[9] MacArthur's understanding of Wesley and Whitefield's role in the history of slavery is shallow and misguided, to say the least. MacArthur denounces *how* to enslave people—he is against the "black slave trade"—but believes that the *institution* of enslaving people is "best," "perfect," and "designed by God for man's good." New Testament scholar Esau McCaulley explains that slaveholders of the antebellum South maintained that the two options were "biblical slavery versus bad slavery. The problem was not slavery itself."[10]

While Wilson's, Wilkins's, and MacArthur's views might represent a fringe opinion among American Christians, few modern people are looking to *any* White Christians to guide society in the right direction regarding race relations. Many people do not trust that White evangelical Christians have learned from their past. James Baldwin explains, "To accept one's past—one's history—is not the same thing as drowning in it; it is learning how to use it. An invented past can never be used; it cracks and crumbles under the pressures of life like clay in a season of drought."[11] Evangelical Christians like me can learn to use our past when we rightly understand the cold facts of our failures alongside the truths of our triumphs. Learning from the past can help us confront modern slavery directly (e.g., human trafficking, forced prostitution, forced labor, forced marriage) as well as learning how and when to be constructively critical of secular and Christian cultural assumptions in our world today.

"MEN OF THEIR TIMES"

I remember sitting in the third-story office of my master of letters graduate program supervisor, looking out the window across the ancient and lush St. Mary's College quad at the University of Saint Andrews. He asked me, "Have you thought about studying the conversion theology of the early evangelicals? It's surprising, but there are many questions in that topic area that haven't been examined." Five years later, I received a PhD in historical and systematic theology from the University of Aberdeen. My thesis was on the conversion theology of John Wesley and George Whitefield.

One of the first steps of PhD research in the United Kingdom is to read *everything* written by the person(s) you are studying. Wesley and Whitefield wrote a lot. This task took me about two years to complete. Prior to my research, I knew very little about Wesley, Whitefield, or any of the other major figures in their era—including Jonathan Edwards.

While I was reading the works of Wesley, Whitefield, and others for the first time, I encountered some things that made me uncomfortable. I remember sitting in the King's College Divinity Library surrounded by walls of modern and ancient books—the college was founded in

1495. As the saying goes, "If only the walls could speak." The walls were quiet that day, but the books spoke loudly. I plodded through the writings of Wesley and Whitefield hour after hour. Reading such a high volume of publications is mind-numbing, but from time to time, something catches your attention and you stop. I stopped because I noticed that Wesley and Whitefield wrote about people groups in racist and demeaning ways. I brought my concerns to my supervisor, and he made no excuses for them—he was just as uncomfortable with the comments as I was.

PhD studies must stay very focused on *one* topic, so I couldn't stop to investigate these disturbing details. My solution was to add footnotes in my thesis. My research was eventually published in my book *Born Again: The Evangelical Theology of Conversion in John Wesley and George Whitefield*, and you can see some of these footnotes there. For example, regarding Wesley's use of the words *heathen* and *Negroland*, I write, "Wesley's terminology is left untouched to present his writing in its original form."[12] Regarding Wesley's use of the word *popery* [often a derogatory term for Roman Catholics], I write, "Throughout this study, my aim is to present Wesley in his own terms and as a man of his day, despite my anxiousness and discomfort."[13]

Historian and activist Jemar Tisby writes, "Many individuals throughout American church history exhibited blatant racism, yet they also built orphanages and schools. They deeply loved their families; they showed kindness toward others. . . . very rarely do historical figures fit neatly into the category of 'villain.'"[14] After studying Wesley and Whitefield, I realized they too didn't fit one category neatly either. And yet I was uncomfortable labeling them "men of their day" and moving on. My academic path led me to study Jonathan Edwards, another early evangelical, and I found that he fit this assessment too. Authors Christina Edmondson and Chad Brennan write, "If an esteemed theologian like Edwards can have such a disconnect in his life, none of us are immune to falling into similar traps."[15] I wanted to learn more about these men and their contemporaries because I knew that they had immense influence on the evangelical legacy I inherited and the life I live.

What does it mean to say that these historical figures were "men of their times"? Neal Conan, host of NPR's *Talk of the Nation*, interviewed Dr. Henry Louis Gates Jr. of Harvard University about Gates's research on Abraham Lincoln.[16] Gates learned that Lincoln hated slavery, but also used the N-word, told racist jokes, and hoped to send America's Black people to Africa. Conan opened his interview by stating, "Intellectually, we know that Lincoln was a man of his times, that attitudes towards race were very different in the first half of the nineteenth century." Gates helped listeners like me see a more complex, and more accurate, picture of Lincoln than before.

Notice, though, how Gates framed his discussion around the phrase "man of his times." People use this phrase to introduce a suspension of judgment because of a chronological gap. When we say someone was a "man of his times," we must also answer what man (or woman) and what time we're talking about. Skeptics like me ask another question: why should we withhold judgment on that person? In Lincoln's case, his legacy of abolishing slavery immediately brings the credibility required for sympathetic consideration, and Gates, the eminent Black historian, is on hand to guide the conversation, so listeners know they are in trustworthy hands.

Will you be remembered as a man or woman "of your times"? We'll return to this question at the end of the book. You might answer that you don't care how you will be remembered. But you *should* care. It's an important question because it isn't really about future generations—it's a question that shapes our present decisions. It helps us think deeply about which beliefs and actions are timeless rather than products of our current location, culture, and era.

Many of us have an older relative whose beliefs and actions we filter. Because they are our relative, we tend to grant more leeway than we would give a stranger. Because we know them better than most, we weigh their strengths against their weaknesses and respond with calculated patience when we encounter their uncomfortable beliefs and actions. This approach is common with family members; it also works for Gates when he learns more about Lincoln.

Considering how we will be remembered shapes us right now more than it shapes how people in the future will remember us. Imagine if you are that older relative (or maybe you are!). Are your beliefs and actions a reflection of your age, upbringing, and culture? Or are they rooted in something deeper, something timeless? Lincoln's racist jokes reflect prejudice common among some White men in his time, but his belief that slavery is unjust is timeless.

In this book, I want to put you in the shoes of John Wesley because Wesley had the gift of time. Wesley lived the longest (by far) of the three men examined in this book, and he eventually played an important role helping Christians and non-Christians alike to advocate for the timeless truth that no human should own another human. Wesley didn't start his life advocating for this, and if his life had ended earlier (as it did for Whitefield and Edwards), Wesley would be remembered differently. Wesley had the gift of time. Will you?

How long will you live? What if your days had ended when you were half your age? What if your days end when you are twice your current age? As I write this today, I am forty-five years old. While I'm not all that different from when I was twenty-two years old, I have changed in some ways. If I had a chance, I would challenge twenty-two-year-old me in several areas, and I'd give myself lots of advice. I can only wonder how ninety-year-old me might challenge me today. Experience tells me that I would be wise to listen to the older me. What if I don't live that long? Or what if I discovered I only had a few years to live?

The lives of John Wesley, Jonathan Edwards, and George Whitefield provide us a wealth of insight about navigating our lives today as we own what happened in the past in order to better own our decisions today. In this book we'll examine the history of slavery and abolitionism through the stories, cultures, ministries, and families of these three men. We will see their horrendous errors regarding slavery and, in Wesley's case, eventual correction—because he lived long enough to do so. Wesley's silence regarding slavery ended when he was seventy-three years old, when he finally shared his *Thoughts upon Slavery*—sixteen years after slave owner Jonathan Edwards died, and four years after slave owner George Whitefield died.

You might think that slavery has nothing to do with you. But it does. By the end of this book my hope is that you will be able to own, with better clarity, the legacy you are writing with your life today.

PART 1

INFLUENCES
BORN INTO
SLAVE SOCIETIES

2

THREE MEN WHO WOULD CHANGE THE WORLD

JONATHAN EDWARDS, GEORGE WHITEFIELD, and John Wesley together provided the foundation of American evangelical Christianity. Consider the highly regarded recent five-volume *A History of Evangelicalism*, of which the first volume is subtitled "The Age of Edwards, Whitefield, and the Wesleys."[1] A thorough discussion of American Christianity, modern British Christianity, and even modern world Christianity requires an examination of these three figures.[2] These men share many similarities, and their stories are interwoven, even as they're also quite different from each other. As this book unfolds, you will see how we must understand all three men together to make sense of slavery and evangelical Christianity in the eighteenth century—and to make better sense of Christianity today.

These three men lived in the same era. In fact, John Wesley was born just 99 days before Jonathan Edwards. While the Atlantic Ocean separated them—except for a brief chapter—the fact that they were born in the same year gives us a plumb line to compare their lives, their influences, their reactions to events in the Atlantic world, and the interactions between England, colonial America, and beyond. We can imagine George Whitefield as Wesley and Edwards's little brother since he was born eleven years after them, in 1714. These three men lived in a dynamic time that is the foundation for all of evangelical Christianity.

A second similarity shared by these three men is their focus. The ministerial focus of all three of these men was clear: conversion. For them, conversion—the evidence of the new birth and of eternal salvation—is the experience through which every genuine Christian must pass; conversion was the "one thing needful."[3] Historian Thomas Kidd writes, "[the] distinctive belief of evangelicals is that the key moment in an individual's salvation is the 'new birth.'"[4] Their focus on the individualistic *experience* of the new birth, generally opposed to a more passive cultural Christianity, is the foundational doctrine that links them and the early evangelical movement together.

A third similarity among these men is their direct and extended relational networks. John Wesley met George Whitefield when Whitefield arrived at Oxford in 1734 and joined the Holy Club. George Whitefield met Jonathan Edwards on Whitefield's second preaching tour across colonial America in 1740. Wesley and Edwards never met face-to-face, yet they read each other's writings, and Wesley even edited and republished five of Edwards's works. (Wesley's assessment of Edwards was dire. Wesley warned that in Edwards's work "much wholesome food is mixt with much deadly poison."[5]) Wesley and Whitefield remained in frequent communication until Whitefield's death. Wesley preached Whitefield's funeral eulogy—near the climax of Wesley's thoughts on slavery, as we will see. Whitefield and Edwards would meet face-to-face a second time, and their ministries brushed shoulders frequently.

Beyond their direct relationships, the networks around these three men formed a "who's who" of early evangelicalism. In recent years, scholars attempting to define evangelicalism have fought for firm criteria. Scholars of early evangelicalism usually start with David Bebbington's quadrilateral of conversion, activism, crucicentrism, and biblicism. Scholars of recent evangelicalism typically highlight the highly political nature of American evangelicalism beginning around 1980 and the fracturing of evangelicalism regarding race; modern politically charged American evangelicalism shares little affinity with the theological and spiritual foundations of early evangelicalism. The relational origins of evangelicalism provide another approach to understanding evangelicalism. Scholar Timothy Larsen explains that an evangelical is one "who stands in the tradition of the global Christian networks arising from the eighteenth-century revival movements associated with John Wesley and George Whitefield."[6]

Apart from their many similarities, these three men each possessed unique gifts—among the most impressive in the entire history of Christianity. Wesley was one of the most effective organizers the church has ever seen. Edwards is among the most powerful Christian thinkers, theologians, and philosophers. Whitefield preached as powerfully and passionately as anyone. Wesley and Whitefield were ministers of the Church of England; Edwards was a Congregationalist. Edwards and Whitefield were Calvinistic in their theology; Wesley was an Arminian. Edwards and Wesley spent most of their lives on their respective home continents; Whitefield made thirteen transatlantic trips.

The popular relevance of each man has waxed and waned over the centuries. Whitefield owned the eighteenth century with his dynamic preaching, boundary-pushing ministry, and celebrity status. Wesley had a significant influence during his lifetime, but nothing compared to the explosive growth and influence of Methodism, the movement birthed out of his ministry, in the nineteenth and twentieth centuries. And the influence of Edwards has been on the rise in the late twentieth and early twenty-first centuries in a way that was hidden earlier.

John Wesley was the first one born and the last one to die among them. His life spans Whitefield's and Edwards's—by a lot. Wesley's life is a lens through which we see how White British and American evangelical Christians in the eighteenth century thought about and engaged in slavery. It is with his story that we will begin. As you read the rest of the chapter, look for the formative influences these men were born into and accepted along the way as we seek to understand and own the evangelical legacy of slavery and how it eventually changed.

INTRODUCING JOHN WESLEY

John Wesley is the central figure of our examination of early evangelicals and slavery because he lived long enough and documented his life
extensively for us to see how one person reacted to several pivotal eras
of evangelical responses to slavery. Wesley is *the* key figure to understanding the past of evangelicals and slavery.

John Wesley rode 250,000 miles on the roads of England, Scotland,
and Ireland to preach 42,000 sermons. He published 233 books. He
grew Methodism from a Bible study of four members to 132,000
people—72,000 in the British Isles and 60,000 in America—by the end
of his life. Modern Methodist churches in America are in decline, but
the ecclesial legacy of Wesley is much wider. Wesleyan origins are
found in a wide range of churches, including United Methodists, Naza-
renes, Free Methodists, Salvation Army, Holiness, Pentecostal, and
Methodist churches around the world that make up 80 different de-
nominations and more than 80 million people worldwide.[7] In 2019,
there were about three times the number of Methodists in Ghana than
in Great Britain and as many in Africa as in the United States.[8]

Wesley's teaching on instantaneous perfection provided the theological and ecclesial roots of Pentecostalism. Methodists stressed the
pursuit of holiness, and some groups understood the gift of tongues as
evidence of a miraculous breakthrough in Christian growth—creating
Pentecostalism.[9] Pentecostalism (and the related charismatic movement)
is the fastest growing form of Christianity, with more than 644 million
adherents in 2020, representing 8.3 percent of the world population.
This includes 68 million people in North America, and an astounding
230 million people in Africa, 195 million in Latin America, and 125
million people in Asia. The total number is expected to surpass one
billion people by 2050.[10] Wesley's influence on not only American
Christianity but world Christianity might be larger than any other
Christian leader in the last three centuries. Even if you aren't aware of
Wesley's direct influence, you are still surrounded by it.

John Wesley was the fifteenth child of Samuel and Susanna Wesley. He was born on June 17, 1703, in the Epworth rectory in Lincolnshire, England. His father was a priest in the Church of England and, like his wife, had come from a long line of nonconformist ministers steeped in the Puritan tradition—which would be relevant to John's formative outlook on slavery.

Samuel Wesley had been a servitor—a servant to rich students—to pay for his education at Oxford. Later, Samuel wrote a weekly newspaper advice column, one time answering the question: "Whether trading for Negroes, i.e. carrying them out of their country into perpetual slavery, be in itself unlawful, and especially contrary to the great law of Christianity?"[11] Samuel's response began by saying that doing so is "contrary to the law of nature, of doing unto all men as we would they should do unto us."[12] The rest of his answer worked through biblical and logical arguments combined to make a clear denunciation of man-stealing and, thus, slave trading. He published these arguments a decade before John's birth.

Susanna's father had been a minister at St. Paul's Cathedral and pastor to Daniel Defoe, author of *Robinson Crusoe*—a story in which the main character is enslaved and later sets out to enslave others. Defoe published a flattering poem about Susanna's father. Thus, John's parents were aware of slavery, the slave trade, and the questions English Christians asked about these issues—though they had no firsthand involvement or contact with enslaved people as far as we know.

Susanna raised her children with discipline, piety, and deep devotion—along with the help of servants she and Samuel employed. Despite their cyclical poverty, the Wesley family employed multiple servants in their house—a common feature in England in those days for landowners and educated families, even if their financial resources were slim. Servants in England during that time should not be confused with "butler" servants, bondservants, and certainly not slaves; the servants in the Wesley house were task-based, paid employees. Susanna embodied the Puritan spirit of her parents for the household management and spiritual leadership of not only her family but also of their servants—effectively she filled the role of master. John Wesley grew up watching his mom and dad provide "master and servant" leadership to the servants in their household.

John's parents managed to secure a scholarship for their son to the Charterhouse boarding school in London, where he spent six years before he was awarded another scholarship to enter as a university student at Christ Church, Oxford. While the triangular slave trade brought few enslaved people to England, consider an advertisement in London just five years prior to John's arrival: "A black Indian boy, 12 years of age, fit to wait on a gentleman, to be disposed of at Denis's Coffee-house in Finch Lane near the Royal Exchange."[13] An ad for "twenty-four sermons" by Richard Lucas surrounded the ad for the twelve-year-old boy.

Three years after John's departure from London to Oxford, the London *Daily Journal* reported, "'Tis said there is a great number of blacks come daily into this city, so that 'tis thought in a short time, if they be not suppressed, the city will swarm with them."[14] From age eleven to seventeen, John Wesley found himself in a place very different from his hometown. He saw the bustle and hustle of London among the elite of a private school, traveling through the city weekly to be with his older brother Samuel, with whom he spent his weekends. John also saw an increasing number of Black people, and inside the coffeehouses in his city, Black people were being sold into slavery.

Early in his years at Oxford, between 1726 and 1727, Wesley read *Othello* by William Shakespeare and *Oroonoko* by Thomas Southerne; a central element of these plays is slavery.[15] One Shakespearean scholar comments that in *Othello* Shakespeare "mixes self-identity, race, and slavery in an unstable and explosive combination."[16] In his play, Southerne depicts an Angolan prince named Oroonoko who enslaves other Africans and sells them to English traders. A climactic moment comes when the slaves are aware that, as slaves, their enslavers would attempt to make them Christians, even if by force. Oroonoko cries out,

"Whip, whip 'em to the knowledge of your Gods, Your Christian Gods, who suffer you to be unjust, dishonest, cowardly, and base, and give 'em your excuse for being so."[17] We can only infer from Wesley's Oxford years what he thought about the institution of slavery and the African slave trade, but it wouldn't be long before Wesley encountered slavery face-to-face.

Four years after enrolling at Oxford, he graduated and a year later was ordained a deacon in the Church of England. Finding success as a scholar, he was elected a fellow of Lincoln College, Oxford, in 1726 and received his MA the following year. For the next three years, John split time between Oxford and the churches at Epworth and Wroot (a town a few miles from Epworth), assisting his elderly father. These years would be the only time in John's life as a parish minister.

The autumn of 1729 became one of several turning points in John's life. That year the rector at Lincoln College requested John to return from his parish ministry. John joined his brother Charles, along with others at Oxford, in regular meetings where they studied the Greek New Testament, read and abridged many devotional and theological works, prayed and fasted regularly, and visited the sick and people in prison. Outsiders mocked their activities and called them "Bible bigots" and "Bible moths." The names for the group that are better known are the Holy Club and the Methodists. While the title was originally intended to mock the group, John Wesley later embraced the label Methodist and defined it as "one that lives according to the method laid down in the Bible."[18]

John Wesley's 1735 failed mission to be the minister to the British colony of Georgia is the next turning point in his life, one we will examine closely later. After leaving Georgia, John wrote, "I went to America to convert the Indians; but O! who shall convert me? Who, what is he that shall deliver me from this evil heart of unbelief?"[19] Six months later, in London on May 24, 1738, Wesley arose at 5:00 a.m. and read in his New Testament of God's "exceedingly great and precious promises." In the afternoon, he went to St. Paul's Cathedral and heard the hymn "Out of the Depths Have I Called You." That night he went reluctantly to a Moravian meeting on Aldersgate street. Around 8:45 p.m., while a leader at the meeting read from Luther's "Preface to the Epistle to the Romans," John wrote, "I felt my heart strangely warmed. I felt I did trust in Christ, Christ alone, for salvation; and an assurance was given me that he had taken away my sin."[20] This moment is so significant that Methodists continue to celebrate May 24 annually as Aldersgate Day or Wesley Day.

Wesley's experience at Aldersgate, alongside many others (such as his brother Charles, who had had a similar experience shortly before, and George Whitefield, who had also experienced something similar three years earlier), led to the widespread appeal for the personal experience of instantaneous conversion—a miraculous moment that brought an inward feeling and certainty that one was forgiven and saved by God. This experience of the new birth would become the hallmark of the evangelical movement and evangelical theology.[21]

With church pulpits closing to Whitefield and Wesley, in April 1739 Whitefield invited John Wesley to preach outdoors in Bristol and to organize small groups for new converts. The first home of the Methodist societies was born in Bristol and met in a small house called the New Room.

Over the ensuing years, Wesley grew the Methodist meetings into societies in London and beyond. These societies typically utilized lay leaders, and Wesley developed rules to ensure consistency and structure—with a key moment being the first Methodist conference in 1744. This occurred shortly after a rift developed with Whitefield over the doctrine of election—on which they never agreed, but they redeveloped a supportive approach to each other amid their differences. Wesley traveled extensively to evangelize and organize. He took forty-two trips to Ireland and twenty-two to Scotland. In 1770, he sent Francis Asbury to America to further develop Methodism there.

Wesley prioritized his health and lived a long, vigorous life. In his eighty-sixth year, Wesley traveled to sixty towns in nine weeks and preached a hundred sermons. Two years later, on March 2, 1791, Wesley died. He left behind a large and growing ministry that, at the time of his death, included 294 preachers in Britain and 198 in America. He did not leave behind a family. He had married Mary "Molly" Vazeille in 1751, but by 1758 it was clear that their marriage was unhealthy. In 1771, Mary finally left John. They had no children together. When Mary died in 1781, John only heard of her death after she was already in her grave.

We will return to Wesley's story in chapter five, but we must first introduce the life of Wesley's most prominent protégé, George Whitefield.

INTRODUCING GEORGE WHITEFIELD

Benjamin Franklin wrote in his autobiography that in late 1739, George Whitefield

> preached one evening from the top of the courthouse steps. . . . Both streets were filled with his hearers to a considerable distance . . . I had the curiosity to learn how far he could be heard. . . . I computed that he might well be heard by more than thirty thousand. This reconciled me to the newspaper accounts of his having preached to 25,000 people in the fields.[22]

This anecdote reveals why Whitefield was "the first transatlantic celebrity of any kind."[23] First, Whitefield's preaching was unique: he was loud, clear, powerful, and often preached outdoors—which was equally scandalous and genius. Second, he was popular—so popular that tens of thousands of people would flock to hear him, and all this before the advent of quick and convenient communication. Third, Whitefield was a Brit in colonial America. You would expect to find Brits in British colonies, but the frequency with which Whitefield made the dangerous trek across the Atlantic was unheard of in his day. Fourth, Whitefield sparked wild curiosity among Christians *and* non-Christians, like Benjamin Franklin—who remained a deist his entire life. Last, Franklin's curiosity and attendance resulted from the publicity Whitefield gathered and created through accounts in newspapers and his own publishing efforts—Whitefield was an early adopter and master of commercial self-promotion. By 1740 Whitefield was the most famous man in America.[24]

To understand George Whitefield, we must grasp what was happening in Bristol—just down the road from his hometown of Gloucester, England—near the time of his birth. When England ended the Royal African Company's African trade monopoly in 1698, Bristol entrepreneurs collaborated quickly, more so than those in London or Liverpool, to make their city a leading slave trade seaport.[25] By the time Whitefield was fourteen years old, forty-five ships per year departed Bristol with goods for Africa to trade for enslaved people to sell in America for raw materials (sugar, cotton, and tobacco) that returned to Bristol with enormous and increasing profit.[26] Bristol merchants expanded their loading port to nearly a mile long as it became the leading slave trade port in England.

Black people were few during this time in Bristol (and throughout England), but those that made it there were a badge of social status for their White owners and a source of cheap labor, often spoken of as objects of evangelism. Consider a cemetery headstone of an African who died in Bristol:

Here

Lieth the Body of

SCIPIO AFRICANUS

Negro Servant to ye Right

Honourable Charles William

Earl of Suffolk and Bradon

Who died Ye 21 December

1720 Aged 18 years

I who was Born a PAGAN and a SLAVE

Now sweetly sleep a CHRISTIAN in my Grave[27]

In 1787, when Thomas Clarkson sought evidence for the Committee for the Abolition of the Slave Trade, he came to Bristol and wrote:

> In my first movements about this city, I found that people talked very openly on the subject of the Slave-trade. They seemed to be well acquainted with the various circumstances belonging to it. There were facts, in short, in every body's mouth, concerning it; and everybody seemed to execrate it, though no one thought of its abolition.[28]

George Whitefield's family was intimately familiar with the servant system in England, as well as the inner workings of Bristol in the seventeenth and early eighteenth century. George Whitefield was born on December 27, 1714, in Gloucester, just thirty-five miles from Bristol and a town which benefited richly from the slave trade economy. Whitefield was born at the Old Bell Inn. The inn was the largest hotel in Gloucester and run by George's parents. George's older brother James was a sea captain and a former merchant in Bristol. While his name doesn't show up on any record as a captain in any slave voyages,[29] he undoubtedly was familiar with the slave trade.[30] Both George's oldest brother, Andrew, and George's grandfather Richard had undertaken apprenticeships—a form of voluntary debt labor, also known as bond-servants.[31] Further, Whitefield's mother grew up in a household being served by a servant named Joane Goodhind and, later, another servant named Elizabeth Cotton.[32]

The Old Bell Inn included a hall in which plays were performed for the public—which certainly influenced Whitefield's future theatrical preaching.[33] When George was two years old, his father died. His mother carried on the business of the inn, and it was here that he spent his youth. Whitefield contracted measles at age four that left him with a lifelong squint, for which he was bullied and teased.[34] Four years later, George's mother married Capel Longden, who mismanaged the inn and destroyed their finances; Whitefield's mother left Longden a few years later.

At the age of twelve, Whitefield enrolled at the school run by his local parish, St. Mary de Crypt. His teachers noticed that he had talent for giving speeches and gave him opportunities to do so. Late at night in his bedroom, Whitefield privately imitated ministers in their reading of prayers. By the age of sixteen, Whitefield was reading the Greek New Testament and had a foundation in Latin, but due to his family's struggling finances, he stopped attending school and for a year and a half took up full-time work at the Old Bell Inn.[35]

At the age of seventeen, Whitefield found entrance as a student to Pembroke College, Oxford, by being a servitor. Shortly before entrance to Pembroke, Whitefield turned to extreme Christian piety through intense fasting, attending worship twice a day, monthly sacrament, and prayer more than twice a day in private. He also had a striking experience where he felt called to preach. At Oxford, he met Charles and John Wesley and a group of likeminded students who became known as the Oxford Methodists. Together they engaged in rigorous spiritual disciplines, including concentrated reading of Scripture, prayer, fasting, self-examination, visiting prisoners and the poor, celebrating the Lord's Supper, and discussing classic books of Christian spirituality. In May 1735, Whitefield experienced the new birth through his conversion, whereby he had a personal experience in which he was assured of his salvation, while deathly sick due to his extreme fasting.[36]

A year after his conversion, Whitefield was ordained as a deacon in the Church of England and began preaching in churches and prisons in London and elsewhere to increasingly large crowds, sometimes as often as four times per day. In Bristol in January 1737, he preached what would become his ministry-defining, breakout sermon: "The Nature and Necessity of our Regeneration or New Birth in Christ Jesus (On Regeneration)." This sermon quickly went into print and became a bestseller. Historian Thomas Kidd writes, "Although the doctrine of the new birth was not new, Whitefield was the most important popularizer of the concept in Anglo-American history, at least until Billy Graham's revivals of the twentieth century."[37]

In a request that would alter his life and the lives of thousands—free and enslaved—the Wesley brothers asked Whitefield to come to Georgia to assist their work there. In the midst of his soaring popularity, Whitefield boarded the *Whitaker* to cross the Atlantic. After a dangerous trip, Whitefield arrived in Savannah, Georgia, on May 7, 1738. Less than two weeks later, Whitefield made a decision that would be his grandest goal and deepest disaster: establishing an orphanage in Savannah. Three months later, he set off back to England to raise funds for the orphanage and to be ordained a priest.

When Whitefield returned to England, he expected to ride his previous wave of popularity. Instead, he met not only increased opportunity but increased opposition too. Whitefield's bold teaching on the new birth rattled the established understanding of salvation—which had generally been assured through infant baptism and bare-minimum church involvement. It didn't help that in his youthful confidence he claimed that many established ministers were not Christians, since they had not experienced the new birth. Whitefield also published his journals, which he later rewrote because the earlier editions of his youth were overly confident and contained self-exalting prose.[38]

For these reasons, many churches closed their pulpits to Whitefield. Closed church doors led Whitefield to explore a new kind of pulpit that expanded his evangelistic reach. On a cold Saturday afternoon in February 1739, George Whitefield and his friend William Seward went to the coal-mining district of Kingswood, near Bristol. Outsiders seldom entered this rough and sometimes violent community, which lacked a school or church for the miners or their families. After gathering about two hundred people, Whitefield stood upon Hannam Mount, on Rose Green, and preached outdoors for the first time. Whitefield returned the following Wednesday and preached to two thousand people. Two days later, he preached to over four thousand, and on Sunday an estimated ten thousand came to hear him preach. In addition to preaching in the open air, he now began speaking without notes.

Whitefield was now holding thirty meetings per week in and around Bristol, but he knew that he needed to prepare to return to Georgia. He asked John Wesley to come and help, and he did. With a bit of reluctance, John Wesley gave his first open-air sermon on April 2.

Whitefield soon set sail for his second trip to America, intending to build an orphanage, but he chose to arrive in Pennsylvania before heading south, in order to learn more about America. He reached Savannah on January 11, 1740, and the next day inspected a site chosen by James Habersham for the orphanage, which he took possession of on January 24, naming it Bethesda, which means "house of mercy." In many ways the cornerstone laid for Bethesda on that day was a turning point in the evangelical history of slavery, as we will see.

Ten months later, Whitefield traveled north and stayed in the home of Jonathan and Sarah Edwards while preaching at Edwards's church. By 1740, the themes and trajectory for the rest of Whitefield's ministry were established, and would continue until his death in 1770.

On November 14, 1741, George Whitefield married Elizabeth James, a widow ten years his senior. They were married twenty-seven years. They had one son, John, who died four months into his life.

Whitefield created and perpetuated evangelistic tactics of mass evangelism, promotion, and media usage that evangelicals continue to utilize. He also imbibed a spirit of independence by pushing beyond the boundaries of the Church of England's control and doctrine in order to accomplish goals that he deemed beyond the scope of his church's constraints—an approach which fit the emerging spirit of independence in colonial America like a glove.

Whitefield's transatlantic travel is the key link between Wesley and Edwards in the story of early evangelicals and slavery. This link brings us to our final key figure.

INTRODUCING JONATHAN EDWARDS

Consider a letter written in 1902 by Mark Twain, after reading Jonathan Edwards's famous work *Freedom of the Will*:

All through the book is the glare of a resplendent intellect gone mad—a marvelous spectacle. No, not all through the book—the drunk does not come on till the last third, where what I take to be Calvinism and its God show up and shine red and hideous in the glow from the fires of hell, their only right and proper adornment. By God I was ashamed to be in such company.[39]

While Twain did not have a high opinion of Edwards, others do. Edwards has been called "America's preeminent thinker,"[40] "colonial America's greatest theologian and philosopher,"[41] and "America's Augustine."[42] If people have heard of Edwards, it is most likely from high school readings of his sermon "Sinners in the Hands of an Angry God." But Edwards has much more to offer than one sermon.

Jonathan Edwards was born on October 5, 1703, in Windsor, Connecticut—a small, relatively unsafe frontier river town. He was the only son among ten sisters. His father was the Reverend Timothy Edwards, and Jonathan's grandfather was the famous Reverend Solomon Stoddard of Northampton, Massachusetts. Jonathan was descended from powerful Puritan ministers who had trekked across the Atlantic from Britain to colonial America.

Enslaving was a part of Jonathan Edwards's family heritage. Both sets of his grandparents were enslavers. Jonathan and his wife, Sarah, grew up in homes where they were served by slaves.[43] An enslaved man named Ansars, and perhaps others, served Jonathan and his parents during his childhood.[44]

By age seven, Edwards was reading and speaking in Latin. He enrolled at what would later become Yale College at age twelve—that was young, but not unheard of in those days. He graduated in 1720, at age sixteen, and delivered the valedictorian speech. Three years later at his master's degree commencement at Yale, he delivered his thesis on the nature and ground of justification disputed between Calvinists and Arminians. While studying for his master's degree, Edwards underwent a religious conversion that reshaped his life. During this time, he also met

Sarah Pierrepont, the daughter of a well-known minister of the New Haven church.

We know now that some of the founders of Yale enslaved Africans.[45] In time, Yale went on to produce more proslavery clergy than any other college in America[46] and became a prominent influence in the pro-slavery movement.[47] We do not know how Edwards's time at Yale impacted his view of slavery, but it likely did little to challenge the view he inherited from his family regarding slavery.

In 1722, a church in New York invited Edwards to lead them, which he did for nearly two years. Edwards's tenure in New York was in the midst of a community entrenched in slavery, laws written against Black people, and fears of slave rebellions.[48]

In September 1726, the congregation in Northampton, one of New England's most prestigious parishes, hired Edwards to serve under his grandfather Solomon Stoddard, who was in his fifty-fifth year of ministry. Three years later, Stoddard died, leaving Edwards in charge. Jonathan married Sarah Pierrepont on July 28, 1727. They had three sons and eight daughters. They also, like their parents, enslaved several people. One of Edwards's children would become an early White abolitionist, though he did so anonymously at first.

We will continue Jonathan Edwards's story in chapter six. What is most important to know now is that modern interest in Edwards has skyrocketed. A critical edition of Edwards's works began at Yale in the 1950s and was completed in 2008 in twenty-six volumes—it continues to be supplemented by digital resources. Pastors and scholars find Edwards's work useful since it was neither fundamentalist nor liberal, with a focus on conversion, spiritual formation, missions, Reformed theology, politics, pluralism, religious violence, beauty, being, and understanding.[49] More than four thousand secondary books, dissertations, and articles regarding Edwards had been published by 2010. Edwards scholars McClymond and McDermott argue that "Edwards has become one of the most studied thinkers in the history of Christian thought and by far the most deeply scrutinized American thinker before 1800."[50]

Over a third of the theological articles in the *Journal of the Evangelical Theology Society* in the 2010s were written on Jonathan Edwards.

No one has sparked modern popular interest in Edwards more than John Piper. Piper is a Reformed theologian, pastor, chancellor of Bethlehem College and Seminary, and a prolific speaker and author. Piper explains, "The person most responsible for my views and for my articulation of those views (under God and the Bible) is Jonathan Edwards.... The impact that Edwards has had on my thinking as it relates to worship and missions (and almost everything else) is incalculable."[51] Piper credited his most famous concept, Christian hedonism, to Edwards.[52] Through Piper and others, current interest in Edwards is at an all-time high. This popularity, though, comes with hard questions about his slaveholding—this book addresses this topic head-on like no other book before it.

A COMMON THREAD: SLAVERY

What might we learn today from these men who shared considerable Christian and social outlooks on life, but whom history has judged very differently?

How is it that Wesley did not participate directly in slavery? How is it that Edwards and Whitefield did?

In England, Christians upheld the ordered family relationship between master and servant (usually a laborer, a fixed-term bond laborer, or an apprentice). English people who came across the Atlantic brought their beliefs with them and expanded the master and servant relationship to include slaves; this included White slaves at first, but eventually—and exclusively—Black slaves.

All sixteen great-grandparents of Jonathan and Sarah Edwards were from England, with most of them being born around 1590–1610. None of them would have grown up in an English slave-owning society because England's participation in the trade came later. The same would be true for the grandparents of Wesley and Whitefield. Six of Jonathan and Sarah Edwards's eight grandparents were born in New England.[53]

Both sets of their parents were slave owners, while their relatives who remained in England were not.

The great-grandparents of Wesley, Whitefield, and Edwards did not enslave people. A primary question that determined whether their grandchildren and great-grandchildren would enslave people is this: Which side of the Atlantic did they live on? Our historical and geographical locatedness profoundly influences our decision-making, including our Christian decision-making.

In the following pages, each of us can find a part of ourselves. We will find parts we like and parts we don't like. Each of these men is a hero on one page and a villain on another. Perhaps our stories are similar. We have over two centuries of distance through which to make our observations of these three men. Only you can evaluate yourself as you work through their histories.

3

WHAT PRECEDED THEM

A BRIEF HISTORY OF SLAVERY

EARLY EVANGELICAL CHRISTIANS did not invent the institution of slavery. They inherited it.

An enslaved person, defined in the broadest sense, is the property of another person, with a will subject to that other person, and whose labor and services are obtained through coercion.[1] The domestication of animals may have provided the basis for slavery. The Latin word *capitale* is the root word for both *cattle* and *capital*, which emerged as the word *chattel*, which is what we find in the phrase *chattel slavery*— treating humans like capital property or cattle.[2]

The ancient history of slavery goes back thousands of years, leading scholar James Walvin to conclude that "slavery was ubiquitous" among ancient societies.[3] Slavery was a feature of civilization that predates formal laws and is found in most ancient societies, including those in Mesopotamia, China, India, Pakistan, Egypt, and beyond.[4] What might be most surprising about the history of the institution of slavery among early evangelical Christians is not that they participated in it, but that they contributed to abolishing it. This dramatic change is one of the reasons we are looking at the long life of John Wesley, while also looking at the shorter lives of Jonathan Edwards and George Whitefield, since it was during Wesley's lifetime that attitudes about slavery among White English Christians began to change.

JUDAISM

Slavery emerges in the Jewish tradition as early as the story of Noah. Noah curses his grandson Canaan to be "the lowest of slaves" and the slave of Shem and Japheth (Genesis 9:24-27). God told Abraham that his descendants would be enslaved and mistreated for four hundred years (Genesis 15:13). Abraham and Sarah had an Egyptian slave, Hagar, whom Abraham slept with and Sarah mistreated. Hagar ran away from them, yet God told her to submit to them (Genesis 16:1-10). The king of Gerar, Abimelek, gave Abraham male and female slaves as property (Genesis 20:14). Later, Joseph's brothers sold him to the Ishmaelites for twenty shekels of silver—the irony of Abraham's descendant Joseph being sold as a slave to the descendants of Abraham's slave Hagar is not lost on attentive readers (Genesis 37:28). The last chapter of Genesis describes Joseph's brothers on their knees before him saying, "we are your slaves" (Genesis 50:18). It is worth noting that this is a reference to African slavery thousands of years before the transatlantic slave trade.

The book of Exodus opens with Egyptian slave masters oppressing the Israelites with forced labor (Exodus 1:11). The Israelites responded by groaning and crying out to God for help (Exodus 2:23). God saw their misery and said, "I am concerned about their suffering" and promised to bring them out from under the yoke of the Egyptians and to "free you from being slaves to them" (Exodus 3:7; 6:6). At no time in any of these narratives is being a slave thought to be a healthy, desirable, or positive situation.

God delivered Israel and highlighted this fact in the beginning of the Ten Commandments: "I am the LORD your God, who brought you out of Egypt, out of the land of slavery" (Exodus 20:2). Instructions about idols and altars immediately follow the statement of the Ten Commandments— perhaps as brief explanations of the first two commandments. Readers might expect the next instructions to explain the rest of the commandments. Instead, the next instructions in Exodus address regulations regarding *how* to enslave people (Exodus 21:1-11). The remainder of the Old Testament imagines slavery as a common component of human societies that is utilized for communal and personal gain and a negative experience that the enslaved person seeks to escape.

GREECE AND ROME

The most documented details of ancient slavery emerge from Rome. The Roman Empire acquired people and enslaved them as the empire grew throughout the Near East, North Africa, and Europe. Slavery became a frequent topic of philosophical and moral debate because of the abuse and management of slaves, yet the institution itself went unchallenged.[5] This is not to say that Roman slaves were content with the institution of slavery, as if being a slave were a harmonious part of a healthy society, as some modern Christians might contend.

For example, in 74 BC, the Roman slave Spartacus led a revolt of slaves. Revolt is not a common feature among people who enjoy their role in society. These slaves won a series of victories against the Romans and grew to form an army of seventy thousand warriors. Rome rallied and defeated Spartacus and his army, killing all but six thousand of the slaves. Roman armies captured the remaining six thousand slaves and crucified one for every 105 feet of the 120-mile Appian Way leading from Capua to Rome, to remind the public of the price for revolting against their slave masters.

EARLY CHRISTIANITY

The earliest Christian communities lay on the eastern outskirts of the Roman Empire. The number of slaves in Palestine was fewer than in the core of the Empire, yet slavery was still common among Jews and Gentiles in early Christian communities.

In 4 BC, a man named Judas led an insurrection in Sepphoris, a town a little less than four miles from Nazareth. The Roman army crushed the revolt, crucified two thousand men near Jerusalem, and sold the entire population of Sepphoris into slavery. New Testament scholar Jennifer Glancy says that "Jesus would likely have been familiar with the fate [of Sepphoris]."[6] Imagine if the government sold an entire town down the street from your hometown into slavery around the time you were born. You would have grown up hearing about it and encountering the relational, economic, and political repercussions.

Modern scholars continue to debate the interpretation of the New Testament on the topic of slavery.[7] Biblical scholar John Anthony Mc-Guckin aptly summarizes the material: "The New Testament literature shows considerable tension in regard to the issue of slavery: never quite feeling confident enough to come out and denounce it explicitly, since to do so would have been tantamount to a declaration of social revolution."[8] New Testament scholar Esau McCaulley writes, "No one in Paul's day or in the centuries that follow ever seemed to envision the end of slavery as an institution."[9] Contrary to popular opinion, Christian interpretation of the Bible did not bring an end to the institution of slavery. Wesley himself explicitly avoided utilizing the Bible as the basis for his eventual antislavery rationale.

The earliest writings of the church fathers—those coming after the New Testament texts—support slavery as an institution. Ignatius, the bishop of Antioch in the late first century, wrote that slaves should "submit themselves the more, for the glory of God. . . . Let them not long to be set free [from slavery] at the public expense, that they be not found slaves to their own desires"—following Paul's admonitions (e.g., 1 Timothy 6:1-2; Titus 2:9-10; 1 Corinthians 7:17-24).[10]

Lactantius—the late third- and early fourth-century North African defender of Christianity and eventual tutor of Crispus, son of the emperor Constantine—taught Christians to punish slaves differently than citizens. He wrote:

> Archytas would be deserving of praise, if, when he had been enraged against any citizen or equal who injured him, he had curbed himself. . . . This self-restraint is glorious . . . but it is a fault not to check the faults of slaves and children; for through their escaping without punishment they will proceed to greater evil. In this case anger is not to be restrained.[11]

Many early church leaders, such as Augustine, advocated for kind treatment of slaves; but Augustine was appalled at efforts to liberate slaves from their plantations.[12] Augustine explained that "nearly all households" owned slaves and that, while unnatural, slavery was the inevitable consequence of humanity's sinful state.[13]

Early Christians supported the institution of slavery while advocating for certain rights. Second-century Pope Callixtus I argued amid opposition from other church leaders that slaves could marry a non-slave in Christian marriage. Callixtus had previously been a slave himself.[14] In AD 306 the Council of Elvira declared that Christian slave owners who used their secular legal right to kill their slaves were excommunicated from the church; specifically, they would be excommunicated seven years if the death was intentional and five years if the death was unintentional.[15] Other Christian leaders, such as John Chrysostom in the early fifth century, campaigned for manumission (releasing) of Christian slaves. The Council of Chalcedon in 451 authorized slaves to become monks if their owners consented.

Early Christian leaders advocated for Christians to be benevolent, kind, and compassionate slave owners. There was an overwhelming consensus that slavery existed in the world as a result of sin and evil, and that the best course of action was to work *within* that system. The only early church leader to challenge the institution of slavery was the fourth-century bishop Gregory of Nyssa in his "Homily on Ecclesiastes," though it appears no other early church leaders heeded his pleas.[16] Gregory writes:

> Since we are created according to the divine likeness and are appointed to rule over the whole earth, then tell me: who is that person who can buy and sell others? Only God can do this . . . Do you delude yourselves that a bill of sale, a written contract, a paltry amount of money, can gain for you possession of the image of God? Oh, what self-deception![17]

Later in the Roman Empire, a transition away from slavery and toward using freemen as laborers arose due to labor shortages. This change brought about the feudal system that characterized the medieval period, and serfdom as an alternative to slave labor. A serf was bound to the land of a land holder rather than bound to an individual; essentially, the serf was "owned" by the land, while the slave was "owned" by a person—though the differences overlap throughout time and locations.[18] Yet slavery persisted elsewhere during this time.

ISLAM, AFRICA, AND BEYOND

Prior to the rise of Islam in the seventh century, slavery already existed in Arabia. Islamic prophet Muhammad owned slaves, and the Qur'an contains detailed teachings regarding the acceptance and regulation of slavery.[19] The practice of slavery was widespread and promoted in Islamic societies. Islam taught that slaves were to be treated well, owners would be rewarded for releasing slaves, slaves could be acquired only through birth or capture in jihad, and under no circumstances were Muslims allowed to be slaves. Slaves, thus, were acquired from outside the Muslim world, typically from central Asia, Africa, and the area around the Black Sea. As we saw earlier, the books of Genesis and Exodus attest to the early presence of slavery in Africa. Slavery continued in ancient Africa but expanded drastically due to Muslim demand for slaves. Islamic slave regulations were widely ignored in Africa; one scholar notes, "principle and practice were frequently at odds."[20] Slave routes across the African Sahara transported nearly four million slaves and lasted from the seventh to the twentieth century.

Muslims were very successful in acquiring slaves in Africa and found additional opportunities for obtaining slaves to the north. The Scandinavian Vikings overtook and enslaved people throughout the modern-day British Isles, Iceland, and Greenland. The Vikings, known in Eastern Europe as the Rus, pushed southeast and overtook the Slavic tribes in what is modern-day Belarus, Ukraine, and western Russia. This expansion developed slave trade routes all the way from Sweden to the Byzantine Empire. These markets intersected with the desires of the prosperous caliphates of the Middle East and beyond.[21]

PORTUGAL AND SPAIN

As the natural resources, especially the gold, of Eastern Europe diminished in the late medieval period, explorers began looking elsewhere. Islamic strongholds blocked routes to the east and south. So explorers took to the seas. With much of northern Africa dominated by Islam, European explorers moved farther and farther south along the western coast of Africa, developing trade routes eventually extending to India and beyond. The natural geographically advantaged leaders of this trade were the Portuguese. In 1419, King Henry of Portugal ordered his ships to explore the African coast. Soon thereafter, the Spanish followed suit, causing disputes between Portugal and Spain over the territory and its resources. In their expeditions, European traders discovered not only vast resources of gold, but also well-established African slave-trading networks developed by centuries of demand from Islamic countries. On January 8, 1455, Pope Nicolas V settled the dispute and granted Portugal the exclusive right to trade, navigate, and use any lands already encountered and any taken in the future. His decree *Bull Romanus Pontifex* declared:

> [Approval] to invade, search out, capture, vanquish, and subdue all Saracens [Muslims] and pagans whatsoever, and other enemies of Christ wheresoever placed, and the kingdoms, dukedoms, principalities, dominions, possessions, and all movable and immovable goods whatsoever held and possessed by them and to reduce their persons to perpetual slavery.[22]

Pope Nicolas V further explained his reasoning for this declaration:

> Many [Africans] taken by force, and some by barter of unprohibited articles, or by other lawful contract of purchase, have been . . . converted to the Catholic faith, and it is hoped, by the help of divine mercy, that if such progress be continued with them, either those peoples will be converted to the faith or at least the souls of many of them will be gained for Christ.[23]

Thus, the pope enabled Portugal to enslave Africans, use their labor, and take their resources because—at least in part—of evangelism, a rationale that would continue for hundreds of years.

Christopher Columbus, sponsored by Spanish monarchs Ferdinand II and Isabella I, voyaged to the Americas to overcome the Portuguese's papal right to African trade and to find a new route to the East for further land, trade, and better agricultural conditions to meet the growing demand for lucrative but labor-intensive crops—especially sugar.

On May 4, 1493, Pope Alexander IV granted Ferdinand and Isabella of Spain all the land west and south of a line in the Atlantic Ocean, beginning just west of eastern Brazil. This decree by the Roman Catholic Church created two initial transatlantic superpowers, evidenced today by most of Latin America speaking Spanish and Brazil speaking Portuguese.

In 1516, Spaniard Bartolomé de las Casas, bishop of Chiapas (modern-day southern Mexico), advocated to end native labor by importing African slave labor. Portuguese developments in Brazil followed las Casas's lead. The additional African slave labor force brought incredible prosperity to their enslavers, especially through the production of European-bound sugar. Thus, the transatlantic triangular slave trade was born: African slave labor sent to the Americas; agricultural raw goods sent from the Americas to Europe; and European money and supplies sent to Africa (to acquire more slaves).

THE DUTCH AND ENGLISH

Henry VIII's marriage to Anne Boleyn in 1534 introduced a new competitor in the triangular trade. When Pope Clement VII and, later, Pope Paul III excommunicated Henry, England no longer considered itself under the limitations of papal decrees. Thus England was now free to enter the lucrative African trade. Thomas Wyndham led the first English trading expedition to the African coast in 1553. Following Wyndham was John Hawkins, who in 1562 hijacked three hundred enslaved Africans from a Portuguese slave ship and sold them in Santo

Domingo—today the Dominican Republic. Queen Elizabeth I was among those who provided Hawkins financial backing and two of her own ships—the *Minon* and the massive seven-hundred-ton *Jesus of Lübek*—to a 1567 slave-trading expedition. Queen Elizabeth profited greatly on her investment and had Hawkins knighted. His coat of arms included an image of a female African slave.[24] Hawkins's final voyage in 1568 ended in disaster, as he faced extreme opposition from existing slave traders. He had set out with six vessels and hundreds of men but returned with only two ships and a few dozen men.[25] England did not participate directly in the triangular trade for nearly a hundred years.

By 1600, the only sustained foreign settlement in what is now North America was Saint Augustine, in modern-day Florida, settled by Spain in 1565. Others attempted to sustain settlements, such as the English Roanoke Colony of 1585 in modern-day North Carolina, but failed. Thus the earliest European transatlantic trade was primarily with Brazil, Central America, and the Caribbean. Then, in the seventeenth century, things changed dramatically. Spain and Portugal committed all of their resources to their existing locations. This provided French, English, and Dutch explorers opportunities to establish sustained settlements on the North American Atlantic coast.

The first Protestant power to dominate Atlantic trade was not the English but the Dutch. The Dutch were under the control of the Spanish Empire until the Dutch Revolt, or Eighty Years' War (1568–1648), during which they also battled the Portuguese. Dutch warships succeeded in overtaking Spanish and Portuguese ships, often filled with slaves. Scholars call this the "incidental slave trade," whereby slaves were captured, defined as contraband, and sold.[26] The English ship the *White Lion* obtained a license from the Dutch to attack Portuguese ships. In July 1619, the *White Lion* captured the Portuguese slave ship *São João Bautista* filled with enslaved Angolans. In late August 1619, the *White Lion* landed in the English colony of Jamestown, Virginia, where Governor George Yeardley and Cape Merchant Abraham Piersey, bought "20 and odd Negroes."[27]

COLONIAL SLAVERY

English settlers in North America sought two things: freedom and money. The two often go hand in hand. The freedom most settlers sought was freedom for the private ownership of land—technically available in England but practically beyond the reach of most people due to generations of a highly hierarchical society. The availability of land for settlers in North America was an opportunity not open to most people in England. The English crown granted the Virginia Company land to be settled and hoped to make money from this land in three ways: trading (furs, skins, and English manufactured goods with native peoples), gold and precious metals (which they eventually realized did not exist in Virginia), and a pathway to the Orient to improve trade (which also was not there).[28] Settlers discovered that the most lucrative crop of the era, sugar, was not successful in the Chesapeake region, but they discovered another crop that grew in abundance in Virginia: tobacco.

Virginians began shipping tobacco to England in the 1610s and demand skyrocketed. Yet there was a problem. Tobacco production requires considerable land and labor. Some might expect Virginian settlers to seek slaves to meet this need, but for decades, they found labor elsewhere. They enlisted additional White Englishmen to cross the Atlantic as indentured servants instead of seeking enslaved Africans for tobacco plantations. Enslaving Africans was not the original intent of the English settlers. By 1660, Africans formed only 3–4 percent of Virginia's population.[29] As English indentured servants became free and began their own endeavors, though, the existing labor force waned. Meanwhile, the children of the small but growing enslaved population were the property of their owners—English owners. These two factors, along with continued rising tobacco demand, contributed to Virginia's transition from a colony dependent on indentured labor to one based on slave labor. In 1705, Virginia codified laws that established three things: perpetual bondage of Africans, a separate penal code for Africans, and a requirement that non-slaveholders protect the property rights of slaveholders. By 1740, Africans accounted for 40 percent of the population of Virginia.[30]

The second successful English settlement in North America, after Jamestown, began in 1620 upon the arrival of the *Mayflower* at Plymouth, Massachusetts. Like the settlers of Jamestown, the Pilgrims on the Mayflower sought freedom, but they did not seek the *economic* freedom the Virginians sought. The Pilgrims sought *religious* freedom from the Church of England. This would have a marked effect on their laws, especially those related to slavery.

Puritans arrived and formed the Massachusetts Bay Colony at present-day Boston in 1630. In 1635, John Winthrop and others (including, later, John Cotton and Nathaniel Ward) gathered a committee to form a set of laws to govern their land. On December 10, 1641, the general court established the Massachusetts Body of Liberties—a set of a hundred laws governing Massachusetts.

The Massachusetts Body of Liberties is the product of the Puritans, who desired to live Christian lives as purely as possible based on the Bible.[31] This fact is evident in law 94, titled Capital Laws, which lists each of the Ten Commandments, supplemented with additional Bible passages to support each. Law 91 of this 1641 document deserves careful attention:

> There shall never be any bond slave, villain, or captive among us unless it be lawful. Captives taken in just wars, and such strangers as willingly sell themselves or are sold to us. And these shall have all the liberties and Christian use which the law of God established in Israel concerning such persons do morally require. This exempts none from servitude who shall be judged thereto by authority.

The Massachusetts Puritans formed their slavery law explicitly on "the law of God established in Israel." They interpreted the Bible to teach that citizens could legally obtain a slave in three ways: first, as a war captive; second, if a person sold themselves into slavery; or third,

via sale by anyone. Notice that these laws make no distinction regarding race or ethnicity. Two years later, Solomon Stoddard, the powerful Puritan minister sometimes called the "pope" of the Connecticut
River Valley (which runs through Massachusetts), and Jonathan Edwards's grandfather, would be born in Boston—and he would be a
slave owner, as we will see later. Stoddard grew up amid the laws and
guidance of the Massachusetts Body of Liberties until they were replaced in 1691.

Northern colonies in the seventeenth century enslaved Africans in
much smaller numbers than the colonies in the South. Slaves in the
north worked on small family farms and within houses, similar to conditions in England. Colonies to the south generally featured agricultural
conditions that favored large plantations, which required massive
numbers of field laborers.

King Charles I granted the original charter for Carolina in 1629. Settlers made little progress until 1663, when Charles II issued a new
charter to eight English noblemen intended to strengthen defenses
against the Spanish presence in Florida. English colonizers came to Barbados in 1627 to plant sugar and quickly turned to enslaved Africans as
a source of labor. The 1661 Barbados Slave Code, officially titled An Act
for the Better Ordering and Governing of Negroes, codified shocking
controls and punishments specifically designated for Black people. The
code made clear distinctions between "White servants" and "negro
slaves"; it used the words *negro* and *slave* interchangeably. White people
were given rights that were denied to Black people.[32]

As land became scarce in Barbados due to increasing development,
Barbadian leaders looked to uninhabited land just to their north, in the
southeast of North America. In 1669, the small island of Barbados had
30,000 slaves, compared to 4,444 in North America.[33] Between 1670
and 1690, more than 54 percent of the new inhabitants of Carolina were
wealthy planters (and their slaves) from the English colony of Barbados.[34] In 1669, the eight English leaders of Carolina adopted the Fun-
damental Constitutions of Carolina—understood to be drafted by John

Locke, the famous English philosopher, who was then secretary of one of the eight Carolina leaders. This constitution installed two governors of what we know today as North and South Carolina. It also authorized slavery. By 1708, enslaved Africans comprised half of the population of South Carolina.[35] This percentage stands in stark contrast to the African population of the northern colonies. By 1765, about 80 percent of North American slaves were in the colonies south of Pennsylvania.[36]

ENGLISH COMMERCIALIZATION OF ENSLAVED AFRICANS

As England formed the colonies of Barbados in 1627, Nevis in 1628, Montserrat and Antigua in 1632, and Jamaica in 1655, English plantation owners recognized a need for additional labor. Dutch traders delivered supplies and enslaved Africans at first, but soon the English recognized a financial opportunity. King Charles II; his brother James Stuart, the Duke of York (who later took the throne as James II); and other prominent shareholders launched the Company of Royal Adventurers Trading to Africa in 1660 and by 1663 declared a monopoly and began trading in slaves across the Atlantic. By 1667, the company had delivered 16,000 African slaves to English colonies. Five years later, it reorganized as the Royal African Company and increased their share of the transatlantic slave trade over the following decade from 33 to 74 percent, overcoming Dutch and French competition.[37]

The Royal African Company failed to meet the increasing demand of plantation owners in the English West Indies and North American colonies. Despite a thousand-year charter given by Charles II to (his) Royal African Company, private slave traders succeeded in weakening the monopoly through illicit competition, campaigning, and political lobbying. Parliament issued the Trade with Africa Act in 1697 to remove the Royal African Company slave trade monopoly. At its peak, the Royal African Company averaged twenty-three slave-trading voyages per year. After breaking the monopoly, independent trade averaged seventy-seven trips per year from 1714 to 1729.[38]

The three men who sparked evangelicalism—Edwards, Whitefield, and Wesley—were Englishmen born in a decade in which England colonies grew quickly due to their adoption and escalation of the transatlantic slave trade. None of them chose to be born in this time, place, or circumstance. The interesting part is what they did about it (and didn't), as we will see.

4

WHAT THEY ASSUMED

ENGLISH CHRISTIAN BELIEFS ABOUT SLAVERY

ON MOST DAYS in the mid-eighteenth century, you would have found George Whitefield awake and alone early in the morning, on his knees with two books laid before him. The first book was his Greek New Testament, which he read regularly, praying over every word and considering every tense. The second book was his cherished copy of Matthew Henry's *Commentary on the Whole Bible*. Consider what the kneeling Whitefield read when he turned to Henry's comments on 1 Corinthians 7:17-24:

> Our states and circumstances in this world are distributions of divine Providence. This fixes the bounds of men's habitations, and orders their steps. God setteth up and pulleth down. . . . But men's outward condition does neither hinder nor promote their acceptance with God. . . . Our comfort and happiness depend on what we are to Christ, not what we are in the world . . . He who is a slave, may yet be a Christian freeman; he who is a freeman, may yet be Christ's servant.[1]

Matthew Henry first published parts of his commentary when Wesley, Edwards, and Whitefield were children.[2] It quickly became a revered resource for Christians and one that these three men utilized throughout their lives. Henry's comments provide a snapshot of widely held English Christian beliefs about slavery in the first decade of the eighteenth century: God controls human circumstances; human circumstances do not restrict access to God; and slaves may be Christians.

Forty years before Henry published his commentary, Richard Baxter, an English Puritan minister and prolific author, released his *Christian Directory*, a work of over a million words which sought to provide a basis for Puritan ethics, families, churches, and politics. Baxter wrote:

> Reverence the providence of God which calleth you to a servant's life, and murmur not at your labour, or your low condition; but know your mercies, and be thankful for them.[3]
>
> [Those] that keep their negroes and slaves from hearing God's Word, and from becoming Christians, because by the law they shall then be either made free, or they shall lose part of their service, do openly profess rebellion against God, and contempt of Christ the Redeemer of souls, and a contempt of the souls of men, and indeed they declare, that their worldly profit is their treasure and their God.[4]

Like Henry, Baxter believed that God's providence directs and orders human roles in society, including those of slaves. Baxter's comments highlight another common theme among Christians leading up to his time—that slave owners should treat their slaves like family. The common approach among Christian leaders in that era was that Christians should be "good Christian slave holders." An issue that arose in the seventeenth century was that some Christians were withholding Christianity from their enslaved people. Baxter charges these slave holders with "rebellion against God," not because they owned slaves, but because they withheld Christianity from them.

Wesley, Edwards, and Whitefield trace their varied theological influences back to the Church of England. *English Christians* in this chapter means Christians originating from the Church of England up to the time of the beginning of the eighteenth century (including those living in the American colonies). This group includes those who conformed to the governance and teachings of the Church of England and those who did not, including separatists and non-conformists such as the Puritans, Presbyterians, Congregationalists, and Baptists. From the founding of the Church of England in 1534 until the time of Wesley, Edwards, and Whitefield, English Christians held four beliefs about slavery and an additional two beliefs that came under question. These themes represent a consensus, not a precise formulation, of belief regarding slavery—exceptions did exist.[5] But these four beliefs, and the additional two under question, help us understand the underlying assumptions, education, and realities that Wesley, Edwards, and Whitefield inherited from their predecessors.

1. SLAVERY IS ORDAINED BY GOD

At the turn of the eighteenth century, English Christians believed that God appointed and ordained slavery as a vocation, office, and proper place in society. They didn't question the institution of slavery because they believed God had created it.

The Church of England's *Books of Homilies* stated in 1547 that God creates and places people in different roles and stations in societies "in a most excellent and perfect order."[6] The sermon states:

> Every degree of people, in their vocation, calling, and office, [God] hath appointed to them their duty and order. Some are in high degree, some in low; some kings and princes, some inferiors and subjects; priests and laymen, masters and servants, fathers and children, husbands and wives, rich and poor; and every one have need of other. So that in all things is to be lauded and praised the goodly order of God.[7]

Richard Hooker, a "founding figure of Anglicanism"[8] and the primary theologian to articulate the contours of the Church of England, expressed the beliefs of the Church of England in his massive *Laws of Ecclesiastical Polity*, the bulk of which was published by 1597. Hooker argued that God created humans naturally free while also placing them under authorities and structures that limit that freedom. Hooker wrote, "God creating mankind . . . is born lord of himself [and] may be made another's servant: and that power which naturally whole societies have, may be derived into many, few, or one, under whom the rest shall then live in subjection."[9] Hooker taught that just as members of a society—he had England in mind—"naturally" live in subjection to the power of the aristocracy, so too servants "naturally" live in subjection to their masters.

William Perkins, sometimes considered the father of Puritanism though he remained a committed Church of England minister his entire life, explained that servants are either free servants or bond-servants, and that these stations in life exist because "God has ordained and allowed it, even by warrant of His own law."[10] Perkins was simply conveying what he had been taught by his church and government—which were one and the same. Another leading English minister, William Gouge, wrote, "God in general ordained degrees of superiority and inferiority, of authority and subjection: and in particular gave to masters the authority which they have, and put servants in that subjection wherein they are." He continued by arguing that these principles "are so clearly and plentifully noted in the Scripture, that any one who is any whit acquainted therewith may know them to be so."[11] Gouge continued the long line of English Christian beliefs that slavery is ordained by God.

In 1674, John Owen, widely considered the premier theologian of Puritan scholastics and Congregational churches, maintained that God ordered roles within societies for their good. "If the authority of parents, masters, and magistrates, did not oblige children, servants, and subjects, unto obedience, the world could not abide one moment out of hellish confusion."[12] Wendy Warren, a historian at Princeton University, wrote, "English colonists in New England knew that God had in fact allowed slavery, just as he had allowed servitude of other sorts, just as he had allowed mastery and ownership. Their world rested on just such an understanding."[13] For English Christians, the servant (or slave) and master relationship existed because of God's design for the world.

In the sixteenth and seventeenth centuries, English churches maintained that God ordained and appointed societies and families to include the institution of slavery. Church leaders saw this as the plain teaching of Scripture, and to depart from this order would lead to "hellish confusion"—as John Owen put it. The divine appointment of the *institution* of slavery is the conceptual hinge on which all subsequent issues turned. If God ordained slavery, then what remains is not *whether* slavery should be a part of Christian societies, but *how* to enslave people in ways that God approves.

2. SLAVERY IS A RESULT OF SIN

English Christians believed that slavery exists within the providence of God, but they also believed that it does so as a result of sin.

William Perkins provides a good early example of this belief. He discusses the relationship between the fall and slavery in his exposition on Galatians 3:28—"In Christ there is . . . neither slave nor free." He explains that prior to the introduction of sin, before the fall, there was no bondage or slavery; humans were "subject for their own good." After the fall, Perkins argues, "Subjection joined with pain and misery follows upon sin," and sin introduces, "the law of corrupt nature, the fruit whereof is bondage."[14] In his comments on Jude 8, Perkins writes that prior to sin there was a civil order by which "man is subject to another for the common good," but the fall initiated "the subjection of a slave or vassal, who is only to seek the proper good of his lord and master."[15] Perkins states this again in his *Christian Economy*, writing, "[servitude] is indeed against the law of entire nature as it was before the fall, but it is not against the law of corrupted nature since the fall."[16] Thus, Perkins believed there was a pure and righteous version of civil order and hierarchy (being subject to someone else), but after the fall this order was corrupted and ruined, with one form becoming slavery.

William Gouge, like Perkins, believed slavery was against human nature, but after sin was introduced to the world, a human could become a "bond-servant to another." He continued, "God hath turned many punishments of sin to be bounden duties; as subjection of wife to husband, and man's eating bread in the sweat of his brow."[17] A generation later, Puritan Stephen Charnock added, "nothing [is] so contrary to man as to enter into slavery."[18] These English Christians acknowledged that slavery and servitude result from sin.

On August 24, 1703 (when John Wesley was almost two months old and Jonathan Edwards was to be born a little over a month later), the acting president of Harvard, Puritan Samuel Willard, wrote a sermon that addressed the relationship between sin and slavery. "All servitude began in the curse," he wrote, "but it is so ordered in the providence of God, as it becomes beneficial to mankind." He continued, "It is very lawful for some to be masters, and some to be servants in a family. . . . It is therefore a condition, in which God may be glorified; and for that reason we are commanded to use it so."[19] Willard is affirming the first point explained above—that God's providence controls all things, including the existence of slavery in the world, and that slavery is due to sin. Willard concludes that the proper course of action for Christians living in a sinful and fallen world is to operate within those realities.

Leading English Christians justified the institution of slavery as a blight in the midst of God's good and sovereign reign as a result of human sin. Slavery could be a direct consequence for sinning, as Mathew Henry explains regarding Israel's enslavement to the Babylonians during their exile. Commenting on Nehemiah 9:4-38, Henry says, "Poverty and slavery are the fruits of sin; it is sin that brings us into all our distresses."[20] Modern historian David Brion Davis writes, "At the time of America's conquest, the Christian view of slavery . . . was contrary to the ideal realm of nature, but was a necessary part of the world of sin."[21]

The institution of slavery was seen as a form of human subjection to other humans as a result of Adam's sin perpetuated throughout humanity, which will remain until sin is vanquished. Until then, English Christians considered slavery an institution to be managed rather than rejected.

3. SLAVE ACQUISITION WITHIN LIMITS

English Christians believed that Scripture outlined proper and improper ways to acquire slaves. The three ways to acquire slaves were to capture a slave through war, to purchase a person or persons selling themselves, or to buy a slave from someone else.

William Perkins understood two sorts of servants: a free servant and a bondservant. A free servant is one that is hired and paid wages—essentially an employee. A bondservant is "a servant bought for money, and is commonly called a slave."[22] Perkins taught that Christians could own slaves if the local laws permitted the practice, but he said to use the practice "with moderation."[23] Perkins permitted three ways to acquire slaves. First, those "who are overcome in war," because "they are saved from death, they owe all that they have to them by whom they are saved." Second, a person can "make sale of himself to another." Third, a person who is "ransomed from his enemy is bound to serve as a slave in lieu of thankfulness." This means that to buy (ransom) a person from another person is an acceptable way to acquire a slave. Perkins added that servitude should "not [be] procured and retained by force, for it is a more grievous crime to spoil a man of his liberty than of his riches."[24]

Nathaniel Ward and John Cotton were raised in Puritan households. They enrolled at Puritan-friendly Cambridge in 1596 and 1598, respectively. While at Cambridge, they sat under the teaching and ministry of William Perkins. John Cotton emigrated to the Massachusetts Bay Colony in 1633, and the following year Ward joined him. In 1635 the colony formed a committee to draft laws, and two sets emerged, one from Cotton and another from Ward. Cotton's draft provided provisions against "mayming or wounding of a freeman," and that "Man-stealing [was] to be punished with death."[25] Ward's draft of what would become the Massachusetts Body of Liberties in 1641 included a familiar familial structure found in Puritan teaching: liberties of freemen (section three), women (section four), children (section five), and servants (section six). This structure follows the New Testament household codes found in Ephesians 5:21–6:9, Colossians 3:18–4:1, and 1 Peter 2:13–3:7.[26]

English Christians engaged increasingly complicated questions as England formally entered the triangular slave trade in the 1660s. A decade later, Richard Baxter published his *Christian Directory*. His section on family duties follows the traditional Puritan discussion progressing through the roles of husbands and wives (chapters one through nine), parents (chapter ten), children (chapters eleven and twelve), and then masters and servants (chapters thirteen and fourteen). In chapter fourteen, Baxter introduces a topic that is new to the traditional ordering of the Puritan home. After discussing "The Duties of Masters Towards Their Servants," Baxter inserts a section titled, "Directions to Those Masters in Foreign Plantations Who Have Negroes and Other Slaves; Being a Solution of Several Cases About Them."[27] Prior to this time a discussion like this was not pertinent to English people because the roles of servants and bondservants were an established and regulated feature of their society, but the growing emergence of chattel slavery created new questions because of England's direct engagement in the transatlantic slave trade.

Baxter permitted slavery where it was allowed by "the laws of nations."[28] A person may be enslaved "as a punishment for his crimes," or if "a man consent[s] to sell himself," or as an "enemy taken in a lawful war."[29] These acquisition methods echo previous Puritan teaching, but Baxter provided new details that pertain directly to the emerging English slave trade:

> To go as pirates and catch up poor negroes or people of another land, that never forfeited life or liberty, and to make them slaves, and sell them, is one of the worst kinds of thievery in the world; and such persons are to be taken for the common enemies of mankind.[30]

Baxter applied the biblical mandate against man-stealing directly, and for the first time, to the acquisition of Black people as slaves. He says that people engaged in this practice, "are fitter to be called incarnate devils than Christians."[31]

While some people might describe Baxter as antislavery, Baxter is clearly proslavery—he approves of the *institution* of slavery. Baxter approves of slavery within limits. Limited slavery is not antislavery. Limited slavery is not abolitionism. Failing to distinguish between the *institution* of slavery and the *regulation* of slavery is a common fault in both popular and academic discussions of slavery, especially among Christians.

In 1703, New England Puritan Samuel Willard delineated four ways a master could rightfully enslave a person. The first three are the ones we've already established, but the fourth, he adds, is "By natural generation . . . men may be born servants, being descended of such parents as are so."[32] Willard made explicit that the children of enslaved people belong to the slave's master—the children were born enslaved. Around the same time, Whitefield's trusted commentator, Matthew Henry, provided generations of Christians similar explanations about how to acquire slaves.[33]

More details were added around the same time England formally entered the slave trade, beginning in the 1660s. Church leaders began explaining differences between enslaving Christians and non-Christians, they commented on man-stealing (which was well known to occur in Africa and elsewhere), and they recognized the implication that evangelism might threaten ownership of enslaved people.

4. SLAVES MUST OBEY; MASTERS MUST BE TEMPERATE

Once Christians acquired slaves, they believed that slaves ultimately must obey God, and after that, slaves must obey their masters, and that masters must be temperate toward their slaves.

"The State of Matrimony," the homily on marriage from the *Books of Homilies*, explained that a husband should not beat his wife, nor his bondservant. It also reveals the cultural normativity of beating slaves, as it explains that it is vile to "entreat [a wife] like a slave."[34] The final homily, "Against Disobedience and Willful Rebellion," was added to the existing corpus in 1571, following the excommunication of Queen Elizabeth I, because the pope urged the English to rebel against her.[35] This sermon warns against the risks of war, which include "perpetual captivity, slavery."[36] It uses Scripture to explain that it is better for servants to obey their masters, even if masters mistreat their servants.[37] Richard Hooker's sermon "The Nature of Pride" chastised people who treated their "servants as if they were beasts, their inferiors as servants, their equals as inferiors," thus simultaneously rejecting mistreatment of others while affirming hierarchical relationships.[38]

In his *Domestical Duties*, William Gouge devoted forty-one pages to the duties of servants (part seven) and forty-eight pages to the duties of masters (part eight). Gouge recognized a difference between a servant (similar to a paid laborer that lives with a family) and a bond-servant (a person owned by the family), but applies the duties to both cases, and that masters had "more absolute power" over slaves (bond-slaves) than servants.[39] Based on Ephesians 6:5-8, Gouge explained that servants should obey and serve their masters with fear and trembling, singleness of heart, conscience to Christ, cheerfulness, readiness, diligence, and faithfulness.[40] Gouge highlights one word "from whence the duties of servants flow . . . and it is one word 'fear,' which is an awful dread of a master."[41] Gouge warns against excess and extreme use of fear, but only for pragmatic reasons, such as that servants might rebel against their masters or give up and would rather die. Then, based on Ephesians 6:9, Gouge explains that masters are to choose good servants, exercise conscience in using them well, and maintain the master's authority.[42] He instructed masters to provide sufficient (but not excess) food, clothing, rest, recreation, and healthcare. Gouge wrote that masters needed to balance their use of power, especially since God is their ultimate authority.

While Richard Baxter, like Gouge, recognized a difference between servants—of whom there was a "contract with them"—and slaves, Baxter's principal directions for both were the same.[43] He told servants to "murmur not at your labour, or your low condition; but know your mercies, and be thankful for them."[44] He added that servants must work hard (as for God), not steal or be lazy, not tell their masters' secrets, not complain about wanting more food, but to pray often and submit to their masters' religious direction.[45] Baxter told masters, "Remember that in Christ they are your brethren and fellow-servants; and therefore rule them not tyrannically, but in tenderness and love."[46]

At the turn of the eighteenth century, Samuel Willard made similar admonitions.[47] English Christians expected servants and slaves to obey their masters in everything, except anything opposed to God, while masters were to rule with fearful authority while avoiding excess and providing adequately for practical needs. Matthew Henry concurred and provided a succinct summary: servants "may be used, but must not be abused" because "their Master is in heaven; and what will they do when he rises up?"[48] In short, a Christian master's position toward slaves must be to use but not abuse.

5. SLAVES DESERVE SPIRITUAL FREEDOM

One of the ways that masters were to provide for their slaves was by offering spiritual freedom because slaves were to be considered as human as anyone else. English Christians believed that all people had two independent statuses that should not be confused or related: spiritual and earthly. A person could be spiritually dead but within civil society a king or a slave. Similarly, a person could be spiritually alive and also be a king or a slave.

The belief that all people have an earthly status (a role on earth) and a spiritual status (Christian or non-Christian) was the strong consensus among English Christians.[49] This belief motivated them to evangelize all people they encountered without concern for how that evangelism might affect a person's earthly status (social, civil, familial). The implications of this belief became increasingly challenging for English Christians, especially at the lay level, as their participation in the transatlantic slave trade increased in the late seventeenth century.

Two critical concepts were introduced into society around the time the English transatlantic slave trade was beginning to escalate. The first was polygenesis. The second was that baptism (possibly) emancipated servants and slaves from their station in life. (We'll examine the second concept in the next section.)

Polygenesis is the belief that there is more than one human race: *poly* (many) *genesis* (origin/production). Monogenesis is the traditional Christian belief that the entire human race originates from one (*mono*) source. Acts 17:26, where Paul says that God "has made of one blood all nations of men," is typically enlisted to support the well-established orthodox Christian view of the unified origin of the human race. French theologian Isaac de la Peyrére introduced the theory of polygenesis to Christianity in 1665 as a way to explain the discoveries of numerous people groups in undiscovered lands in the fifteenth and sixteenth centuries.

Morgan Godwyn, a Church of England minister, served in the English colonies of Virginia and Barbados beginning in 1665. Upon his return to England in 1680, he published a scathing 174-page book titled *The Negro's and Indians Advocate, suing for their admission to the church, or, A persuasive to the instructing and baptizing of the Negro's and Indians in our plantations*. Godwyn explained that he encountered enslavers who justified their trade because, "they strain hard to derive our Negroes from a stock different from Adam's. . . . [They] infer their Negroes brutality; justify their reduction of them under bondage; disable them from all rights and claims, even to religion itself."[50] The surge in English enslavement of Black people occurred at the same time as the introduction of the racist and anti-Christian ideology of polygenesis. Godwyn observed that English slaveholders used this concept to withhold Christianity from Black people because they believed in their innate incapacity for salvation.

A close look at the writings of Cotton Mather exposes many of the English Christians' tensions regarding slavery. Mather is especially helpful to examine because he was born a generation before Edwards,

Whitefield, and Wesley; he provides a timely look into their world. Mather's first name, Cotton, honors his grandfather John Cotton, who was educated at Cambridge, emigrated to the Massachusetts Bay Colony in 1633, and helped form the proslavery Massachusetts Body of Liberties. Cotton Mather was one of the most celebrated New England writers of his day and a founder of Yale University. Like Edwards, he was a Congregational minister and a Puritan, with roots in the nonconformist tradition. Mather subscribed to the Puritan ideal of household governance by parents of children and servants. He illustrated this approach in his 1699 work *A Family Well-Ordered*.[51]

In 1698, Mather wrote *A Pastoral Letter to the English Captives, in Africa, from New England*, in which he addresses 203 English people captured and enslaved by Barbary pirates in Morocco.[52] This was a common occurrence from the sixteenth to the nineteenth century by Barbary pirates—Muslim captors operating along the Mediterranean coast. In this letter he tells his fellow Englishmen to stand strong in their Christian faith (not to convert to Islam) and explains that their enslavement is "by the providence of God put upon you."[53] Five years later, in his work *The Glory of Goodness*, Mather celebrates the escape of these people from their Muslim enslavers.[54] Scholar Richard Fowler comments that "nowhere in *The Glory of Goodness* does an explanation appear for why slavery is an injustice when suffered by White New England sailors but is acceptable practice to inflict on Black Africans."[55]

Fowler's point is taken, but what Fowler fails to take into account is how Mather understands the role of servant and slave in the scheme of the Christian household. Mather likely would have little reluctance if the 203 English people had been made servants or slaves in a *Christian* household—Mather was upset that Christians were made servants and slaves in *Muslim* households. This distinction helps us understand the English Christian mindset Wesley, Edwards, and Whitefield were born into—the role of servant or slave is a God-given station in life; the issue is the proper *Christian management* (including the Christian nurture) of servants and slaves, not the *institution* of servanthood or slavery itself.

Mather believed that all people, including Black people and Indians, are descendants of Adam, have souls, and deserve spiritual opportunity. Mather opened his 1706 work *The Negro Christianized* by writing, "An opportunity there is in your hands, O all of you that have any Negroes in your houses; an opportunity to try . . . of converting, the blackest instances of blindness and baseness, into admirable candidates of eternal blessedness."[56] Mather explained that people of all colors are human, adding, "The biggest part of mankind, perhaps, are copper-colored." Additionally, he wrote, "The God who looks at the heart, is not moved by the color of the skin, is not more propitious to one color than another."[57] This work concludes with a three-question "Shorter Catechism for the Negros of a small capacity." The first question asks, "Who made you and all the world?" and answers, "The Great God made me, to serve him."[58]

Mather's own household attests to his belief in the propriety of enslaving Black people within a Christian household. In June 1706, Mather published *The Negro Christianized*, of which he hoped "every family of New England, which has a Negro" would have, but also those in the [West] Indies.[59] Six months later, Mather opened his diary and wrote:

> This day, a surprising thing befell me. Some gentlemen of our church, understanding (without any application of mine to them for such a thing), that I wanted a good servant at the expense of between forty and fifty pounds, purchased for me, a very likely slave; a young man, who is a Negro of a very promising aspect and temper, and this day they presented him to me . . . I put upon him the name of Onesimus; and I resolved with the help of the Lord, that I would use the best endeavors to make him a servant of Christ.[60]

Over the next ten years, Mather struggled with Onesimus's behavior. In July 1716, Mather recorded in his journal, "My servant Onesimus, proves wicked, and grows useless." Mather wrote of "my disposing of him, and my supplying of my family with a better servant."[61] Mather allowed Onesimus to buy his release, and Mather used the money to enslave a Black boy he named Obadiah.[62]

Mather, the prominent minister and educator who "wrote the book" on how to Christianize enslaved Black people, was unable to do so himself. Yet Mather's efforts illustrate his belief, following his Puritan tradition, of the responsibility and possibility of converting slaves and Black people to Christianity. The English Christians that Wesley, Whitefield, and Edwards followed believed that all humans, regardless of their skin color or station in life, deserved to hear the gospel, respond to it, and grow in their faith.

6. SLAVE CONVERSION DOES NOT EMANCIPATE

The preface to the 1662 edition of the *Book of Common Prayer* explains that the adult baptismal rite was added because of the rise of Anabaptism (i.e., those who had been persuaded to forgo infant baptism), and also because it "is now become necessary, and may be always useful for the baptizing of Natives in our Plantations and others converted to the Faith."[63]

English Christians generally believed that spiritual and social statuses were separate categories, and thus baptism did not emancipate a slave. Yet during the rise of the English slave trade in the late seventeenth century, a growing number of English slave owners began excluding their slaves from being exposed to Christianity, in part because of anxiety that becoming a Christian, formally marked through baptism, would change their civil status from slave to freeperson.

This belief that baptism would emancipate slaves may have stemmed from the Old Testament teaching that the Hebrews were not to own another Hebrew as a slave, but only as hired workers (Leviticus 25:39-43) and that they were to be released after six years (Exodus 21:2; Deuteronomy 15:12). The concern was that if a slave was baptized as a Christian, the slave then was no longer a foreigner, but a peer as a Christian—akin to being a fellow Hebrew spiritually.[64]

Richard Baxter's 1673 *Christian Directory*, as discussed earlier, captured this worry:

> Those therefore that keep their negroes and slaves from hearing
> God's Word, and from becoming Christians, because by the law
> they shall then be either made free, or they shall lose part of their
> service, do openly profess rebellion against God, and contempt of
> Christ the Redeemer of souls, and a contempt of the souls of men,
> and indeed they declare, that their worldly profit is their treasure
> and their God.[65]

Baxter condemned those who withheld the gospel from their
slaves because they feared they would lose their "profit." Emancipation of slaves upon baptism was not the law of the land, but Baxter
hoped it would be. He wrote, "It is therefore well done of princes who
make laws that infidel-slaves shall be freemen, when they are duly
Christened."[66] Baxter is an outlier among English theologians on
this topic.

In 1680, Morgan Godwyn wrote against slave owners' "refusal of the
Christianizing of their slaves."[67] Godwyn wrote that slave owners made
the "common affirmation, that the baptizing of their Negroes is the
ready way to have all their throats cut . . . without any great show of
reason to make it out."[68] He encountered masters who claimed that if
they let their slaves be baptized, the slaves would consider themselves
equal to their masters and, in turn, kill them. Godwyn had not heard
any reports of baptized slaves attacking their masters, but he highlighted an instance quite the opposite. He recalled a story of a slave that
received "baptism upon a Sunday morning at his parish church." When
his overseer found out about his baptism, it "cost [the slave] an afternoon baptism in blood . . . as in the morning he had received a
baptism with water."[69]

Godwyn believed that the Bible upheld the institution of slavery. He
wrote, "Bondage is not inconsistent with Christianity."[70] But he was per-
plexed at the slaveholder's worries because he insisted that Scripture

taught that Christians slaves were instructed to obey their masters—a Christian slave should be expected to be *more* obedient upon baptism. Further, Godwyn cited laws in Virginia and Maryland that explicitly stated that baptism did not affect the status of the enslaved.[71] Godwyn wrote another tract the following year against those who "refused to make their Negro's Christians."[72]

Cotton Mather understood that Christian enslavers were worried that "if the Negroes are Christianized, they will be baptized; and their baptism will presently entitle them to their freedom; so our money is thrown away."[73] To this claim, Mather responded:

> But it is all a Mistake. There is no such thing. What law is it that sets the baptized slave at liberty? Not the law of Christianity: that allows of slavery; only it wonderfully dulcifies, and modifies, and moderates the circumstances of it. Christianity directs a slave, upon his embracing the law of the Redeemer, to satisfy himself, that he is the Lords free-man, tho' he continues a slave. . . . The baptized then are not thereby entitled to their liberty.[74]

Godwyn and Mather were not alone among English Christians in denying that baptism emancipated slaves. In the early eighteenth century, the Church of England and the Society for the Propagation of the Gospel in Foreign Parts (SPG) agreed that baptism did not alter earthly status.[75] Yet hesitancy to evangelize slaves remained.

Slavery in the era of Wesley, Edwards, and Whitefield was largely race-based physical exploitation which often withheld Christian instruction for fear of rebellion or emancipation. Many English Christians attempted to confront the violence, lack of access to Christianity, and unjust acquisition of slaves while being blind to the racial nature of slavery. English Christians believed that slavery was ordained by God; that it existed due to the realities of an unavoidably sinful world, in which slaves could be acquired by certain biblically permitted means; and that slaves were to obey their masters, and masters were to treat their slaves "ethically." English Christians sought to return to what they

understood as a proper biblical approach to slavery while not considering the propriety of the institution of slavery itself.

We now focus our attention on Wesley, Edwards, and Whitefield. It's
worth stopping to ask two questions. First, given that they were born
in this situation, how would you expect them to think about slavery?
Second, how would you think about slavery if you had been born in
this era?

PART 2

PARTICIPATION

PARTICIPATING IN SOCIETY

5

WESLEY IN GEORGIA

ENCOUNTERS SLAVERY

I WOKE UP IN SAVANNAH, GEORGIA, early one Sunday morning to drive to a small church at the end of a back road. I stopped at a Waffle House for their famous All-Star Special. Stuffed, I drove farther and farther into the woods. Near the end of the road, a little sign appeared in the distance. As I drove closer, the church sign came near enough to read:

Jerusalem Lutheran Church

Organized in 1734

Built in 1767–69

Sunday School 9:45 a.m.

Worship Service 11:00 a.m.

After a vibrant service, Robert Peavy, assistant curator of the living history museum next to their church, gave me an unscheduled and in-depth three-hour personal tour. Inside the museum, I sat on a creaky wooden pew older than my grandparents. The ancient wooden walls of the museum reverberated with Robert's voice as he sang for me a few verses of the Salzburger "Exile Song" with unrestrained gusto. After the tour, we walked the grounds outside and headed down toward the river, where they have a rustic yet functional meeting area with an old rugged cross on a dirt stage under a canopy of cypress trees. Mr. Peavy kindly offered to take a picture of me behind the weathered outdoor wooden pulpit. That's when he said, "Sean, right behind you is the Savannah River, and on the other side of the river is South Carolina."

I still think about that moment. The river was wide, but not too wide. I could have thrown a ball across it. In the 1730s and 1740s that gap—that river—made a world of difference for Black people.

GEORGIA: THE SOLE COLONY (INITIALLY) WITHOUT SLAVERY

The Colony of Georgia, chartered in England in 1732 and established in Savannah in 1733, was the thirteenth and final English colony of what was known as British America—with one major distinction. Georgia was the *only* colony established that outlawed slavery from its inception. On first impression, we might say, "Yes, something for Americans to be proud of." But that would be a mistake.

On June 9, 1732, King George II approved a charter for a colony, politely named for him: *Georgia*. The charter was designed for "many of our poor subjects . . . but also strengthen our colonies and increase the trade . . . [because] our provinces in North America have been frequently ravaged by Indian enemies; more especially that of South Carolina . . . the whole southern frontier continueth unsettled, and lieth open."[1] England placed Georgia under the care of a group called the "Trustees for establishing the Colony of Georgia in America," the same group that initiated the charter. One of the trustees was the Reverend John Burton.

On January 9, 1734, Burton and the other trustees brought before the king "An Act for rendering the Colony of Georgia more Defensible by Prohibiting the Importation and use of Black Slaves or Negroes into the same," also known as the "Negro Act."[2] The king approved the trustees' request on April 3, 1735, along with two other key requests for Georgia: first, no un-approved trade with American Indians; second, no rum; and third, no slaves.

The trustees learned from other colonies that they needed to regulate trade because colonists were taking advantage of and infuriating the American Indians.[3] The trustees prohibited rum (and brandies) because they wanted to curb drunkenness among the British and the American

Indians.[4] The trustees prohibited hard liquors, yet ale, beer, and wine were staples of strategic importance for the colony. In 1738, James Oglethorpe, one of the trustees, wrote to the others, "We want beer extremely. I brought over twenty tons of beer, which I believe will be gone before I can receive a supply . . . since beer's being cheap is the only means to keep rum out of the colony."[5]

The third appeal of the trustees was to outlaw slavery in Georgia. The reasons Georgia initially outlawed slavery are crucial to understand—laws are often only as strong as the rationale on which they are founded. The primary reason the trustees outlawed slavery was due to the threat of war with Spanish Florida. They believed that only non-slaves would be compelled to defend the British colony of Georgia, and they worried that slaves might join forces against their enslavers. They envisioned a colony with no Black people at all. The Negro Act says, "all and every black or blacks negroe or negroes which shall at any time then after be found in the said Province of Georgia . . . shall and may be seized and taken . . . and are hereby declared to be the sole property of and to belong only to the said trustees and their successors and shall and may be exported [and] sold."[6] The trustees equated Black people with slaves: Black people were slaves, and slaves were Black people. If any Black person was seen in Georgia, they would be apprehended by the colony of Georgia and sold elsewhere.

This provision was intended to defend Georgia from an African revolt, and from war with Spanish Florida. Further, the geographic location of Georgia served as a buffer for the other English colonies (which were all to the north), so that a slave from any other colony that fled southward to Florida would be immediately identified in Georgia as a runaway and apprehended—the Negro Act made this reason explicit.[7] On April 3, 1735, the king and his court stated, "His Majesty . . . is hereby pleased . . . to declare his approbation of the said act [and it is] hereby confirmed finally enacted and ratified accordingly."[8]

It is difficult to reconcile the motto taken up by the trustees for the colony of Georgia, *non sibi sed aliis* (not for self, but for others), when the *self* and *others* they had in mind were only White people.

GEORGIA: WE NEED MINISTERS AND EVANGELISM

The entire initial Georgia Board of Trustees was composed of men from a group called Doctor Bray's Associates.[9] This association carried out the vision of the Reverend Dr. Thomas Bray, an Oxford-educated Anglican minister who founded the Society for the Promotion of Christian Knowledge (SPCK) and the Society for the Propagation of the Gospel in Foreign Parts (SPG). When Bray became ill in his final years, he established a group of "associates" to carry out his initiatives and vision.

In 1710, Christopher Codrington, a wealthy English plantation owner in Barbados, died and left the SPG two plantations and several hundred slaves.[10] The SPG had been attempting to convince slave owners that they should not fear the evangelization and baptism of slaves; instead, they argued that Christianizing their slaves would result in harder-working and more obedient slaves. The SPG saw their inheritance of the Codrington plantations and slaves as an opportunity to showcase their approach as an example for other slaveholders. Yet from 1717 to 1726, the SPG failed to convert even one person among their slaves in Barbados. In 1732, a Codrington attorney recommended that the SPG stop branding the chests of newly purchased slaves with the letters *S-O-C-I-E-T-Y*. Should it surprise us that newly enslaved Africans were not keen to respond to the Christian gospel when their chests were scabbed over and permanently marked with shorthand for their new owners: the *SOCIETY* for the propagation of the gospel? David Brion Davis concludes, "Instead of providing a model for others to follow, the agents of the SPG conformed to whatever local policies and usages seemed to promise the greatest profits."[11]

The first minister the trustees sent to Georgia became sick and died. A minister named Samuel Quincy contacted the SPG to be a missionary "in the plantations" (probably in the SPG's work in the Caribbean), but they suggested he go to Georgia to fill the unexpected opening instead. Upon arrival, he became sick, encountered other difficulties, and made plans to leave Georgia.[12]

Around this time, in mid-1734, leading trustee James Oglethorpe traveled back to England with Chief Tomochichi and a small party of his tribe, the Yamacraw Indians, who lived in the area near the Georgian colonists. Tomochichi had taken an interest in Christianity and furthering relationships with the English. During the trip, Tomochichi and his group met with the archbishop of Canterbury, King George II, and other church leaders. After this trip, Georgia gained support for not just one individual minister but, instead, a group of ministers to be sent to Georgia.

GEORGIA CALLS JOHN WESLEY AND OTHERS

The search for ministers for Georgia was accelerating. By November 1734, Oglethorpe and Samuel Wesley, John's father, began corresponding about mission work in Georgia. Samuel Wesley lamented that he was too old for such a task but recommended not his son John Wesley, but his son-in-law John Whitelamb for the job. Samuel died a few months later, and Whitelamb did not go to Georgia.

At the same time, Oxford professor, SPG member, and Georgia trustee the Reverend John Burton took notice of the members of the Holy Club as people well suited for the difficult work needed in Georgia. On August 28, 1735, Burton recruited John Wesley for Georgia and ten days later wrote to Wesley more details about ministering there. Later that month, Burton wrote, "One end for which we were associated was the conversion of negro slaves. As yet nothing has been attempted in this way. But a door has been opened, and not far from home. The Purrysburgers have purchased slaves; they act under our influence, and Mr. Oglethorpe will think it advisable to begin there."[13] In this letter Burton indicates what we saw earlier: his advocacy for the conversion of slaves, rather than keeping them from Christianity, as was the approach of other slave owners. At this time, Georgia had outlawed slaves, so Burton mentions evangelism opportunities in Purrysburg, a small settlement about twenty miles from Savannah, across the border in South Carolina, where slavery was legal.

In Wesley's response to Burton, Wesley does not address the topic of slavery. His focus is on his own salvation and evangelizing the Native Americans.[14] While Wesley was in America, he spent only a short time in South Carolina. Part of Burton and Oglethorpe's recruitment of Wesley included evangelization of enslaved Africans; Wesley was not ignorant of the details surrounding English enslavement of Africans.

Less than two months after being recruited by Burton and Oglethorpe, John Wesley boarded the *Simmonds* for Savannah, along with his brother Charles and two other members of the Holy Club, Benjamin Ingham and Charles Delamotte. At eight in the morning on Friday, February 6, 1735, they stepped on American ground in Georgia and kneeled down to thank God. The next morning at 7:45 a.m. they smashed the barrels of rum aboard the ship—abiding by the new laws of Georgia.[15]

WESLEY'S FIRST ENCOUNTER WITH SLAVES—AUGUST 1736

When Wesley and his companions arrived in Georgia, less than a thousand people had been sent to the colony, with only 518 people living in Savannah shortly thereafter.[16] The leading occupation of the people of Georgia during that time was "servant."[17] Though slavery was formally outlawed in Georgia, the English social classes remained a prominent feature in colonial Georgia.

For instance, a man named Walter Thomas arrived in Georgia a year after Wesley. Thomas's profession was listed as "servant."[18] Other interesting anecdotes of these people provide snapshots of Wesley's realities. A man named Patrick Mackay came to Georgia fleeing Scotland due to a felony charge. The trustees provided Mackay five hundred acres of land on September 3, 1735, where he "keeps serv[ants] on it." The note adds, "But has also a planation on the Carolina side of the River Savannah, on which he keeps Negroes, which is of bad example to our Planters."[19] A later complaint, and one that increased, was that there were not enough servants to do the work needed in Georgia.[20] Wesley did not encounter slaves in Georgia, but he did when he crossed the Carolina border, just a few miles north of Savannah. Georgia, in theory,

had no Black people, while in South Carolina Black people outnum-
bered White people by well over two to one.[21]

John's brother Charles, upon his arrival in Georgia, struggled immediately with his health and working relationship with Oglethorpe.
Charles resigned and headed to Charleston, South Carolina, accom-
panied by John, where he tried to find passage to England.

John preached the day after he and his brother arrived in Charleston.
In his journal he wrote, "I was glad to see several Negroes at church."[22]
John Wesley encountered an African slave in America for the first time
that day. Wesley served Communion to about fifty people and "one
Negro woman."[23] He described an encounter with an African woman
in terms of her knowledge of Christianity—he was silent regarding the
institution of slavery.

The next day he hoped to visit the plantation of a Mr. Skene, who was
the first planter to allow SPG missionaries to evangelize his slaves. This
was one of the purposes for which the trustees had recruited John. He
believed there were now fifty "Christian Negroes" on the property, but did
not have time that day to visit the Skene plantation.[24] A leading historian
of Wesley's time in Georgia says, "Wesley's comments on slavery are rather
bare at this point; he seems to be more interested in the spiritual state of
these individuals rather than their legal or physical state.... [It] represents
a missed opportunity to oppose an institution that he later condemned."[25]

John's purpose for traveling to South Carolina was to accompany his
brother Charles for his departure back to England. John was with his
brother until at least August 4.[26] It is curious that John does not
comment on what Charles records in his own diary on August 2, which
I quote at length due to the level of detail—it is difficult to imagine that
John was unaware of these specifics. Charles wrote,

> I had observed much, and heard more, of the cruelty of masters
> towards their negroes; but now I received an authentic account of
> some horrid instances thereof. The giving a child a slave of its own
> age to tyrannize over, to beat and abuse out of sport, was, I myself

saw, a common practice. Nor is it strange, being thus trained up in cruelty, they should afterwards arrive at so great perfection in it; that Mr. Star, a gentleman I often met at Mr. Lasserre's, should, as he himself informed L., first nail up a negro by the ears, then order him to be whipped in the severest manner, and then to have scalding water thrown over him, so that the poor creature could not stir for four months after. Another much-applauded punishment is drawing their slaves' teeth. One Colonel Lynch is universally known to have cut off a poor negro's legs, and to kill several of them every year by his barbarities.

It were endless to recount all the shocking instances of diabolical cruelty which these men (as they call themselves) daily practice upon their fellow creatures; and that on the most trivial occasions. I shall only mention one more, related to me by a Swiss gentleman, Mr. Zouberbuhler, an eye-witness, of Mr. Hill, a dancing-master in Charlestown. He whipped a she-slave so long, that she fell down at his feet for dead. When, by the help of a physician, she was so far recovered as to show signs of life, he repeated the whipping with equal rigour, and concluded with dropping hot sealing-wax upon her flesh. Her crime was overfilling a tea-cup.

These horrid cruelties are the less to be wondered at, because the government itself, in effect, countenances and allows them to kill their slaves, by the ridiculous penalty appointed for it, of about seven pounds sterling, half of which is usually saved by the criminal's informing against himself. This I can look upon as no other than a public act to indemnify murder.[27]

John Wesley rejected slavery thirty-eight years later, in 1774. We must recognize here that when Wesley first encountered slavery face-to-face on August 1, 1736, his comments reveal that he spent his energies on evangelism while the injustice of slavery stared him right in his face. He missed it. His enthusiasm for evangelism blinded him to the evil institution in front of him.

Wesley made a small note in his private diary less than two weeks after his arrival back in Georgia. On August 20 from 11:15 a.m. to 1:45 p.m. he read *Negro's Advocate*.[28] This refers to Anglican minister Morgan Godwyn's 1680 publication cited in chapter four, titled: *The Negro's and Indians Advocate, suing for their admission to the church, or, A persuasive to the instructing and baptizing of the Negro's and Indians in our plantations . . .* This work focuses on the necessity of evangelizing enslaved people. The timing of Wesley's first encounter with enslaved people and his reading of Godwyn does not seem unrelated and is an extension of Wesley's focus on evangelization, it is not a reflection of any interest in challenging the institution of slavery itself.

Two months later, from November 18 to December 1, Wesley read more works by SPG associates that stressed the importance of evangelizing enslaved people. None of Wesley's reading or writing at this time challenged the institution of slavery. His interest was evangelizing slaves, not liberating them.[29]

WESLEY'S SECOND ENCOUNTER WITH SLAVES—APRIL 1737

On April 12, 1737, Wesley made his second and most extensive trip across the Savannah River into slaveholding South Carolina, to meet with Anglican clergy. After arriving and preaching in Charleston, Wesley read Cotton Mather's "Epistle to the Christian Indians"—a fourteen-page evangelistic document urging Native Americans to respond to the gospel.[30]

On his way back to Savannah, Wesley stopped at Reverend Thompson's house the following day in Ponpon, South Carolina, Wesley met "a young Negro there, who seemed more sensible than the rest," her name being Nanny.[31]

Wesley learned that Nanny had grown up from childhood as the slave of a minister in the English colony of Barbados but had been in Carolina for two or three years. Nanny grew up going to church every Sunday "to carry my mistress's children." When Wesley asked her what she learned at church, she replied, "Nothing: I heard a [great] deal, but did not understand it." When Wesley asked her what her minister-enslaver and mistress taught her at home, she replied, "Nothing."

Remember, Nanny had grown up in Barbados during the same time the Church of England empowered the Society for the Propagation for the Gospel to brand their slaves on their chests with *S-O-C-I-E-T-Y*. Wesley engaged Nanny in a conversation about God as Creator of heaven and earth. He told her, "He made you to live with himself in the sky. And so you will, in a little time—if you are good. If you are good, when your body dies your soul will go up, and want nothing, and have whatever you desire." Wesley continued his gospel promises by saying, "No one will beat or hurt you there."[32]

Wesley's diary indicates that he talked with Nanny for one hour that night and over two hours the following night.[33] The encounter shows that Wesley was well aware of the physical abuse and suffering of enslaved Black people, but instead of challenging the institution, he tried to leverage it as an evangelistic tool. His sole concern was Nanny's spiritual salvation.

Wesley traveled farther south and made it to Hugh Bryant's plantation for dinner. Nearly forty years later in his *Thoughts upon Slavery*, Wesley mentioned Bryant:

> Have you tried what mildness and gentleness would do? I knew one that did; that had prudence and patience to make the experiment; Mr. Hugh Bryan[t], who then lived on the borders of South Carolina. And what was the effect? Why, that all his Negroes (and he had no small number of them) loved and reverenced him as a father, and cheerfully obeyed him out of love. Yea, they were more afraid of a frown from him, than of many blows from an overseer.[34]

Wesley's time on Bryant's plantation, which had many enslaved people, left a positive impression on Wesley—so positive that Wesley included it in his (eventual) antislavery tract! Wesley commends Bryant for not mistreating his slaves, which sadly shows that such behavior must have been unusual—especially in contrast to Charles Wesley's reports. Yet John's compliment of Bryant affirms, at minimum, Wesley's residual support for the *institution* of slavery even late in his life.

Wesley traveled farther south to a plantation at Tillifinny and met "an old Negro who was tolerably well instructed in the principles of Christianity . . . and who, as well as his fellow Negroes and a half-Indian woman, seemed earnestly desirous . . . of further instruction." The man explained that in his previous location he had gone to church every Sunday, but now was too far away from a church to attend. He said, "if there was any church within five or six miles, I can't walk, but I would crawl hither."[35]

Wesley also met another Black person who was "capable and desirous of instruction." Wesley's mind hummed not with considerations for the plight of their enslavement, but with strategies for evangelism.

> I can't but think, the easiest and shortest way to propagate Christianity among the American Negroes would be, first, to find out some of the most serious planters, and then, having inquired which of their slaves were best inclined, to go to them from plantation to plantation, teaching some to read, and instructing others without, as in particular cases should appear most expedient.[36]

The following day Wesley returned to Savannah, concluding his second trip to South Carolina and the closest he ever came face-to-face with slavery in his life.

WESLEY RETURNS TO GEORGIA AND FLEES AMERICA

Wesley returned to Savannah and continued his ministry just as he had before his trip to South Carolina. With his brother gone, the mission in Georgia needed further ministerial assistance. The person who emerged to fill this gap was Wesley's Holy Club protégé, George Whitefield.

When Wesley returned to his ministry in Georgia he also returned to a growing and problematic personal issue: his broken heart for a young woman named Sophy Hopkey. It is a complicated and sad tale. Shortly after arriving in Georgia, Wesley had become romantically involved with Hopkey but had dragged his feet. Hopkey got fed up with Wesley and within a week became engaged to another man and married him in March 1737. This fiasco occurred shortly before Wesley's second trip to South Carolina—in fact he went there to confront the clergy there, since Hopkey had eloped with her new husband in South Carolina.

In August 1737, Wesley denied Hopkey and her husband Communion and got himself in deep trouble: Hopkey's husband brought charges against Wesley for defaming their reputations. The charges sought £1000 in damages—twenty times Wesley's annual salary. By the end of November, tensions spilled over, and Wesley snuck out of town after evening prayers. He headed north toward Charleston, South Carolina, for his third trip into the slave colony, getting lost in the woods and swamps, but finally arriving safely. On December 22, 1737, he boarded the *Samuel* for England and never returned to America.

Wesley was not the only person preparing to cross the Atlantic. He would soon cross paths with George Whitefield. Whitefield's time in Georgia would be quite different from Wesley's.

Prior to his time in the American colonies, Wesley knew of slavery, but when he came face-to-face with it, he doubled down on his efforts to evangelize enslaved people. While Wesley's participation in slavery at home in England and abroad in the colonies constituted a failure to engage the injustice of the institution of slavery, we will see that Whitefield participated in slavery in much more direct ways.

6

WHITEFIELD IN GEORGIA

ENCOUNTERS SLAVERY AND ENSLAVES OTHERS

WE ALL FACE MOMENTS when we encounter something that reveals our previously dormant beliefs. The days, months, and years after these encounters often show us many things about us—some of which we like, others that we regret, and still others that are a bit of both. George Whitefield faced a moment like this on May 7, 1738, when he took his first step in Savannah, Georgia. Every step after that revealed more and more of what he really believed about race, culture, class, the Bible, and Christianity.

Less than two years later, Whitefield announced his plans to purchase Black people as his slaves. Three decades later, Whitefield listed his "assets" in his will and to whom he would give them, including the forty-nine people he enslaved. What had lain dormant in his beliefs was now in plain sight.

WHITEFIELD CALLED TO GEORGIA

George Whitefield was twenty-two years old, and his life was changing quickly. A year earlier, Whitefield had been a lonely and sickly college student hoping with all his heart to simply be sure of his personal salvation. His closest friends and mentors from the Holy Club had left him to travel across the Atlantic and minister in Georgia. George received updates from them and determined that if they needed him, he was ready to help. But he heard nothing back—at first. So Whitefield

took holy orders as a deacon and filled in for two months as the minister at the Tower of London, preaching only once. While there, he
received another letter from Georgia which "made him long to go
abroad for God."[1]

Transatlantic communication was slow in the eighteenth century,
and Whitefield didn't know what had happened over in the colonies.
But things were happening that would alter his life forever. Charles
Wesley, frustrated with his job and his health, departed Georgia while
Whitefield was sitting in the Tower of London wondering about his
future. Charles's departure created a void that increased the need for
another minister in Georgia.

After completing his time in London, Whitefield moved to the lowly,
overlooked rural town of Dummer, southwest of London, to fill another
role as a temporary minister. Then, in early December, Whitefield and
his friends received a remarkable letter from John Wesley, sent from
across the Atlantic three months earlier:

> Do you seek means of building up yourselves in the knowledge
> and love of God? I call the God whom we serve to witness, I know
> of no place under heaven where there are more, or perhaps so
> many, as in this place. Does your heart burn within you to turn
> many others to righteousness? Behold, the whole land, thousands
> of thousands, are before you! I will resign to any of you all or any
> part of my charge. Choose what seemeth good in your own eyes.
> Here are within these walls children of all ages and dispositions.
> Who will bring them up in the nurture and admonition of the
> Lord, till they are meet to be preachers of righteousness? Here are
> adults from the farthest parts of Europe and Asia, and the inmost
> kingdoms of Africa. Add to these the known and unknown na-
> tives of this vast continent, and you will have a great number
> which no man can [count].[2]

John Wesley's plea was full of promises and adventure in which
Whitefield had already expressed interest, and it made his ho-hum

ministry in Dummer pale in comparison. Notice too that John high-lighted adults from "the inmost kingdoms of Africa" now in America. Charles Wesley, now in England, told Whitefield that he was seeking laborers for Georgia.

To cap it off, Whitefield received another letter that month from John Wesley: "Only Delamotte is with me, till God shall stir up the hearts of some of his servants, who, putting their lives in their hands, shall come over and help us, where the harvest is so great, and the labourers so few. What if thou are the man, Whitefield?" The Wesley brothers did every-thing they could to get Whitefield to go to Georgia. Whitefield wrote, "I at length resolved within myself to embark for Georgia."[3] But it didn't happen quickly.

Whitefield departed Dummer and made his way to his hometown of Gloucester. While there, he began preaching more regularly and, in his words, "began to grow a little popular."[4] Whitefield's friends began asking him if he might stay in England, instead of going to Georgia, since he was drawing increasingly large crowds to his sermons. He declined, saying, "none of these things moved me." He made his way to London to be interviewed by James Oglethorpe and the trustees of Georgia.

When Whitefield arrived in London in March 1737, he passed a strict examination by the trustees and waited to join Oglethorpe on his next trip to Georgia. While he was waiting for Oglethorpe, Whitefield preached. The more he preached, the more people came. Due to popular demand, Whitefield began printing his sermons—they quickly became bestsellers. Whitefield was growing into a sensation, preaching nine times a week. He leveraged his popularity to raise funds for the people of Georgia before finally departing for Georgia on December 28, 1737.

WHITEFIELD'S DREAM: AN ORPHANAGE

The idea of an orphanage in Georgia originated with the Georgia trustees. Transatlantic travel and the difficult circumstances of the Georgian colony took the lives of many of its first colonists, leaving many children orphaned. Progress was slow in Savannah, in part due

to the number of orphan children.[5] The trustees asked Charles Wesley
to "draw up a scheme for an Orphan-house" on November 2, 1737.[6] Five
days later Wesley opened his copy of *Pietas Hallensis* and "desired our
Orphan-house might be begun in the power of faith."[7]

In 1695, August Herman Francke, a German Lutheran minister and
theologian, had founded an orphanage in Halle, Germany. In 1701, he
wrote *Pietas Hallensis: An Historical Narration of the Wonderful Foot-
steps of Divine Providence in Erecting, Carrying On, and Building the
Orphan House.* The Holy Club long admired Francke's book and his
orphan-house. The Wesleys read Francke's account in 1734 and Whitefield read it in 1736. Later, when Whitefield arrived in Georgia in 1738,
he befriended a group of German pietists who had established a community named Ebenezer near Savannah; this group was connected to
the Francke Foundation from Halle, Germany. Many years later Whitefield reflected on Francke's orphanage, "whose memory is very precious
to me, and whose example has a thousand times been blessed to
strengthen and encourage me in the carrying on this enterprize."[8]

While the orphanage wasn't originally Whitefield's idea, it became
his passion. Before he departed America, he explained to the trustees
that he "resolved, in the strength of God, to prosecute it with all my
might."[9] Whitefield went on to call the orphanage his "darling" and his
"beloved Bethesda."[10]

Whitefield knew from the start that his first trip would be brief because he was only yet a deacon in the Church of England. In order to
exercise all the duties of a minister, such as presiding over the sacraments, he would need to be ordained a priest under the hands of a
bishop—all of whom were in England. Thus Whitefield's purpose for
his first journey was to survey what was needed in Georgia before returning to England.

Whitefield's long-term intentions for the orphanage were clear
before his first trip. Colonists in Georgia had been requesting a schoolmaster since late 1736. Whitefield recruited one of his recent converts,
a London merchant named James Habersham, to be schoolmaster for

his orphanage. Whitefield convinced the trustees to pay for Habersham's travel. When Whitefield headed back to England for his ordination and to raise financial support for the orphanage, he left Habersham in Georgia.

Whitefield returned to England and found himself much more of a celebrity than when he left. His previous preaching and publishing had increased the public's curiosity, as well as the ire of many ministers—which served to create even more public interest. While thousands flocked to hear his preaching, some churches rescinded their offers and denied him their pulpits. Whitefield responded by taking his preaching outdoors. This tactic created audiences that weren't limited by building size and served to make him increasingly famous (with common people) and infamous (with church leaders).

Whitefield used these opportunities to raise money for his fledgling orphanage. Six months after his return to London, the trustees granted Whitefield five hundred acres for the orphanage, after which he made his plans to return to Georgia—eventually. Instead of traveling directly from England to Georgia, Whitefield traveled from England to Pennsylvania and preached his way southward, requesting donations along the way for the orphanage.

Whitefield arrived in Savannah in January 1740 and examined the progress Habersham had made in his absence. Habersham had secured the five-hundred-acre plot, begun clearing the land, and started building the orphanage. He showed Whitefield the site on January 24, and Whitefield said, "I called it Bethesda, that is, the House of Mercy,"[11] the English translation of the Aramaic word *Bethesda*. Because the house was not completed, Whitefield rented a large house in Savannah and began housing orphans there.

When Whitefield laid the ceremonial first brick of the great house at his orphanage on March 25, he wrote, "Nearly forty children are now under my care, and nearly a hundred mouths are daily supplied with food from our store." Whitefield plotted to expand his work to form the first college in Georgia.[12]

Whitefield's project was thriving; the trustees were covering all of the initial costs for the orphanage, Whitefield's collections of donations were ready and waiting in reserve, children and workers were being added every day, and the construction project had made him the number one employer in Georgia.[13] But darker days awaited.

WHITEFIELD'S NIGHTMARE: THE ONGOING COSTS OF AN ORPHANAGE

In colonial Georgia, land was plentiful, but laborers were few. The trustees made land readily available, making many people landowners and leaving few people to be land workers. To the north, South Carolina landowners found a cheap source of labor: enslaved Africans. But slavery was illegal in Georgia, and the available labor source (White laborers) was more expensive on an ongoing basis than enslaved labor. As the initial funds for Whitefield's orphanage were depleted, he and Habersham needed to develop a sustainable revenue source to pay for their ongoing expenses. They needed cheap laborers and profitable commodities to sell; both were hard to come by.

Whitefield and Habersham planned on two sources of cheap labor: indentured servants and orphans. The trustees initially assigned to Bethesda about a dozen White laborers who had become indentured servants because the trustees paid for their travel to Georgia.[14]This worked for a while, but all the agrarian colonial economies faced a similar problem: once the term of the indentured labor was completed, the labor was gone. It is a vicious, shortsighted economic cycle that set up many American landowners to make labor decisions they had never envisioned.

As the indentured servants departed, Bethesda was left to depend on their orphans for free labor. Casual readers of the history of Whitefield's Bethesda might scratch their heads when they see Whitefield hoping to add more and more orphans despite going further and further in debt. One might think Whitefield should lower his expenses by limiting or reducing the number of orphans, but given the circumstances,

Whitefield did the opposite. The only (legal) hope of making Bethesda's cashflow positive was by increasing outside donations and increasing free labor by adding more orphans.

For example, when Peter and Charles Tondee, two of Bethesda's orphans, grew up, left the orphanage, took apprenticeships, and took up residence with their new boss, Whitefield objected. Whitefield "thought it would be a great hardship to have that boy taken from him, now he is grown capable to doing him some service, after living so long with him when he could do him none."[15] When orphans grew old enough to work, Whitefield didn't want them to leave, even if they had families to join or careers to begin. He needed them to contribute to the orphanage. Whitefield appealed to the rights the trustees had given him that authorized his care for orphans and brought Peter and Charles back to Bethesda.

Bethesda also struggled to find a profitable commodity to produce. They began planting cotton, hoping that the small hands of orphans would be well suited to removing the small seeds from the difficult strain of cotton that grew in the area. When that didn't work, they found more success, like others in the area, growing rice and indigo. Habersham put the children to work cutting firewood, clearing fields, digging potatoes, and sowing grain anytime they weren't doing their schoolwork.[16] While Habersham was trying every practical means he could dream up, Whitefield offered sermonic promises of providence in place of practical solutions.

Nine months after the grand celebration of laying the first brick of the great house at Bethesda, Whitefield announced that he was five hundred pounds sterling in debt (several times an annual wage for a minister) due to the losses incurred at Bethesda. Two weeks later, Whitefield left Bethesda and did not return in person for six years, leaving Habersham to operate Bethesda alone.

Over the ensuing months, things got worse. Exasperated, Habersham wrote, "Negroes not being allowed, and labour among us so expensive, we can make but little improvement in farming."[17] Later that year, Whitefield added, "As for manuring more land than the hired servants and great boys can manage, it is impracticable without a few negroes. It will in no wise answer the expense. I am now upwards of eight hundred pounds in debt, on the Orphan-house account."[18] A month later Habersham added, "As we are denied the use of Negroes . . . we are obligated to employ white Men in Planting, who are not able under the present Footing to defray their Wages and Victuals [food and provisions]."[19]

With mouths to feed and food scarce, Habersham and Whitefield made explicit what many Georgians had been pleading for years. A year later, Habersham left the orphanage, started his own successful mercantile in Savannah, and purchased plantations in South Carolina (and, in due time, Georgia). When he died, he was the third-wealthiest person in Georgia.

Much of Habersham's wealth came on the backs of slave labor. Whitefield had a solution for Bethesda's financial woes too.

WHITEFIELD'S SOLUTION: SLAVERY

Whitefield had arrived in Savannah on May 7, 1738; he later commented about his arrival, "The people (says he) were denied the use of both rum and slaves" and added, "in reality, to place people there on such a footing, was little better than to tie their legs, and bid them walk. The scheme was well meant at home; but, as too many years experience evidently proved, was absolute impracticable in so hot a country abroad."[20] Whitefield sensed that the Georgian heat would make physical labor difficult. This immediately brought to his mind the need for hard labor that he believed only Black slaves could provide. Despite later evidence to the contrary (for instance, the hardworking White Salzburger community near Savannah), Whitefield remained committed to his opinion for the rest of his life.

Shortly after his arrival, one of Whitefield's letters mentions working with ten servants, as does another letter a few weeks later. Whitefield's comments about servants during this time help us understand the categorical distinctions he made, along with others in his era, regarding servants and slaves. Servants were paid laborers, and being a servant was a freely chosen job; slaves were not at liberty to choose their job, nor their place in life.

Whitefield spent only three short months in America on his first trip before returning to seek his ordination and to raise support for the orphanage. Whitefield arrived back in London on December 8, 1738. The next day, a Georgian group known as the Malcontents submitted their petition to the trustees to legalize slavery in Georgia. Concurrent with Whitefield's first trip to Georgia, a strong contingent from there were convinced that the colony would not succeed without the use of slave labor.

Shortly before Whitefield returned to America, he stayed with the Delamotte family. This family was connected to the Holy Club and included a young woman Whitefield would later offer his hand to in marriage (unsuccessfully): Elizabeth Delamotte. Biographer Thomas Kidd writes that Whitefield spent "much of his time" at Blendon Hall, near London, the estate of Thomas Delamotte, "a sugar merchant who traded with Caribbean slave plantations. . . . The Delamottes had become something of a second family for him."[21] Whitefield's "second family," earned their wealth through the transatlantic slave trade. He tried to join this family via marriage and spent extensive time with them immediately prior to returning to America. Had romance worked differently, Whitefield's financial woes would have been solved through Caribbean slave plantation profits.

On his second trip to America, Whitefield landed in Pennsylvania so he could work his way south to Bethesda on a preaching and fundraising mission. Six weeks after his arrival, Whitefield came to a town called Seals Church, Virginia, to lodge at a house. The homeowner was not there, but the overseer of the slaves was, and he hosted Whitefield and those with him. Whitefield complimented the food, the accommodations, and the conversation. Unlike a letter Whitefield published a month later, all of his comments were glowing with praise for this slave master.[22] Two weeks later, while in North Carolina, he visited a house and "afterwards I went, as my usual custom is, among the

Negroes belonging to the house." Whitefield ministered to the family and commented that the children said their prayers with "a proficiency as any White people's children," leading him to desire to begin a school for "young Negroes."[23] Two days later, Whitefield wrote to a friend in London explaining that slaves were much on his heart.[24]

Four days later, Whitefield entered South Carolina and found himself worried for his life. Whitefield and his party lost their way and found a fire and a "hut full of negroes." Whitefield's friends went up and asked for directions, but the men in the hut said they didn't know the house Whitefield's friends were looking for, and that they were "new comers." Whitefield's friends "inferred" that the Black people "might be some of those who lately had made an insurrection in the province, and were run away from their masters."

The Stono rebellion had occurred three months earlier in that area. One hundred Black slaves had risen up and begun marching south to freedom toward Spanish Florida, chanting "Liberty!" as they went. They had also killed twenty White people. The White militia had caught them, killed them, and decapitated most of them. Given these recent events, Whitefield and his party thought it best to "mend our pace." They eventually found their way to the plantation where they were staying. A few days later Whitefield's journey came to an end as five slaves rowed him in a boat from Charleston to Savannah.[25]

Two weeks later, Whitefield published a blockbuster open letter titled, "A Letter to the Inhabitants of Maryland, Virginia, North and South-Carolina."[26] This became one of the earliest formal proslavery publications in print.[27] He opened the letter explaining his sympathy for slaves but also that he wasn't ready to say whether he thought slavery should be legalized. But Whitefield was sure of two things. First, he argued that slaves needed to be treated better. Whitefield attacked those who treated their slaves as animals; he shared anecdotes of slaves that had been cut with knives, stabbed with forks, and whipped to death. He was surprised that, given such abuse, there had not been more suicides or rebellion among them. Second, Whitefield attacked anyone who kept

Christianity from slaves. He added that a properly Christianized slave would be more obedient to their master.

Two weeks after laying the first brick for the great house at Bethesda, Whitefield was on a new mission as he headed back north to Pennsylvania. On April 7, he addressed a letter to the SPG about starting a "Negro school," writing, "To me Pennsylvania seems to be the best Province in America for such an undertaking. The Negroes meet there with the best usage, and I believe many of my acquaintance will either give me or let me purchase their young slaves at a very easy rate. I intend taking up a tract of land far back in the country."[28] Two weeks later, Whitefield purchased five thousand acres on the forks of the Delaware river and ordered a large house to be built for the "instruction of these poor creatures."[29] A few days later Whitefield wrote to his "Friends in London" of his intent to purchase land in Pennsylvania and "young ones I intend to buy."[30] Three months earlier Whitefield had written that he was unsure of the legality of owning slaves, but now, only three months later, it was clear that Whitefield had perfect clarity regarding the propriety of buying slaves, including "young ones."

Over the next few months Whitefield returned to Savanah but headed back north on a preaching tour. On this trip, on October 17–20, Whitefield took the invitation he received to minister at the church of Jonathan Edwards. Whitefield visited extensively with Jonathan and Sarah Edwards. As we will see in the next chapter, their home included a house slave. Whitefield stayed the night at Jonathan's parents' home— another home that included a house slave.

WHITEFIELD'S EFFORTS TO LEGALIZE SLAVERY IN GEORGIA

When Whitefield returned to London, Whitefield attended the parliamentary hearing of Thomas Stephen and Lord Gage's pleas to legalize slavery in Georgia. During these hearings Lord Gage called on Whitefield to testify for their case, but the conveyors forbade Whitefield to speak.[31] Later that year Whitefield authored an account of Bethesda, writing, "it is impracticable without a few negroes."[32]

A few months later, Whitefield returned to Parliament to testify for the allowance of slavery in Georgia. Again, the conveyors would not allow him to speak because "many expressed their dislike at examining an enthusiastical madman as they call him, and thought it demeaned the dignity of the house."[33] The parliamentary efforts were effective at removing the prohibitions on rum and titles to land on Indian territory, but they had not made headway on the legalization of slavery in Georgia. Whitefield wrote, "And if they should see good hereafter to grant a limited use of negroes, it must certainly, in all outward appearance, be as flourishing a colony as South-Carolina."[34]

For the next few years neither Whitefield nor anyone else was able to legalize slavery in Georgia. Yet the financial challenges continued at Bethesda, and so did Whitefield's rhetoric for legalization. On December 24, 1745, Pastor John Martin Bolzius, the leader of the German Salzburgers in Ebenezer, Georgia, wrote a long letter to George Whitefield responding to four arguments Whitefield made for the legalization of slavery.[35]

First, Whitefield argued that the climate in Georgia was too hot for White people. He believed only Black slaves were able to work in these conditions. Second, Whitefield claimed that the enormous financial investment in the colony would go to waste because the colony was sure to fail if slaves were not allowed. His third argument was similar, stating that his efforts at Bethesda would be wasted because he could not continue without slave labor. The fourth argument, a common one in proslavery rhetoric, was that introducing slaves to Georgia would bring more Black people to the saving knowledge of Jesus Christ. Bolzius refuted each of Whitefield's claims, but to little avail.

WHITEFIELD'S FUNDS FROM HIS SLAVE PLANTATION IN SOUTH CAROLINA

Since Whitefield's efforts to legalize slavery in Georgia were failing and his expenses continued at Bethesda, he found a different way to make money. On March 15, 1747, he wrote a letter explaining his new source of income.

> It is impossible for the inhabitants [of Georgia] to subsist them-selves without the use of slaves. But GOD has put it into the hearts of my South-Carolina friends, to contribute liberally to-wards purchasing a plantation and slaves in this province; which I purpose to devote to the support of Bethesda.—Blessed be GOD, the purchase is made . . . One negroe has been given me.—Some more I purpose to purchase this week.[36]

Whitefield was now the owner of a South Carolina slave plantation just north across the Georgia colony line. He named his plantation Providence.

In a letter penned to John Wesley a few months later, Whitefield wrote, "I have news of the awakening of several negroes at my new plantation, lately purchased at South-Carolina."[37] The success of the plantation motivated Whitefield to write to the trustees to tell them that unless slavery was legalized, he was planning on moving his Bethesda orphanage to South Carolina.[38]

WHITEFIELD'S SOLUTION LEGALIZED: SLAVERY LAWFUL IN GEORGIA

The turning point came on May 19, 1749, when the trustees petitioned the king of England to repeal the prohibition of slavery. The Malcontents, who had repeatedly lobbied to legalize slavery, answered several key questions the trustees put forward regarding regulations "if" slavery was made legal. Eventually, the trustees were persuaded of the good intentions and plans of the Malcontents.[39] Over the next year and a half a group was formed to create the specifics of the slave code that was introduced when slavery was legalized on January 1, 1751.

During that gap of time, Whitefield employed slaves illegally. A letter dated October 20, 1749, explains that five Black people were preparing a plantation at Bethesda. A White resident named George Geare wrote,

"Bless God he had been pleased to send negros to Bethesda one man two children two women . . . they are now clearing of land for a plantation . . . trust the Lord will yet bless Bethesda."[40]

Three months after slavery was legalized in Georgia, Whitefield wrote a letter detailing his justification of slavery. In it he explained that "the time for favouring that Colony seems to be come." He urged slave owners to be good to their slaves. Eleven years earlier he asked the question, "Whether it be lawful for christians to buy slaves . . . I shall not take upon me to determine." He now wrote, "As for the lawfulness of keeping slaves, I have no doubt."[41]

Whitefield justified enslaving Black people because of his reading of the Bible. He wrote that liberty is "best," but that slavery "not be so irksome." He repeated his rationale that Black slavery was required in Georgia because of the intense heat, and he added that he was eager to "purchase a good number of [slaves]." He concluded his letter by explaining that the opportunity of hearing about Christ outweighed the "temporal inconveniences" of being a slave.

With slavery now legal, Whitefield proceeded to enlarge his slave-holdings in order to make his "beloved Bethesda" sustainable. He named his plantation next to his orphanage Ephratah, which means "fruitful" in Hebrew. By the end of the year, Whitefield enslaved twenty Black people who worked at Ephratah.[42] During the first week of 1753, Whitefield decided to sell his Providence plantation in South Carolina as soon as possible, even if he lost money, in order to accelerate his efforts at Ephratah.[43] In the ensuing seventeen years leading up to Whitefield's death, he purchased more slaves to fund his orphanage. We will pick up that story later. For now, consider a prayer Whitefield published, titled "A Prayer for a Poor Negroe":

> O Righteous Father, who hast made of one blood all nations under heaven . . . Blessed be thy name, for bringing, me over into a Christian country . . . Make me contented with my condition, knowing, O LORD, that thou hast placed me in it. Let me never be

tempted to rebel against my master or mistress; and enable me to be obedient. . . . Keep my hands from picking and stealing, and suffer me not to behave unseemly on the LORD's-day. Bless my master and mistress, and my labours for their sake.[44]

We can see how Whitefield came to be a slave owner. As an Englishman of that era, a dominant social class system was well entrenched. As a Christian of Puritan heritage and influence, he understood the Bible to detail the nature and legitimacy of the relationship between masters and servants, as well as masters and slaves. As an early evangelical, he prioritized spreading the gospel and the message of the new birth above all else and at nearly any cost. In these ways he was no different from John Wesley. The situation that revealed Whitefield's outright approval of the institution of slavery was his need to support his "beloved Bethesda." Further to the north, however, another early evangelical enslaved people not to support an orphan house but to support his own house. The man was Jonathan Edwards.

7

EDWARDS IN MASSACHUSETTS

ENSLAVES OTHERS

ON A THURSDAY NIGHT in November 1726, the citizens of Northampton, Massachusetts, held a town meeting, approving "the invitation of the Reverend Mr. Jonathan Edwards to assist our Reverend Pastor: Mr. Stoddard in the work of the ministry."[1] Edwards had just celebrated his twenty-third birthday, completed his education, and gained a few years of scattered pastoral experience. His new job was a big one. Historian George Marsden comments, "To move to Northampton was to move into the seat of family power."[2]

In 1653, English settlers arrived in the land of the Pocumtuc Native Americans, on the west side of the Connecticut River in modern-day western Massachusetts, to form the town of Northampton. Seven years later the town had grown to about three hundred people. The settlers collaborated to call their first minister; a year later they built their meeting house. Upon the death of the first pastor, the town called the eminent Solomon Stoddard to be their pastor in 1672. The eminent? Yes.

Stoddard was the son of a wealthy Boston merchant, nephew of Sir George Downing (of Downing Street—of London fame), and his mother was niece to Massachusetts Governor John Winthrop. Stoddard was a graduate of Harvard and its first librarian. Biographer Perry Miller writes, "Stoddard belonged, if anybody did, to the aristocracy of New England."[3] He was a studious, thoughtful, powerful Puritan pastor who never missed a sabbath or lecture in the fifty-nine years of his ministry.[4] His pastoral work in the Northampton church elevated the already elite credentials upon which he came to be known as the "Puritan Pope of the Connecticut River Valley."[5] In addition to his ministerial acumen, Stoddard amassed a sizable financial estate and land holdings and left a "servant man" in his will to his wife.[6] (One doesn't just "leave" an employee in one's will; the "servant man" was enslaved by Stoddard.) Solomon and his wife, Esther, had twelve children and many grandchildren—including Jonathan Edwards, who replaced his grandfather as pastor in Northampton.

The church granted Jonathan a suitable salary, fifty acres of land, and finances for a home to be built that was later described as a "Mansion home, barn, and home lot."[7] The first year Jonathan lived in Northampton, he lived with his grandfather Solomon and his uncle Colonel John Stoddard.[8]

While Solomon was the spiritual leader of Northampton, his son Colonel John Stoddard was the political, military, and financial leader of the town. John was a graduate of Harvard and a decorated military man. He leveraged his role as a government surveyor early in his career for inside information to acquire newly opened land grants.[9] When he died, John was one of the wealthiest men in Massachusetts and was known for his opulence. He was the owner of Northampton's first gold watch, teapot, teakettle, cups and saucers, as well as other items which aligned with his elite social status as "an aristocrat of the aristocrats."[10] John enslaved a Black woman named Bess, who was left in his final estate. When John's wife, Prudence, died in 1764, her estate included one female "negro" (perhaps this woman was Bess).[11]

As Jonathan settled into the massive shadow of his grandfather in the first year of his ministry, he lived with two of the richest and most powerful people in the community—his uncle and his grandfather. Their home was filled with luxurious goods. They were served by at least one Black slave, just as Jonathan had been served as a child by Ansars, the man his parents enslaved.[12] As Jonathan waited for his home to be built, he knew that his aging grandfather's pastoral capacities were in decline. Jonathan was young and had little, but plenty of opportunities were on his horizon.

CULTURAL NORMS

The first century of New England Puritans underwent a transformation in some of their cultural norms. They had brought with them across the Atlantic a theological understanding of social hierarchy based upon their biblical and theological assumptions. Alongside these beliefs were cultural norms that taught people to avoid presenting themselves in extravagant ways that might elevate their sense of superiority. They believed that God had ordered families in a hierarchical pattern, and the discrete family units joined together to form community church congregations. But they believed that broader social stratification beyond the family unit—putting one family above another because of riches, power, prominence, etc.—was to be avoided. Thus, any efforts to elevate oneself in the community were initially frowned on. Puritan Richard Baxter explained in 1675 that clothing was a consequence of sin but served to preserve people from shame, cold, and physical hurt. He warned "that we imitate not the fashions of light and wain persons . . . bestow no needless cost upon our attire. . . . Thus must apparel be used: the cheapest that is warm and comely, according to the fashion of the gravest persons of our rank, and the lower of them."[13] He added, "Excess in apparel, is the very sign of folly, that is hand'd out to tell the world what you are."[14] He also wrote, "A poor self-denying, humble, patient, heavenly Christian, is worth a thousand of these painted posts and peacocks."[15]

Baxter captures the negative attitude of Puritans in England toward public and private displays of opulence. Meanwhile, across the Atlantic, Puritans in colonial America were in the midst of a cultural shift. Historian Richard Bushman writes, "By 1765 the Yankee spirit had replaced the Puritan. . . . The avid pursuit of gain, partly condemned in 1690, was largely acceptable in 1765. The rulers, having failed to contain ambition, accommodated it."[16] Generational distinctions emerged among Puritans in America. The early generations retained the prevailing notions of England, while later generations of Puritans in America began legislating formal distinctions based on wealth, education, and social class—and utilized the Bible to justify these cultural distinctions. These changing cultural accommodations justified by their understanding of the Bible will help us see later in this chapter the relevance of Jonathan Edwards's being born into an era where distinctions in social strata shape his understanding of slavery.

Jonathan Edwards arrived in Northampton as a highly educated man from an exalted family, a new landowner, and a minister. He was immediately a member of the upper echelon of Northampton society. One unusual practice of Edwards's ministry shows explicitly how he understood his place in society: he wore a wig.

Jonathan's grandfather Solomon, as a gatekeeper of the older generation, was no fan of wigs. Biographer Patricia Tracy explains, "Stoddard had no patience with status seeking. He was tireless in denouncing the fashions of a would-be leisure class, especially wigs and extravagant clothing."[17] Yet his grandson was a wig-wearer. Paintings of Edwards show him wearing a wig and at least one of his church members criticized him for wearing it as a display of superiority over his congregation.[18] While it might seem trivial to criticize Edwards for wearing a wig, it was in direct defiance to his grandfather's expectations. In wearing it, Jonathan was making a conscious and visible effort to present himself as a member of the aristocracy of his community. Edwards scholar Ken Minkema writes, "That wig tells us much about Edwards. [It] reflected his aristocratic attitudes. As a minister and member of a prominent extended family, he expected deference from his 'inferiors,' and he defended the prerogatives of his profession and class."[19]

Less than a year after getting settled in Northampton, Jonathan was ordained as pastor and married Sarah Pierpont, whose father was a prominent physician, a founder of Yale, and a descendant of the Reverend Thomas Hooker, the founder of the Connecticut colony.

Seven months later, in February 1729, Solomon Stoddard died. The moment was perfectly primed for Jonathan to take the helm.

Jonathan preached a sermon a few months later that derided his congregation on their pride and vanity. He asked, "How excessively do many affect to make a flaunting appearance in their buildings and apparel and way of living, many going far beyond their condition or what would be suitable for them?"[20] He was comfortable distinguishing himself from others in his town, and warned people of a lower class to not go "beyond their condition"—an aristocratic lifestyle was appropriate for him, but not for others. Marsden writes, "At twenty-six, Edwards was now a man of authority. He was an aristocrat in the hierarchical society that took aristocracy for granted. He was much aware of the authority of his office and the deference it should command."[21]

VENUS

By June 1731, Jonathan and Sarah settled into their new home and were living on a recently increased salary of £140 per year.[22] They were the proud parents of two daughters: Sarah, who was about to turn three years old; and Jerusha, who had recently turned one. Jonathan and Sarah may have already had an intuition that eight months later they would meet their third child, Esther. Their ministry and home life were growing and getting busier.

On Thursday, June 7, 1731, Jonathan sat down at a table in Newport, Rhode Island, having traveled 130 miles from his hometown, and paid eighty pounds, over half of his annual salary, to buy Venus, a Black slave around the age of fourteen.[23] A copy of the receipt for Venus exists today and specifies that Jonathan and his heirs owned Venus "forever."[24]

Edwards's purchase of Venus is shocking today; it is also an example of a man participating in the cultural and religious norms he was born into. Jonathan and his wife, Sarah, had grown up in houses and among extended families that enslaved Black people. Jonathan and Sarah's theological forebears affirmed a hierarchical family and societal order which specified the place and function of servants and, eventually, slaves. Jonathan descended from a line of elite aristocracy. Jonathan and Sarah now had a house, children, a prominent role in their community, and the financial means to acquire a slave (barely), and they did so. They were not alone in their purchase. Minkema writes, "Within Northampton, a small but growing number of elites typically owned one or two slaves—a female for domestic chores and a male for fieldwork."[25]

After this account, there is no further mention of Venus in any remaining records. She may have been traded, been sold, died, or run away. Alternatively, five years later the Edwards family owned a woman named Leah, which may have been a new name given to Venus, perhaps following the occasional tradition of receiving a new name after Christian baptism.[26]

In November 1740, Jonathan and Sarah traveled to New Haven to execute the will of Sarah's recently deceased mother, Mary Pierpont. Mary's will manumitted "Jethro Negro and his wife Ruth" who were her former slaves. Jonathan and Sarah signed as guarantors of financial support for them.[27] Jonathan and Sarah were certainly aware of the possibility of manumitting slaves, and in particular the slaves Sarah grew up with in her house. It further shows that Sarah (and Jonathan) chose not to follow her mother's example in their own will, since they chose not to manumit their slave, Titus, upon their own deaths.

DRAFT LETTER ON SLAVERY

A year after the Edwardses helped manumit Jethro and Ruth, Jonathan sat down to write on already-used scraps of paper his only known direct comments about slavery.[28] Ken Minkema found these notes while working on a separate project and published them in 1997.[29] What we have are scraps of notes on two salvaged letter covers—not a complete letter, but a draft letter.

Edwards wasn't intending to write about slavery: he was addressing it incidentally because of a different topic. The Hampshire County ministerial association had asked Edwards to write an official reply to defend a minister named the Reverend Benjamin Doolittle of

Northfield, Massachusetts, a town thirty miles away. Doolittle's congregation was upset about his demands to increase his salary and to pay for his firewood. Edwards's defense of Doolittle is surprising because Doolittle reportedly held to Arminian theology, which Edwards repeatedly attacked and described as "plainly absurd." Doolittle also had three well-paying jobs (as a doctor, proprietor's clerk, and minister), and was known to have questionable character.[30] Doolittle enslaved a man named Abijah Prince, and his congregants seem to have taken issue with the propriety of slaveholding as part of their attack on Doolittle. So Edwards, on being asked to defend Doolittle's request for a salary increase, drafted his only known writing on the topic of slavery, and in doing so, explained how he justified the institution of slavery.

Minkema's analysis of Edwards's cryptic draft letter is that Edwards believed slavery was a necessary evil that served "some positive good in the natural order that God had decreed."[31] The clearest and largest part of the draft argues that if slavery is unjust, Doolittle's congregation is equally guilty through partaking of the *benefits* of slave labor. Edwards wrote, "Let them also fully and thoroughly vindicate themselves and their own practice in partaking of negroes' slavery, or confess that there is no hurt in partaking in it."[32] The idea is that those who do not own slaves but enjoy the end products of slavery—such as cheaper food and merchandise—are just as complicit as slave owners. (Some Quakers and others would use this argument not *for* but *against* slavery.) Here, however, Edwards uses this logic to support slavery. He believes "there is no hurt in partaking" of the benefits of slavery, in part because of the overall benefits of slavery for society at large.

Meanwhile, Edward's draft letter argued to forbid the transatlantic *trade* of slaves. He wrote against nations that "have any power or business to disfranchise all the nations of Africa."[33] So Edwards supported the *institution* of slavery but was against unjust acquisition of slaves, which implied the capture of Africans by transatlantic slave traders. This contradicts Edwards's earlier purchase of Venus in 1731, who had been taken from Africa.[34]

A few years after he defended the institution of slavery related to Doolittle's congregation's frustrations about his salary and lifestyle, Edwards's church grew increasingly frustrated with his own lifestyle. In 1744 church members called for him to account for his supposed extravagance. Edwards wrote, "I perceived that much fault was found by some persons with our manner of spending, with the clothes that we wore and the like, from which, together with some mistakes of matters of fact, there manifestly appeared a considerable degree of disgust in many."[35] Edwards offered to give an account of his expenses to the church. Church members were suspicious of the family's jewelry, chocolate, Boston-made clothing, children's toys, gold chain, silver patch box—and slaves.[36] While tensions over his salary were never resolved, the church retained Edwards as their pastor. Two years later, Jonathan and Sarah searched for a new maid, presumably a slave, one with a "good hand at spinning fine linen."[37] Their taste for the finer things in life remained. A year later, Edwards bragged "that he was the highest-paid minister in New England outside the city of Boston."[38] The following year, though, things would change abruptly for the Edwards family.

STOCKBRIDGE

Jonathan must have had a terrible feeling in his stomach when 230 men cast their vote on June 22, 1750, to determine whether they would retain him as their pastor. Twenty-three years before, he had stepped into the bright spotlight of the Northampton church as heir apparent, and soon successor, to his grandfather, the "Puritan Pope of the Connecticut River Valley." Over those two decades, the church experienced profound waves of revival that were publicized throughout America and across the Atlantic. But amid the highlights, many challenges had arisen too. Tensions over his salary, his handling of indecency among the young men in his congregation, tragedy in his community, as well as his stances on church membership and access to the Communion table, had upset his congregation, and in a Congregational church, that put his job in continual jeopardy. Of the 230 who cast their vote, 207 voted against him. Jonathan was fired.[39]

A year later, Edwards was installed as pastor in Stockbridge, Massachusetts, fifty-five miles west of Northampton. He inherited a ministry that historian Rachel Wheeler describes as "quite simply a mess."[40] Less than two decades earlier John Stoddard, Solomon's son and Jonathan's uncle, thought that the area would serve as a missionary outpost to the Stockbridge Indians, an indigenous Mohican tribe.

When Edwards arrived, there were 218 Mohicans and about a dozen English families.[41] Within the next two years, an additional ninety Mohawks of the Iroquois Six Nations arrived.

Edwards served as pastor at Stockbridge for seven years. The pastoral demands were quite different from Northampton. On most Sundays, Edwards provided four church services, two for the English and two for the Native Americans.[42] But he also had more time than ever to devote himself to his studies and writing—some of Edwards's most enduring and significant work emerged during his time in Stockbridge. This is not to say that his pastoral work was easy. For instance, in 1754 a band of Schaghticoke Indians attacked and killed three White congregants on a Sunday morning.

Jonathan's only son, Jonathan Edwards Jr., was six years old when the Edwardses moved to Stockbridge. He grew up among the Mohican children of the village. The younger Jonathan later explained, "The Indians . . . were my daily school mates and play-fellows. Out of my father's house, I seldom heard any language spoken, beside the Indian . . . I knew the names of some things in Indian which I did not know in English; even all my thoughts ran in Indian."[43] The younger Jonathan Edwards's childhood among the Mohicans and Mohawks exposed him to people with a very different culture from his own.

SLAVERY AS GOD'S HARMONY

When Jonathan and Sarah moved to Stockbridge, they brought with them Rose, a woman they enslaved. Rose is understood to be the first slave in Stockbridge. An account in 1854 says that Rose "is said to have been stolen from Africa when a child, as she was getting water at a spring."[44] Rose lived with the Edwards family when they moved to Stockbridge in 1751 but is not listed in Jonathan's 1753 will. Jonathan officiated the wedding of Rose and a free Black man named Joab Benny in 1756. A year before his marriage to Rose, Joab had purchased fifty acres from a Stockbridge Mohican named John Skushawmh in the southeast corner of Stockbridge. Though it isn't clear, it is possible that Rose was not enslaved by the Edwards family at the time of her marriage; it is possible that Joab purchased Rose's freedom. It is also possible that Edwards could have freed Rose, though that would be unprecedented in his dealings with enslaved people.[45] Joab and Rose went on to have six children, and she became a full member of the Stockbridge church in 1771.

On May 24, 1756, three weeks before Joab and Rose's wedding, the Edwards family purchased a three-year-old boy named Titus. The reasons the Edwards family purchased a three-year-old slave are not clear.

During his time in Stockbridge, Edwards produced one of his most significant writings: *The Nature of True Virtue*. George Marsden calls it a "masterpiece in the larger history of Christian literature."[46] Mark Noll writes that *True Virtue* is "an unusually fitting capstone to his theological career."[47] Edwards wrote it to be read together with his work *Concerning the End for Which God Created the World*, of which Edwards argues God "makes himself his end."[48] In *True Virtue*, Edwards explains that, contrary to humanistic moralism, Christian virtues find their origin and end, like the creation of the world, in God.

In *True Virtue*, Edwards proposes an ethical framework to understand how and why to make moral choices. He does not discuss slavery in this work. Instead, Edwards provides what can now be seen as his undergirding logic to the place and function of slavery in God's world. In short, Edwards understood slavery as an example of God's harmony and order for the world.[49]

Edwards hinted at this social ordering when he preached his first sermon in the new meetinghouse in Northampton on December 25, 1737. As he stood in front of the congregation, all of the parishioners were seated according to their wealth—the richest were closest; the poorest were further away. He preached, "There are sufficient and suitable accommodation for all the different souls of persons that are in the world: for great and small, for high and low, rich and poor, wise and unwise, bond and free; persons of all nations, and all conditions, and circumstances."[50] He explained that in the palace of heaven there are many apartments, "some are more stately and costly than others, according to the degree of dignity. There is one apartment that is the king's presence chambers. There are other apartments for the next heir to the crown. There are others for other children, and others [for] his attendants and the great officers of his household—one for the high steward, and another for the chamberlain—and others for the meaner officers and servants."[51] Edwards challenged his congregation to seek the highest places in heaven while accepting their places and stations in life on earth.

His sermon "Of God, The Father" in 1746 provided a theologically rich and nuanced explanation of the Trinity: "Each person [of the Trinity] has his distinct part and, as it were, sustains a distinct character and charge in that affair [of redemption]. They not only are all concerned as joint actors and co-workers in an affair of common concern, but each one has his distinct part in the affair assigned him, as what more especially belongs to him, rather than to either of the other persons of the Trinity."[52] Edwards understood God's work of redemption as a positive example of a structured hierarchy since each of the parts are "assigned"—this implies that one person of the Trinity "assigns" while others are "assigned."

In *True Virtue*, the key concept to understand this harmony and order is how separate things work together to form a cohesive whole; these things on their own are incomplete and thus need each other in order to be beautiful. Edwards writes, "This kind of beauty is not entirely different from that beauty which there is in fitting a mortise to its tenon."[53] The logic Edwards applies here makes slavery beautiful on its own when paired with other stations in life.

After establishing how disparate things in the world work together for God's glory and beauty, Edwards explains how this applies to human societies. He writes, "There is a beauty of order in society . . . which is of the secondary kind. As, when the different members of society have all their appointed office, place, and station, according to their several capacities and talents, and everyone keeps his place and continues in his proper business."[54] For Edwards, the stations in life, places in a community, and offices people hold are all ordered by God for the glory of God. He continues:

> There is some natural agreement of one thing to another . . . some equality and proportion in things of a similar nature, and of a direct relation one to another. So it is in relative duties; duties of children to parents, and of parents to children; duties of husbands and wives; duties of rulers and subjects; duties of friendship and good neighborhood: and all duties that we owe to God.[55]

For Edwards, the duties of rulers and subjects—which are biblically akin to masters and slaves—are examples of the class-based duties owed to God for the glory of God. Edwards wrote *True Virtue* during his first few years in Stockbridge, likely in 1753–1754, but it was not published until seven years after his death.[56] *True Virtue* advances the theological and ethical social codes he inherited from his Puritan predecessors by framing them in the scheme of God's glory and beauty refracted in the world. Edwards writes, "all the beauty to be found throughout the whole creation, is but the reflection of the diffused beams of that Being."[57] In *True Virtue*, there was an underdeveloped concept that redefined this moral order.

Edwards articulated disinterested benevolence as the key ethical mandate to glorify God. He writes, "True virtue most essentially consists in benevolence" to God and "will seek the good of every individual being unless it be conceived as not consistent with the highest good of Being in general."[58] Edwards believed that true virtue is seeking the ultimate good of another person, without consideration about how it benefits or does not benefit yourself. Edwards did not develop this idea fully, but his later followers, the Edwardseans, would develop it into the concept of *disinterested benevolence*, a key conceptual foundation for their abolitionism.[59]

SARAH SEEKS MORE SLAVES

In the midst of Jonathan's new pastoral duties and writing projects, Sarah was seeking more slaves for their Stockbridge household. Rose's marriage to Joab likely left the Edwards family without a maid in their house. The Edwardses were used to having a slave in their house ever since they purchased Venus, over thirty years before—it seems that Sarah was persistent in finding a replacement or an additional slave for their household.

On February 28, 1744, Jonathan Edwards wrote a letter to Joseph Bellamy. Bellamy was one of his previous theology students and a pastor fifty miles away in Bethlem (later called Bethlehem),[60] a new settlement in rural Connecticut. Edwards wrote to him because Bellamy was considering taking a new role in New York. Edwards wrote, "If it should finally so come to pass that you should remove to New York, my wife desires to buy your Negro woman, as she supposes she will do better for the country than the city. She will probably come along through your place some time in April, when she will talk with you about it."[61] Bellamy stayed in Bethlem and presumably kept his slave. Samuel Hopkins, another disciple of Edwards, convinced Bellamy to release a slave (as we will see later), but we don't know the exact timing of this account, or whether Bellamy may have acquired another slave after releasing the person Hopkins convinced him to release.[62]

Three years later, on November 20, 1757, Jonathan wrote a letter to his daughter Esther shortly after the death of her husband, then-president of Princeton College, Aaron Burr Sr. Esther and Aaron owned a slave named Harry (they may have also called him "Old Mingo").[63] Edwards wrote, "If you think of selling Harry, your mother desires you not to sell him, without letting her know it."[64] At that point Jonathan and Sarah owned Titus, but he was just four years old. It is clear that they were looking to buy another slave—likely a person able to help the household. Following what we learned from Jonathan's draft letter on slavery in 1741, we may infer that Jonathan did not try to purchase a slave from the slave market, presumably directly from Africa, as he had with Venus in Providence, Rhode Island. Instead he may have tried to buy a slave who was already enslaved in America—perhaps to distance himself from the transatlantic slave trade.

PRINCETON: JOSEPH AND SUE

Aaron Burr's death left a presidential vacancy at Princeton, which was offered to his father-in-law, Jonathan Edwards. He accepted the role and moved to Princeton. Shortly after arriving, he and his family underwent inoculation against a recent smallpox outbreak. Jonathan became ill and died on March 22, 1758, less than two months after arriving at Princeton. Seven months later, Sarah Edwards died of dysentery.

After Jonathan and Sarah died, their estate inventory listed their slave, Titus. Titus ended up being connected closely to Jonathan's oldest son, Timothy, throughout his life. The final Edwards estate also included a married Black couple named Joseph and Su (Sue). Their inclusion in the Edwards estate raises further questions. Why were Joseph and Sue not listed in the Edwards family estate inventory created ten days prior to their sale in the final Edwards estate?

As soon as Edwards could afford to enslave a Black person, he did, and this pattern continued for the rest of his life. He enslaved Black people as what he understood to be appropriate to his standing as a member of the New England aristocracy and as an extension of his theology of the glory of God reflected in the harmony created by the various roles and social stations in life, including slavery. While his congregants often pushed back on how he spent his salary and his acquisition of expensive items, neither he nor they questioned the institution of slavery.

Edwards, unlike some of his contemporaries, affirmed that there is just one human race; a careful reading of his works and life, especially based on his time spent in Stockbridge, reveals a subtle antiracist trajectory that his followers eventually expanded.[65] Yet for all that, the loudest evidence of Edwards's view regarding race as it relates to slavery is that he only enslaved Black people.

Edwards's beliefs about *how* to acquire a slave did seem to change over time. He acquired his first slave, Venus, knowing that she had come directly from Africa, and thus was stolen. Yet later, in his draft letter and implied in other correspondence, he deemed this method of acquiring slaves inappropriate. Jonathan's ownership of Rose and her subsequent marriage to Joab, which Jonathan officiated, gives a partial glimpse into his relationship with one of his slaves—though what can be inferred is very limited. When given the opportunity to provide instructions in his will to offer Titus his freedom, Edwards instead indicated how to continue his family's enslavement of the young boy.

Of the three men we're examining in this book, Jonathan Edwards lived the shortest life. He died at the age of fifty-four. Whitefield lived only one year longer, but died in 1770, which was a much more dynamic time for early abolitionism. When Edwards died in 1758, few if any of his White New England Congregationalist and Puritan peers would have questioned his enslavement of Black people. Sadly, given the family he came from, they would have expected it.

8

WESLEY'S THIRTY-SEVEN-YEAR SILENCE

CAPTAIN HUGH PERCY prepared his ship the *Samuel* for passengers on the shores of Charleston, South Carolina, on Thursday, December 22, 1737. John Wesley lined up with the others and boarded. Four days after they departed for England, Wesley "began instructing a Negro lad in the principles of Christianity."[1] Twelve days later, Wesley noted that he continued his discussions with this boy and that "another Negro who was on board desired to be a hearer too."[2] The captain, Hugh Percy, was known to use the *Samuel* for trade and travel between Rotterdam, London, Pennsylvania, and South Carolina. Wesley doesn't elaborate further on their discussion, nor about the status of the young Black person—though it was not uncommon for transatlantic captains to have a Black cabin boy as a part of their crew. Wesley never comments about these Black people again.

SILENCE: RETURNING TO ENGLAND (1738)

During John Wesley's time in Georgia, he had heard from his brother and seen firsthand the atrocities of slavery in the colonial South— particularly in South Carolina. John and Charles received accounts of slaves being killed as well as a slave being nailed up by his ears, beaten, and then doused with scalding water, leaving the slave unable to "stir" for four months. They knew of a slave owner who cut off the legs of his slave. Charles reported a story about a Mr. Hill who whipped his "she-slave" to the brink of death, but had a physician available to revive her so that he could repeat the whipping before "dropping hot sealing-wax" on her flesh.

John Wesley eventually became an abolitionist. But it's critical to note (and I urge you to carefully ponder this point) that Wesley had clear knowledge of the evils of slavery as early as 1736, but the earliest we can observe any real change in his position is in 1774, thirty-seven years later. Accounts of Wesley's life and approach to abolition fail to make an adequate account of this gap. Instead, they minimize his silence.

Unlike Whitefield and Edwards, Wesley never owned slaves. But if Wesley had died in 1773, at the ripe old age of seventy, we could easily classify his *beliefs* about slavery as comparable to Whitefield's and Edwards's. Up to 1774, the primary differences among Wesley, Whitefield, and Edwards weren't their beliefs about slavery but where they lived. Edwards lived his entire life in colonial America. Wesley lived the rest of his life in England. Whitefield lived in both countries and owned slaves in colonial America but did not own slaves in England. In England, Wesley and Whitefield believed and acted in the same way regarding slavery—it was only when Whitefield spent time in colonial America that he had the opportunity and context to enslave people. So what did Wesley do with his knowledge and experiences with American slavery when he returned to England?

That is what we will learn in this chapter, while also remembering that during this period the slaveholders George Whitefield and Jonathan Edwards made arguments similar to Wesley's—never challenging the *institution* of slavery, but focusing instead on *how* Christians ought to enslave Black people.

John met Moravian leader Peter Böhler six days after landing in England. John and Peter's discussions relating to faith, the new birth, and conversion culminated in Wesley's heart being "strangely warmed" at Aldersgate Street five months later on May 24, 1738. This story dominates biographies about Wesley—and it is indeed a life-changing focal point of his life. In this whirlwind of life-changing spiritual moments, Wesley's Georgia experiences quickly fade into the background.

Less than a month after Wesley's Aldersgate experience, he traveled to Germany for three months to visit the Moravians, meeting their leader exiled leader Count Zinzendorf in Marienborn before continuing on to the Moravian Herrnhut community.[3] Seven years earlier, a former slave from the island of St. Thomas (in what is now the US Virgin Islands) named Anthony Ulrich came to the Moravians and pleaded for them to send missionaries to the island—but added a key condition: Ulrich told the Moravians that slaves would only listen to other slaves, so the missionaries needed to become slaves themselves to earn a hearing among the slaves. Two men, Leonard Dober and David Nitschmann, volunteered for the task. Despite their best intentions, nothing went as planned. They later learned that White people were not allowed to be slaves in the West Indies. Nonetheless they went to St. Thomas as missionaries. They soon learned that Ulrich had other plans as well. He came to St. Thomas in 1734 and bought his own plantation and a slave of his own.[4]

A year later, Dober and Nitschmann traveled back across the Atlantic to Herrnhut with two young boys, Jupiter and Oly-Carmel—their newly acquired slaves.[5] The following year the Moravians sent Fredrick Martin to St. Thomas. Martin bought an estate, financed by the Moravians in Herrnhut, that included nine slaves. These slaves made it possible for him to pursue his missionary work on the island. He named the endeavor New Herrnhut.[6] Zinzendorf himself visited the plantation in January 1739. New Herrnhut grew to sixty-nine acres and included 250 slaves; the original church and slave quarters remain today.[7] When Wesley immersed himself among the Moravians immediately after returning to England, he learned from a group that not only understood slavery to be a condition ordained by God, but that also financed and perpetuated slave ownership.

Wesley returned to England, as did Whitefield a few months later. Whitefield had returned to England to be ordained a priest and to make formal arrangements for his orphanage back in Georgia. Remember, Whitefield already believed that the heat in Georgia made work "absolutely impracticable" for White people and that slaves would be needed for the colony to progress.[8]

Wesley and Whitefield collaborated in the bold, controversial, and groundbreaking task of open-air preaching. The evangelical revival was now under way. It was during this era that Wesley developed small group meetings called societies, and attended to the practical and educational needs of the community—this became known as the "People called Methodists" and the Methodist societies. It was during this time that Wesley created what became known as the Foundry—a chapel, meetinghouse, and school in London. That was when John Wesley met Silas Todd.

Silas Todd had grown up in Bristol, a leading hub of the transatlantic slave trade. Todd had taken to the seas at the age of fourteen and entered the world of the slave trade. About ten years later, convicted by God and haunted by what he had done, he left the slave trade in order to be with his wife and begin his career as an educator. In 1740, Todd heard Wesley speak and joined his cause. Todd became one of the schoolmasters of the Foundry in 1744 and served for the Methodists for several decades. In 1787 and 1788 Wesley's *Arminian Magazine* published the autobiography of Todd.[9]

Todd's autobiography does not reject the institution of slavery, but it does reject the violence of the slave trade. It speaks glowingly of the infamous Bristol merchant, slave trader, and philanthropist Edward Colston.[10] (Colston's statue would later be dragged into the Bristol harbor by protesters in June 2020, due to his extensive involvement in the Bristol slave trade.) Wesley spent several decades working with Todd, a remorseful ex–slave trader, without ever rejecting the slave trade. Wesley published Todd's story only after publishing his 1774 *Thoughts upon Slavery.*

The month before Wesley met Todd, Wesley made a small note in his personal diary. He wrote, "collected for the Negro school."[11] Wesley does not specify which school he sought to assist—what seems most likely is that the collection was for Whitefield's recent endeavor in

Pennsylvania, where, in April 1740, he purchased five thousand acres of land to build a school for Black children in collaboration with the Moravians. Wesley was certainly concerned for the proper *education* of slaves well before he was concerned with the *institution* of slavery.

When Wesley returned from his firsthand experience of seeing slavery in the American colonies, he did not rush back to England to campaign for change. Instead, he focused on his own personal spiritual growth and the growth of his ministry. While he did this, he continued to work with and amid people actively involved in the slave trade.

SILENCE: EDUCATE THE SLAVES (1755)

When Wesley was in Georgia and South Carolina, he had worked to educate everyone he came into contact with before he departed in 1737. In 1740, South Carolina passed the Negro Act, which made it illegal to teach a slave to read or write; the fine for doing so was one hundred pounds.[12] In 1755, Georgia passed a similar statute.[13] The general sentiment among slave owners was that literacy raised the risk of independence and rebellion among slaves. They believed it was an unneeded skill and dangerous.

Samuel Davies was born in Delaware and became a Presbyterian minister in Virginia in 1747. He was educated under a man who graduated from William Tennent's famous "Log College." Davies partnered with Tennent's son Gilbert Tennent on a trip to Britain to raise money for the fledgling College of New Jersey (which would become Princeton University). Davies made many contacts on his trip, including Whitefield and Wesley. Later, Whitefield made a trip to Davies's town to preach. When Davies returned to Virginia, he began writing to his English contacts requesting funds to educate slaves.[14]

Wesley recorded a letter he received from Davies on July 27, 1755. Davies wrote, "The poor negro slaves here never heard of Jesus, or His religion, till they arrived at the land of their slavery in America, whom their masters generally neglect." Davies added that three hundred Black slaves had attended his church and that a hundred of them had been baptized. He continued, "There are multitudes of them in various parts who are eagerly desirous of instruction. They have generally very little help to read."[15] Davies penned a sermon addressed to the London-based Society for Promoting Religious Knowledge among the Poor. He wrote, "Certainly he that can lay our forty or fifty pounds to purchase a slave, is able to spare a few shillings to furnish him with a few books for his instruction. . . . The Relation you bear to your Negroes as their Masters obliges you to instruct them in the Christian religion."[16] Davies never challenged the institution of slavery, but he did campaign for the Christianization and education of slaves.

Wesley supported Davies's campaign by sending materials across the Atlantic. Davies responded to Wesley several months later. Davies wrote, "When the books arrived, I gave public notice after sermon, and desired such Negroes as could read, and such White people as would make good use of them, and were not able to buy, to come to my house. . . . All the books were very acceptable. . . . Such of the Negroes as can read already, are evidently improving in knowledge."[17]

At the same time Wesley was providing reading materials to Black slaves in America, he was also releasing his *Notes on the New Testament*, in 1755. Wesley's comments regarding the passage in 1 Corinthians 7:21-24, which discusses whether a servant or slave should seek freedom, indicate that a slave should not seek to change their status "without a clear direction of Providence."[18] Wesley's comment on slave passages such as Ephesians 6:5-8, Colossians 3:22-24, 1 Timothy 6:1-2, Titus 2:9-10, and 1 Peter 2:18 consistently translate the Greek word *doulos* as *servant* instead of *slave*.

Regarding Paul's letter to Philemon, Wesley wrote that this epistle "gives us a specimen how Christians ought to treat secular affairs from higher principles."[19] His comment on 1 Timothy 1:10, where Paul writes against "man-stealers," indicates further that Wesley was concerned about *how* to enslave, not *whether* enslaving others was proper for Christians. Wesley wrote, "Man-stealers—The worst of all thieves, in comparison of whom highwaymen and housebreakers are innocent!

What then are most traders in Negroes, procurers of servants for America, and all who [en]list soldiers by lies, tricks, and incitements?"[20] Wesley's parallel with unlawful acquisition of military soldiers is telling. Wesley believes there is nothing wrong with being a soldier; Wesley's complaint is *how* soldiers are conscripted. Similarly, Wesley is against improper *methods* of acquiring slaves, not against slavery itself.

Like Davies, Wesley believed education, including literacy, was an essential responsibility of Christian slave owners. Wesley, like Davies and others, was pushing against the prevailing culture which sought to limit or eradicate illiteracy among Black people, such as in South Carolina and Georgia.

SILENCE: CHRISTIANIZE THE SLAVES (1758)

When Nathanial Gilbert landed in England in 1758, another opportunity arrived on Wesley's doorstep to take a stand against slavery. Gilbert arrived from the British colony of Antigua with his wife, four daughters, and three slaves (two Black and one described as "mulatto"), seeking to improve his health. The "mulatto" woman was probably named Mary Alley, and the other two slaves were probably named Sophia Campbell and Bessie.[21] Gilbert had descended from a long line of wealthy Antiguan plantation overseers and owners. Antigua was an island filled with enslaved Black people—in 1744, Antigua had 3,538 White people and 27,892 slaves.[22] In 1746, Gilbert's father bought a plantation that included 227 Black slaves.[23]

Upon Gilbert's arrival in England, Wesley preached where Gilbert was staying on Tuesday, January 17, 1758. Wesley recorded that the three slaves "appear to be much awakened."[24] Eleven months later Wesley baptized two of them (one we later learn was named Bessie), and he rejoiced in knowing an "African Christian."[25] Nathanial Gilbert, his family, and his slaves returned to Antigua in late 1759. When they returned, Gilbert did not free his slaves, even while ministering to freed Black people.[26] Further, Gilbert held a political office with influence over the laws in Antigua, including the laws related to slavery. One person commented that the slave laws in Antigua were "the most diabolical passed by any man."[27] Despite these conditions, Gilbert and others established Methodism in Antigua and worked to convert slaves to Christianity—all while staying in correspondence with John Wesley.[28]

In 1765, Wesley also corresponded with John Newton, the famous author of "Amazing Grace" and ex–slave trader. Wesley wrote to Newton after reading Newton's autobiography. In this work, Newton wrote extensively of his previous participation in the slave trade. In their correspondence Wesley made no comment about slavery; their discussions concerned Newton's challenges to obtain ordination because of his association and beliefs related to Methodism.[29] Newton waited until 1787 to denounce the slave trade, in his work *Thoughts upon the African Slave Trade*, to help William Wilberforce's campaign against slavery.

As Methodism grew in the British Isles, Methodists emigrated abroad, including to colonial America. An Irish Methodist named Robert Strawbridge moved to Maryland in 1765 and delivered one of the earliest Methodist sermons in America. A freeman named Caleb Hyland, who was Black, supplied a table for Strawbridge to stand on during his first sermon.[30] The Methodist message of free grace appealed to many people, including, and perhaps especially, to "the least of these," people on the fringes of society. By 1774, the superintendent of the Methodists in America reported that a quarter of all Methodist members in America were slaves or former slaves.[31] Despite the growth of Methodism in America among free and enslaved Black people, Wesley provided no further word in this era on the institution of slavery.

SILENCE: CELEBRATE WHITEFIELD—THE SLAVE OWNER (1770)

Robert Keene, one of the managers of Whitefield's Tabernacle in Moorfields, London—a church Whitefield's followers built—once asked Whitefield, "If you should die abroad, who shall we get to preach your funeral sermon? Must it be your old friend, the Reverend John Wesley?" Whitefield replied, "He is the man."[32] Whitefield died in 1770, and so it was.

John Wesley and George Whitefield were friends, enemies, and off-and-on coworkers for over three decades. Some were surprised by Whitefield's choice to have Wesley preach his eulogy. Many people wanted to celebrate Whitefield's life, and people were curious to hear what Wesley had to say about his sometimes-foe.

Wesley arrived at the funeral two and a half hours early. The church was already full. There was no reason to delay, so the funeral began nearly two hours earlier than planned.

When Wesley climbed the pulpit to deliver his eulogy, he chose to speak about Whitefield's life, his character, and what to learn from him.[33] Wesley had plenty he could say about Whitefield's well-publicized and dynamic life—about his thirteen transatlantic adventures, his legendary thundering voice that pierced crowds of thousands clamoring together in an open field, and his prolific authorship of bestselling sermons and personal journals. Wesley discussed all of those topics and more, but he kept returning to one particular passion of Whitefield's life, something that had spanned the entire timeline of his ministry and occupied much of his energy: Bethesda, Whitefield's orphanage in Savannah, Georgia.

Wesley explained that shortly after Whitefield's first step on American land, he committed to helping the poor orphans of Georgia. He retraced how Whitefield obtained the land and initial finances, then laid the cornerstone of the house for the orphans and other workers. Wesley eulogized Whitefield's piety, virtue, faithfulness, charity, tenderheartedness, and commitment to "moral duty." Wesley believed that Whitefield's Bethesda orphan house illustrated the "integrity which was inseparable from his whole character, and regulated all his words and actions."[34] Wesley closed his eulogy urging his hearers to respond to Whitefield's example of "catholic love"—his universal love for all people.

After Whitefield's funeral, critics wrote that Wesley underrepresented Whitefield's Calvinistic theology. But no one criticized Wesley's evaluation of Whitefield's life and character.

A funeral is not the proper time to dwell on a friend's failures. Still, did Wesley really believe that Whitefield's orphanage was an example of "moral duty" to every person who arrived at Bethesda, or just for some people? Was Whitefield's orphanage good news for everyone who heard about it or stepped foot on the property?

John Wesley was completely aware of Whitefield's slaveholding. On August 30, 1747, Whitefield wrote to Wesley, commenting, "I have news of the awakening of several negroes at my new plantation, lately purchased at South-Carolina."[35] A few years later, on March 22, 1751, Whitefield wrote Wesley a longer letter explaining in detail how he justified his support for slavery; this is the letter we examined earlier where Whitefield wrote, "As for the lawfulness of keeping slaves I have no doubt."[36] On the same day, Whitefield composed a similar letter to another friend, providing biblical justification for owning slaves.[37]

Wesley was aware, too, of Whitefield's efforts to expand his Georgia plantation into a college. One month prior to Whitefield's death in February 1770, Wesley wrote Whitefield a pointed and firm admonishment against Whitefield's hopes to expand the Bethesda property to house five hundred college students. Wesley's letter was full of advice about how to utilize the land and financial resources at Bethesda differently.[38] But Wesley was silent on one topic: the source of Whitefield's funding, which Wesley knew came through slave labor.

Whitefield's plans for a large college did not come to fruition. Instead, eight months before his death, Whitefield's orphanage housed fifteen boys and one girl. Meanwhile, to support the sixteen children, Whitefield enslaved twenty-four men, eleven women, and fifteen children as his personal property.[39]

In the year of Whitefield's death, his orphanage—his life-dream, which Wesley lovingly eulogized at length—served sixteen children and enslaved fifty people through the practice of chattel slavery. Just imagine the cost of supporting a college of five hundred students. Wesley's letter to Whitefield in 1770 shows that he wasn't concerned about the cost of what was happening at Bethesda, but about Whitefield's choice to prioritize academic prestige above the needs of orphan children.

A few months after Whitefield's death, his estate was inventoried. This account includes a list of his twelve head of cattle, various garden tools, acreage, and then lists an "account of negroes." This included Dick, Oxford, Adam, Abner, Thomas, Luke, Simon, Old Will, Toby, Jacob, Scipio, Cato, Benjamin, Peter, Jonathan, Davy, Matthew, Cyrus, Titus, Job, Jeremy, Abraham, Abigail, Fanny, Sarah, Beck, Bet, Mary, Nanny, Phoebe, Susan, Hannah, Amoretta, Nat, Gearge,[40] Sampson, Saul, Sam, Daniel, Joe, Paul, Isaac, London, Aaron, Old Sambo, Rachel, Esther, Ruth, and Dinah. These forty-nine humans—one less than the count several months earlier—were purchased and owned by George Whitefield at a value of £2,197, which made up 74 percent of the entire value of his Bethesda endeavor.[41] Whitefield did not free any of these enslaved people but willed them instead to his wealthy benefactor in England.

A month before this inventory, on November 29, 1770, Wesley wrote to a friend about the "excellent institution the Orphan House in Georgia."[42] Five months after the inventory, Wesley wrote another friend about "that good man Mr. Whitefield."[43]

Despite Wesley's firsthand knowledge of the evils of slavery in Georgia, he did not speak against the institution of slavery. If anything, he further equipped enslavers to continue doing their work. He provided books to educate enslaved Africans. He advocated for the Christianization of enslaved Africans. He celebrated his friend and enslaver George Whitefield. This forces us to question Wesley's letter near the end of his life, when he wrote to Granville Sharp in 1787, "Ever since I heard of it I felt a perfect detestation of the horrid Slave Trade."[44] Perhaps Wesley "felt" a certain way about slavery, but we have seen that he waited many decades to say anything about it.

As of 1772, nothing distinguished Wesley's and Whitefield's beliefs about slavery. Both believed in educating slaves, both believed in Christianizing slaves, both were against violence toward slaves—and both affirmed the institution of slavery. What distinguished Whitefield from Wesley was only that Whitefield owned and operated property in colonial America that required labor. Wesley had no plantations in America. If he had in this era—up to around 1772—I believe he would have purchased slaves. Yet a small, unusual, and vocal group of people were gaining more and more attention from Wesley and others.

PART 3

ACTION
ACTION AGAINST SLAVERY

9

UNLIKELY VOICES

QUAKERS

LATE ON A RAINY NIGHT IN SAVANNAH, Georgia, the director of the Beach Institute, an African American cultural center, asked me a question. "Sean," he said, then paused for a long moment. "Do you know who the first abolitionist was?"

He had given me a private and in-depth three-hour tour after the museum was closed to others. He had stayed even longer to talk with me and educate me. He was asking me what I thought was a simple question with a simple answer.

I confess that in my mind I quickly assembled a list of people—but none of them was the right answer. Fortunately, I knew I was there to learn, not to educate him, so I kept my mouth shut. He knew what he was doing, and I'm grateful he was so gracious to me. After I let the silence echo for a few moments, he answered his question for me. He said, "The first abolitionist was the first enslaved person."

A few months later, I shared this story with a friend who told me the Black museum director was wrong. He told me there were times in history when slavery wasn't all that bad. He suggested that some people were fortunate to be enslaved. I couldn't disagree with him more—and I told him so.

In the next two chapters we will look at the influences that helped persuade John Wesley to speak up publicly about slavery. One of the primary catalysts for Wesley was what he learned from Quaker abolitionists. This chapter will highlight Quaker abolitionism, but their cause would not exist if enslaved people themselves had not already sought freedom.

Simply put, the well-deserved credit that Quakers receive for their abolitionism comes only because of the brave cries for freedom from enslaved people themselves. Historian Manisha Sinha writes, "Slave resistance . . . lay at the heart of the abolition movement. . . . The story of abolition must begin with the struggles of the enslaved."[1] Far too often the story of abolitionism begins with "White heroes" because, as Toni Morrison wrote, "Definitions belong to the definers, not the defined."[2]

The voices of enslaved people in the era of Wesley, Edwards, and Whitefield were rarely repeated in print and seldom loud enough to be heard across the Atlantic, where Wesley lived. The voices of the enslaved needed messengers, which they fortunately found.

WHO ARE THE QUAKERS?

The Society for the Relief of Free Negroes Unlawfully Held in Bondage had its first meeting in April 1775 in Philadelphia. Seventeen of the twenty-four men who first attended were Quakers. When the Society for the Abolition of the Slave Trade first met in James Phillips's small printshop in London in May 1787, nine of the twelve people in the room were Quakers.

Why were Quakers, a small sect in Britain and America, such an overwhelming majority of the early abolitionists? The answer begins over a century earlier.

The political upheavals of mid-seventeenth-century Britain led to the growth of an array of religious groups in England, including the Baptists and the Quakers. During this time, George Fox, who had grown up in a devout Anglican family, increasingly followed an inner voice from God that troubled him but also led him to preach publicly as he studied the Bible further.

Fox's teaching included several important beliefs. First, and centrally, Fox believed that every person has access to a direct inner encounter with God. Second, following the first principle, he taught of the spiritual equality of every person. Third, because of equal access to God's voice, he believed the church is not led by individual voting but by corporate guidance. And fourth, on the basis of human equality, he insisted on a commitment to peace, pacifism, and nonviolence. Due to his belief in equality, Fox did not hesitate to challenge authority—for which he was repeatedly imprisoned.

In May 1652, Fox felt led by God to climb 1,300 feet up Pendle Hill in northwest England, where he had a vision of a "great people to be gathered." This led him to form a monthly meeting of a "Society of Friends," who responded and gathered around his teaching. This group later became known as the Quakers, presumably as those who tremble at the Word of God.

It's easy to see how the seeds of Fox's beliefs could sprout into abolitionism. First, Fox believed that God's vision for humanity required a radical nonhierarchical spiritual and natural equality of all people—equality among men, women, White, Black, brown, rich, poor—absolutely every human. This belief stands against the unequal owner-slave relationship foundational to slavery. Second, because of a commitment to nonviolence, the inherent violence in the vast majority of owner-slave relationships was also not only morally but spiritually reprehensible. And third, because of a radical commitment to equality, Quakers did not hesitate to challenge anyone's authority, including the king and his government—and that is what got them in trouble the most. Yet the group continued to strengthen, growing to fifty thousand members by the end of the seventeenth century.[3]

While Fox's principles laid the foundation for later abolitionism, he did not reject the institution of slavery itself. Mirroring the emphases of other Christians we've already discussed, he focused on obedience of slaves to their masters, proper education of slaves, and their Christianization. The apparent contradiction between his principles and their application created division among Quakers regarding slavery for nearly a century. When Fox traveled to Barbados in 1671, he recommended (but did not insist) that slaves be freed after a certain term of service.[4] He told them "to be sober and fear God, and to love their masters and mistresses, and to be faithful and diligent in their masters' service and business."[5] While in Barbados, Fox's focus was not on liberating slaves, but on dispelling rumors that Quakers were inciting slave revolts; his goal was to soothe slave owners' worries.[6]

In 1666, at the age of twenty-two, William Penn joined the Quakers and began traveling with George Fox throughout England and Europe. William Penn leveraged his family's legacy to design his "Holy Experiment," an English colony of religious freedom founded in 1682 and undergirded by Quaker principles. He called it Pennsylvania to honor his father. The Holy Experiment quickly ran into challenges, one of which was the issue of slavery. Penn mimicked Fox's position on slavery—Penn owned slaves and sought to treat them "ethically." It was during this time that a group of four Pennsylvania Quakers authored the 1688 Germantown Petition. Despite its frequent appearance in modern discussions of early antislavery activism, the Germantown Petition made little or no impact on the Quakers or on the institution of slavery.

Five years later a Pennsylvania Quaker named George Keith produced one of the earliest antislavery tracts, a six-page work titled *An Exhortation & Caution to Friends Concerning Buying or Keeping of Negroes* which argued for "inward and outward" liberty for all people "without exception."[7]

In September 1738, a fifty-six-year-old hunchbacked man who stood a little over four feet tall wobbled from his home (he lived in a cave) with his tiny cane into the Quakers' Philadelphia yearly meeting. Beneath his overcoat, he wore a military costume with a sword hidden at his side. He made his way to the front of the meeting and said, "Oh all you Negro masters who are contently holding your fellow creatures in a state of slavery . . . you might as well throw off the plain coat as I do," which he did. He then continued, "It should be as justifiable in the sight of the Almighty . . . if you should thrust a sword through their hearts as

I do through this book!" Then he drew his sword over his head and thrust it through a Bible he had brought with him.

The Bible had been hollowed out, and inside was a bladder full of blood-red pokeberry juice. The juice splattered "blood" all over the Quakers near the front of the meeting. The members picked the man up and carried him out of the building—but he had made his point clear. His name was Benjamin Lay, and he was a Quaker man of action— action against the institution of slavery.[8]

A year before his "blood Bible" protest, Lay, who had been in Barbados and witnessed the horrors of slavery firsthand, brought unorganized portions of letters, extensive reflections on biblical passages, history, autobiography, and arguments against slavery to his Philadelphia friend Benjamin Franklin. Franklin offered to organize, edit, and print the material, which ended up forming a 277-page book.[9] The book was called *All Slave Keepers That Keep the Innocent in Bondage, Apostates*.[10] The book made an impact, especially on generations of abolitionists, including Thomas Clarkson and Benjamin Rush. Lay's writing and activism did not create any immediate official change among Quakers, but he inspired many others, including a Quaker who was likely present in the assembly for Lay's 1738 "blood Bible" protest: John Woolman.[11]

Woolman grew up in a devout Quaker family near Philadelphia. For nearly thirty years he traveled through the colonies to undertake missionary work and constantly advocated for the rights of slaves. Woolman's work among the Philadelphia Quakers and their annual meeting in the mid-1750s became a turning point for the splintered opinions and practices of Quakers regarding slavery. In 1755, a year after publishing Woolman's key work, the Philadelphia annual meeting published their own work, *An Epistle of Caution and Advice, Concerning the Buying and Keeping of Slaves*, which argued against not just the slave trade, but the institution of slavery itself. This work was sent across the Atlantic to the London yearly meeting and influenced their decision in 1758 to formally condemn the slave trade.[12] Woolman's essay caught the eye of another

Philadelphia Quaker who would have an enormous impact on John Wesley. Before we get to that, we need to take a step back and realize what non-Quakers thought of them in the eighteenth century. It's easy to esteem Quakers today as pioneers of English and American abolitionism, but in the eighteenth century, they were an unlikely voice for Christians to listen to.

QUAKERS AS UNLIKELY INFLUENCES ON WESLEY AND OTHERS

As we look back and admire the (eventual) abolitionist stance of the Quakers, it's difficult for us to realize how eccentric their sect was among Christians and society at large. They were an odd and unlikely voice to listen to—their beliefs had little authority or sway outside themselves. Very few non-Quakers were saying, "The Quakers make a good point! We should listen to them."

The primary reason the Quakers were a fringe group among Christians and society stems from their foundational belief of the primacy of the inner light of God inside every person. While this same belief undergirded their commitment to equality, which led to their abolitionism, it also caused much pushback.

Because of the Quaker primacy of the inner light as the leading of God's Spirit inside every person, they rejected many traditional Christian beliefs. Quakers taught that Scripture was secondary to this kind of direct revelation. For Quakers, the Scriptures are "a secondary rule, subordinate to the Spirit . . . for as by the inward testimony of the Spirit we do alone truly know them."[13] For Quakers, the inner work of the Spirit speaks to all humans and can overrule established Christian norms that are formed by Christian tradition. This means that first-order Christian doctrines found in the creeds, such as the Trinity, are not a formal part of Quaker beliefs. The Quakers' emphasis on the inner work of God also negated the need for external sacraments. These views were a significant departure from traditional Christian belief and practice and made traditional Christians skeptical of their sect and opinions.

Jonathan Edwards spoke against Quaker beliefs many times. For example, in a sermon about Satan, Edwards wrote, "As a false teacher, [Satan] plies doctrines of salvation 'under color of divine truth,' convincing Muslims that Mohammed is a 'true prophet,' Catholics that they serve the interests and kingdom of Christ, and Quakers that their inner light is indeed the Holy Spirit."[14] Edwards's rejection of the Quakers continued what he received from his Puritan forefathers, who spoke against Quaker theology and persecuted them.[15]

We would expect George Whitefield, as a Church of England priest, to reject the Quakers too, due to their rejection of some central beliefs of orthodox Christianity. But because Whitefield emphasized the power of the Holy Spirit moving through the mind, emotions, and experiences of people, he was open to accepting how God might move outside the formal boundaries of his own church. For instance, in his journal on March 23, 1739, Whitefield wrote, "Dined with many Quakers at Frenchay, who entertained me and my friends with much Christian love; but we could by no means agree about the disuse of the two outward signs in the Sacrament, nor of their absolute refusing to pay tithes. But I think their notions about walking and being led by the Spirit are right and good."[16] Whitefield collaborated and worked with Quakers, but he also worked to convince them of aligning to traditional beliefs, such as baptism.[17]

Similarly, John Wesley also stressed the importance of the Holy Spirit's direct influence on the lives of people. Wesley and Whitefield spent their formative years together in the Holy Club at Oxford and pioneered the evangelical revival using similar beliefs about the work of the Spirit. At the outset of the formal organization of Methodism, Methodist leaders met in 1744 to discuss a list of questions, including "What can we adopt from . . . the Quakers?"[18] The following year, Wesley wrote, "There is still a wider difference in some points between us and the people usually termed Quakers."[19]

Wesley, like Whitefield, sought to convert Quakers to traditional beliefs and practices—in fact, there were many Quaker converts to

Methodism. Wesley appreciated how his Quaker friends were attentive to the leading of the Spirit and their commitment to personal holiness, but "a wider difference" remained and was never resolved between Wesley's creedal and ecclesiastical theology and that of the Quakers.

The Quakers isolated themselves theologically and politically, and outsiders generally were content for Quakers to stay away. They were a fringe voice. It would have been difficult for most eighteenth-century Christians to receive the antislavery message from Quakers due to their beliefs and practices, which to this day remain on the fringes of Christianity. Yet eventually, John Wesley was willing to listen—especially to one particular Quaker.

ANTHONY BENEZET—THE QUAKER
OUTSIDERS STARTED LISTENING TO

The Benezets immigrated to Philadelphia from London in 1731 after coming into contact with the Moravians and Quakers. In the ensuing years, John Stephen Benezet hosted Moravian bishops August Spangenberg and Nicolaus Zinzendorf in his Philadelphia home. In April 1740, George Whitefield purchased five thousand acres located seventy-five miles from Philadelphia, naming it Nazareth, with the intention of relocating Moravians from Georgia to the property and forming a school for Black children. John Stephen served as a manager and collector of donations for Whitefield's Nazareth, though Whitefield's project never came to fruition. By this time John Stephen's son Anthony had married a Quaker woman, who was herself a Quaker minister. Anthony spent time working as a proofreader in a printshop (a skill that would become very useful later in his life) and began his lifelong career as a schoolteacher.

Anthony's time in the Philadelphia Quaker community brought him into contact with early abolitionists Benjamin Lay and John Woolman. These relationships, combined with his father's efforts to form a school for Black children, help us understand why, in 1750, Anthony began teaching Black people in the evenings in his home. Benezet lived in the center of the slave-trading area of Philadelphia and saw daily the challenges and lack of resources they faced. An advertisement in the *Philadelphia Gazette* on October 3, 1751, read, "SOLD, A Parcel of likely Negroes, very reasonable. . . . Said Negroes may be seen at a Free Negroe Woman, in Chester Street, opposite to Mr. Anthony Benezet."[20] When Anthony opened the door of his Philadelphia house, he and the Black children he educated saw just across the street a place where slaves were sold.

While Benezet's most important publication would come in 1771, his work in 1766 became the catalyst for a series of events that grew his influence well beyond his Philadelphia Quaker circles. That year, Benezet authored what historian and editor David Crosby calls "a user's manual for antislavery activists," titled *A Caution and Warning to Great Britain and Her Colonies*.[21] Benezet argued for ending the slave trade by imploring the king and his government to act because the king and government were being taken advantage of by greedy and morally despicable merchants. His evidence included several pages of George Whitefield's descriptions of the inhumane treatment of slaves in Maryland, Virginia, and the Carolinas.[22]

By evaluating Benezet's subsequent publications, we can see that his antislavery strategy originated primarily with rationale based on the Bible but increasingly depended on historical accounts, interviews, moral philosophy, and rhetorical strategies to motivate readers to action. These tactics proved to be successful in abolishing the slave trade but unsuccessful in resolving the exegetical and hermeneutical tensions Christians faced when they turned to individual Bible passages that discuss slavery.

Anthony Benezet's publications attracted attention beyond the Quakers, and sometimes in surprising ways. In 1767, Granville Sharp, a self-taught antislavery lawyer, was rummaging through books in a London book stall when he "accidentally met with a copy" of Benezet's 1762 work *A Short Account of that Part of Africa Inhabited by the Negroes*.[23] At this time Sharp was wrapping up defending the rights of

Jonathan Strong, a Barbadian enslaved man whose owner had taken him to London and beaten him to the point of death. Later, when the enslaver saw Strong still alive, he attempted to recover his "property." Sharp intervened, educated himself in law, and became the foremost antislavery lawyer of the eighteenth century.[24]

When Sharp found Benezet's publication, he reprinted it in London, despite Sharp's description of Benezet being "involved in the errors of Quakerism" and without asking for permission. (This practice, while bold, was not improper in that era.)[25] Two years later, in 1769, Sharp authored a summary of his legal arguments titled *A Representation of the Injustice and Dangerous Tendency of Tolerating Slavery*—the first tract in England attacking slavery. In an ironic twist, though the two had not met each other, nor corresponded, Benezet discovered Sharp's publication and reprinted it himself in Philadelphia.[26] It wasn't until May 1772 that Benezet and Sharp corresponded directly, when Benezet wrote to Sharp a letter which begins, "I have long been desirous to advise with such well-minded persons in England, who have a prospect of the iniquity of the Slave Trade, and are concerned to prevent its continuation."[27] Benezet enclosed several publications with his letter— including his 1771 work we will discuss below. Benezet also spoke of his correspondence with "my friend, J Wesley" and Wesley's intention to create antislavery publications.[28]

Benezet believed that his previous publications were not making the impact he had hoped for. He felt he needed to produce something better, and he did just that when he wrote *Some Historical Account of Guinea* in 1771. Abolitionism scholar David Crosby wrote that it "became a kind of bible for later abolitionists in England and America. . . . It also became the standard early-nineteenth-century source for African history, with parts of it incorporated whole into early editions of the *Encyclopedia Britannica*."[29]

In *Some Historical Account of Guinea*, Benezet argued that West Africa is inhabited by people who are sociable, capable, and fully human, who lived amid a commendable government and economy, in which "they might have lived happily if not disturbed by the Europeans."[30] Near the end of his work Benezet presents a plan for gradual emancipation.[31] At the end, Benezet included four extracts of additional works: first, Granville Sharp's 1769 publication; second, writings on natural law by Wallace, Hutchenson, and Foster included in earlier works; third, an antislavery address by Arthur Lee to the Assembly of Virginia; and fourth, a sermon by Bishop Warburton included in Benezet's previous work. None of the supplements included at the end of Benezet's most well-known work were written by Quakers. The inclusion of these sources illustrates that by 1771 the Quakers were not alone in their antislavery crusade in England and America. Though at that time, Benezet couldn't have imagined the boost that his campaign would receive from his new friend across the Atlantic.

10

WESLEY SPEAKS
ABOUT SLAVERY

As John Wesley concluded his eulogy for George Whitefield and stepped down from the pulpit of Tottenham Court Road Chapel in London on November 18, 1770, he knew that Whitefield had operated the orphanage on the backs of slave labor—slaves owned by Whitefield himself.

Within months after writing Whitefield's eulogy, Wesley began writing an altogether different eulogy—a eulogy for his silence on slavery. It would spark a new passion that Wesley would embrace for the rest of his life: antislavery.

While Wesley was writing his eulogy for Whitefield, across the Atlantic, Anthony Benezet was putting the finishing touches on his publication *Some Historical Account of Guinea*. Fifteen months later, Wesley read Benezet's work, prompting Wesley to open his journal and write, "I read a very different book, published by an honest Quaker, on that execrable sum of all villainies, commonly called the 'slave trade.' I read of nothing like it in the heathen world, whether ancient or modern."[1]

Wesley had long been aware of the atrocities of the slave trade, but had been silent on this topic. Reading Benezet's work, however, was a tipping point which prompted Wesley to speak up and use his voice and platform regarding political, ethical, and social issues on which he had previously been silent.

These concerns did not arise in his mind overnight. Many of them had been there for many years. Had he waited too long to speak up?

ONE INFLUENCE: METHODISM IN AMERICA

In the years leading up to Wesley's reading of Benezet's letter in 1772, several major changes occurred in Wesley's world. In the previous decade, Wesley's people, called Methodists, and their societies had spread well beyond the British Isles and into places where the atrocities of slavery were a daily part of life. Remember, because Wesley had lived in the British Isles since his departure from Georgia in 1737, he was insulated by the Atlantic from most of the harsh realities of slavery.

The first Methodists arrived in America in 1760, and three years later Robert Strawbridge formed a Methodist class in Maryland. In 1766 the first Methodist congregation in America was established. Before the end of the decade, Wesley sent two missionaries to America. By the time of the American revolution there were twenty-two preachers and nearly three thousand Methodists in the American colonies—primarily in Maryland, Virginia, Pennsylvania, and New York.[2] Francis Asbury was one of these ministers. He arrived in 1771, became co-superintendent, and eventually bishop of Methodism in America.

Methodism also took root in the West Indies. It took root in Antigua in 1759 through slaveholder Nathaniel Gilbert and his brother Francis (as we saw in chapter eight). Wesley was in frequent contact with the Gilberts and, in 1768 and 1773, published separate books about the lives and unfortunate deaths of Nathaniel's daughters Mary and Alice. In the midst of Wesley's correspondence with Gilbert, on October 29, 1768, Gilbert wrote to Anthony Benezet, "Your tracts concerning slavery are very just, and it is a matter I have often thought of even before I became acquainted with the truth. Your arguments are forcible against purchasing slaves, or being anyway concerned in that trade."[3] Gilbert came into contact with Benezet's writings over three years before Wesley did— one wonders if Gilbert introduced Wesley to Benezet's works. Benezet would later call Gilbert "much esteemed" and "my dear friend."[4] Still, despite Gilbert's friendship and compliments to Benezet, Gilbert continued his activities in the slave trade.

While Methodism was growing in the Americas, America's evolving political situation occupied more and more of Wesley's attention. The Stamp Act of 1765 imposed taxes on American colonists and increased tensions with Britain, as did the occupation of Boston by British troops in 1768—leading to the Boston Massacre in 1770. Wesley wrote and published a letter to a friend in 1768 titled *Free Thoughts on the Present State of Public Affairs*. Wesley wrote, "I am no politician; politics lie quite out of my province."[5] He went on to argue, however, that the colonists are "deprived of that liberty which their ancestors bought with so much treasure and blood."[6] Wesley defended the king's authority over his people but blamed the turmoil on his political appointees in the colonies.

Four years later, leading up to the moment when Wesley read Benezet, Wesley wrote two important political tracts: *Thoughts upon Liberty* and *Thoughts Concerning the Origin of Power*. In the former work, Wesley's first lines are: "All men in the world desire liberty; whoever breathes, breathes after this, and that by a kind of natural instinct antecedent to art or education. . . . The love of liberty is then the glory of rational beings."[7] Wesley's concern at this point is not slavery, but it is clear that the increasing tension and issues in the American colonies provided an opportunity for Wesley to think, write, and publish his beliefs and teachings on liberty.

Wesley wrote this on February 24, 1772, just twelve days after reading Benezet's works about slavery. Wesley does not write directly about the slave trade, as Benezet does, but we can see that the topic is in his mind as he writes about "the liberty of taking, when we see best, the goods and chattels of our neighbors."[8] He continues, "God did never give authority to any man, or number of men, to deprive any child of man thereof, under any colour or pretence whatever."[9] Wesley's publication later that year explores who should have power "over our liberty and property."[10] Mimicking what we will see in what Wesley read in

Benezet's work, Wesley discusses what the "first adventurers to America found."[11] Wesley concludes that power "belongs to every individual of the human species," which includes men, women, younger people, and those of all economic statuses.[12] The circumstances in the American colonies paved the way for Wesley to reflect deeply on the nature of liberty and equality for all humans.

In 1772, Granville Sharp, whom we met in the last chapter, was arguing the famous Somerset case before Lord Mansfield regarding the rights of enslaved people. On the day when Sharp won his case, which secured the freedom of the previously enslaved man named James Somerset—and by inference stated that in England slavery had no legal basis—Sharp received a letter from Benezet that discussed his "friend" John Wesley's desire to work with Sharp to publish a weekly publication on the "origin, nature, and dreadful effects of the slave trade."[13] Wesley must have reached out to Benezet several months earlier, due to the pace of transatlantic communication. When Sharp received his letter from Benezet, it was not Sharp's first introduction to Wesley. The reason Wesley had Benezet's works in the first place was that Wesley had written Granville Sharp regarding his desire to write against the slave trade, of which Sharp "furnished him with a large bundle of Books and Papers."[14] These resources formed the basis for Wesley's *Thoughts upon Slavery*.

The following year, Wesley's antislavery journey was heightened when two enslaved brothers—Little Ephraim Robin John and Ancona Robin Robin John, of the Efik clan in Africa, members of the ruling family of Old Town, Calabar, Nigeria—arrived in Bristol, England. They had previously been in Virginia, where they had learned of Methodism and the Wesley brothers, so they sought them out upon their arrival in Bristol. After spending a month or so catechizing them, Charles Wesley baptized them on January 23, 1774. The following month John wrote his brother Charles about Ephraim and Ancona Robin.[15]

The growth of Methodism in America by the late 1760s and early 1770s brought questions about freedom, liberty, and direct engagement with slavery to John Wesley's world in a way that he had not experienced before. But that wasn't the only influence that was percolating in Wesley's mind, leading him toward his eventual antislavery advocacy.

ANOTHER INFLUENCE: WESLEY'S MATURING ESCHATOLOGY

While external circumstances were changing in John Wesley's world, his internal thinking about how God was shaping the present world was changing too. In his younger years, Wesley held to a view that Christians were to not expect too much from the imperfect political rulers and the imperfect church—he believed that Christians were to wait for the true king (Jesus) to return to fully restore the true church.[16] Consider Wesley's 1765 comments on Isaiah 60:18, where the Scripture states, "No longer will violence be heard in your land, nor ruin or destruction within your borders, but you will call your walls Salvation and your gates Praise." Wesley writes, "All this will be fulfilled during the thousand years wherein Christ shall reign upon earth."[17] Wesley eventually believed God might begin that process sooner. He believed increasingly that God's immediate intentions were to change not only souls, but also our bodies; not only individuals, but also our societies; not only humans, but all of creation—now, rather than waiting until "later."[18]

In his younger years, Wesley could have viewed the plight of slavery with disdain and abhorrence, seeking, like many of his peers, to regulate a "benevolent" form of slavery in the midst of a broken and imperfect world which would never be corrected until the return of Christ. But beginning in the late 1760s, Wesley's theology of the end times changed the way he understood the role Christians played in political and social issues. Rather than sitting on his hands, Wesley began getting his hands dirty in the difficult social issues of the day. An example of this is found in his primary publication immediately prior to *Thoughts upon Slavery*, called *Thoughts upon the Present Scarcity of Provisions*. In this publication he asked, "Why are thousands of people starving, perishing for want, in every part of the nation?"[19] He also asked, "Why are so many thousand people, in London, in Bristol, in Norwich, in every county, from one end of England to the other, utterly destitute of employment?"[20] Wesley provided specific answers for his Christian readers to put into action. As 1774 drew near, not only was Wesley's world changing through the expansion of Methodism, but his theology was changing in a way that motivated him to focus further on political and social causes—including slavery.

SPEAKING UP: WESLEY PUBLISHES *THOUGHTS UPON SLAVERY*

In the months leading up to 1774, John Wesley took up his winter residence in London and began compiling his sources and ideas for a new publication against slavery. In February 1774, Wesley released the results of his work: *Thoughts upon Slavery*.

Wesley's *Thoughts upon Slavery* contains five sections. The first three sections are compilations of publications from three authors. They include an introduction by lawyer Francis Hargrave, followed by details from Anthony Benezet and Granville Sharp on West Africa and how Africans are captured by enslavers. In the fourth and fifth sections, Wesley reveals his own thoughts, discusses whether slavery can be defended, and concludes by providing practical applications.

Wesley's editorial abridgment in the first three sections is the primary genius of *Thoughts upon Slavery*. The publications by Sharp and Benezet were thorough and comprehensive. They were also very lengthy and so were mostly read only by people who had both time and money to devote to a rather unpopular topic. These tended to be people already committed or leaning toward antislavery. Wesley's abridgment of these materials made this information accessible to a broader audience, since it dramatically brought down both the length and the price of this material—the majority of Wesley's prints of *Thoughts upon Slavery* sold for a mere two pence each.[21]

The last two sections of *Thoughts upon Slavery* display Wesley's original contribution. They form about half of the publication. Wesley begins by asking, "I would now inquire, whether these things can be defended?"[22] Interestingly (and of supreme importance for issues that will plague his legacy and that of much of the Christian antislavery movement), Wesley declares that he will make his arguments from "heathen honesty," by which he means natural law, logic, and philosophy, rather than from biblical rationale—Wesley writes, "setting the Bible out of the question."[23] Wesley does not explain why he made the decision to use secular arguments rather than biblical ones. A charitable speculation would be that Wesley wanted his argument against slavery to appeal to Christians and non-Christians alike, and to avoid intramural squabbling over specific Bible passages. A more ominous speculation would be that Wesley was not prepared to tackle the challenge to resolve the tenuous scriptural teaching on slavery—a challenge that remained for later Christians.[24]

Wesley's answer to whether slavery can be defended is no: "I absolutely deny all slave-holding to be consistent with any degree of natural justice."[25] He supports his argument by examining several common justifications for slavery. First, he rejects the idea that capturing a slave in war, buying a slave selling themselves into slavery, and keeping the children of slaves are legitimate ways to enslave someone. Instead, he explains that these reasons are "built upon false foundations."[26] Next, he writes against those who insist on enslaving Black people because they are supposedly more suited for work in hot climates—an argument George Whitefield used.[27] Wesley shows that this is a false claim and gives firsthand evidence from his time in Georgia as one of his proofs. Last, he shows the absurd belief that Black people are "stupid" compared to White people. Wesley writes, "Certainly the African is in no respect inferior to the European."[28] Wesley further explains that if any educational deficit appears among enslaved Black people, it is because their masters have withheld educational resources and opportunities, not because of any inherent disability.

Wesley closes *Thoughts upon Slavery* with a section on application. Wesley argues for a "bottom-up" solution rather than "top-down." At this point of his career, Wesley believed the "top-down" approach of petitioning Parliament to be ineffective. "So many things, which seem of greater importance, lie before [Parliament], that they are not likely to attend to this."[29] Wesley published this work in 1774; this was a time when the British government was navigating an increasing revolutionary crisis in their transatlantic colonies. Instead, Wesley argues for a "bottom-up" approach, calling on individual ship captains, with similar words for merchants and plantation owners, to "Immediately quit the horrid trade: At all events, be an honest man."[30] In his closing statements, Wesley writes, "Liberty is the right of every human creature. . . . Let none serve you but by his own act and deed, by his own voluntary choice."[31]

Wesley's *Thoughts upon Slavery* was an incomplete argument against slavery (as we'll see in a moment), but it also was a major step forward in the antislavery movement, and in Wesley's life. Until this point, Wesley had not openly and clearly denounced the slave trade and the institution of slavery. For thirty-seven years he had been aware of the horrors, injustice, and inhumanity of slavery and had not spoken up about it. Now, finally, loudly, and bluntly, Wesley states, "I absolutely deny all slave-holding."[32]

Wesley's publication is as interesting for what it left out as for what it said. Wesley drew much of it from Benezet's *Some Historical Account of Guinea*, but he chose to discard several important topics Benezet included. First, unlike Wesley, Benezet chose to engage Scripture and theology, discussing how slavery related to the Mosaic law, the theology of Richard Baxter, and additional engagement with Scriptures from Genesis, Jeremiah, and Luke.[33] Wesley, on the other hand, chose only to engage natural law. It is a bit odd, to say the least, that the Quaker author engaged more Scripture and theology than Wesley on this topic. Additionally, Benezet provided detailed proposals for gradual emancipation of slaves; Wesley provided no guidance on this topic. Last, Benezet provided an extract of a sermon from Bishop Warburton preached to the slaveholding Society for the Propagation of the Gospel— Wesley provided no sermon.[34]

Across the Atlantic, Benezet acquired a copy of Wesley's *Thoughts upon Slavery*. Benezet wrote Wesley on May 23, 1774, that Wesley's publication "afforded me much satisfaction. I was the more especially glad to see it, as the circumstances of the times made it necessary that something on that most weighty subject, not large, but striking and pathetic, should now be published."[35] Benezet enjoyed Wesley's work, especially as an accessible abridgment. He explained to Wesley that he reprinted Wesley's work in Philadelphia. In this new edition, Benezet added lengthy additional footnotes, an afterword, and addenda—increasing its length by 85 percent.[36] Benezet added a section explaining how a slave could purchase their freedom from their master and, once again, included the Warburton sermon extract.[37]

Benezet didn't feel that Wesley provided enough practical and explicitly Christian details to reprint as it was. Wesley's *Thoughts upon Slavery* may have been a turning point in his life, but it was an incomplete work—and Wesley's antislavery work had really just begun.

AMERICAN LIBERTY DIVERTS WESLEY'S ANTISLAVERY EFFORTS (1775–1783)

When he published *Thoughts upon Slavery* in 1774, Wesley hoped to abolish "all slavery."[38] Any momentum he created, however, was diverted a year later when, on April 19, 1775, the shot heard round the world was fired at the battles of Lexington and Concord in Massachusetts, initiating the Revolutionary War.

Four months later, Wesley published *A Calm Address to Our American Colonies*, where he asked, "'Who then is a slave?' Look into America, and you may easily see. . . . Vainly do you [those in American colonies] complain of being 'made slaves.' Am I or two millions of Englishmen made slaves because we are taxed without our own consent?"[39] Wesley attacked Americans who justified their rebellion by equating their taxation under monarchical rule to slavery. He continued this attack on November 7, 1775, in his sermon *National Sins and Miseries*: "All those who are either passionately or dolefully crying out 'Bondage!

Slavery!' while there is no more danger of any such thing than there is of the sky falling upon their head, are utterly distracted; their reason is gone; their intellects are quite confounded."[40] Wesley explained to the Americans, "You and I, and the English in general, go where we will, and enjoy the fruit of our labours: This is liberty. The Negro does not: This is slavery."[41]

A few months later, Wesley called on the British to take responsibility for their role in enslaving Africans abroad. He wrote, "One of the greatest evils of Britain is slavery . . . the blood that we have shed in Asia, Africa, and America. . . . [It is] iniquitous from first to last. It is the price of blood! It is a trade of blood, and has stained our land with blood!"[42] Later that year, and two months before the American Declaration of Independence, Wesley returned to his rhetoric of comparing actual slavery of Black people to American revolutionaries who claimed they were enslaved to the king of England. Wesley wrote, "Slavery is a state wherein neither a man's goods, nor liberty, nor life, are at his own disposal. Such is the state of a thousand, of ten thousand, Negroes in the American colonies. . . . This is slavery; and will you face us down that the Americans are in such slavery as this?"[43]

By 1776, Wesley had redirected his efforts from abolishing the slave trade to correcting what he saw as flawed arguments by American revolutionaries regarding their "slavery" to the king. Wesley's antislavery passion was further muted because the dangers of the Revolutionary War put a temporary pause on the transatlantic slave trade. On April 4, 1777, while Wesley was in Liverpool, one of the largest slave-trading ports, he gazed on the transatlantic ships that remained in port and wrote, "Since the American War broke out, there is no demand for human cattle."[44] Nearly a year later, Wesley celebrated the continued pause in the trade. Wesley wrote, "'We have also lost our Negro trade.' I would to God it may never be found more! that we may never more steal and sell our brethren like beasts; never murder them by thousands and tens of thousands! . . . Never was anything such a reproach to England since it was a nation, as the having any hand in this execrable traffic."[45]

The war temporarily abolished the slave trade more than Wesley's pamphlet could have ever done.

American Methodists, however, did engage the issue of human slavery directly, as we'll see in the next chapter. And with the conclusion of the American Revolution, Wesley would advocate more strongly than ever for the abolishment of slavery in all its forms, for the final decade of his life.

PUBLISH AND PREACH: WESLEY'S LAST
STAND AGAINST SLAVERY

In the nine years leading up to Wesley's *Thoughts upon Slavery*, 316,943 slaves were brought to mainland North America and the Caribbean from Africa via English ships. In the following nine years, this number was halved to 164,060 slaves. From 1779 to 1782, no slaves were imported via English ships into mainland North America, as the Revolutionary War put a temporary stop to the importation of slaves.[46]

After the Treaty of Paris in 1783, the English slave trade returned to the Americas, especially the Caribbean, stronger than ever—this brought Wesley back to focus on his efforts in abolishing the "horrid trade." He wasn't alone. A horrendous catalyst to renew the war against the slave trade originated in a terrible Atlantic tragedy.

In September 1781, the slave ship *Zong* departed Ghana for Jamaica with twice the number of people aboard as it could safely carry: 422 slaves. Due to navigation errors, the ship was low on fresh water, and many of the people aboard were sick and diseased. Over the course of three days, Captain Luke Collingwood selected 133 slaves and threw them overboard while still in their chains. When the ship finally arrived in Jamaica, there were still 420 gallons of fresh water on the *Zong*.

This horrific incident would have likely never come to the public's attention except that the owners of the *Zong* had taken out an insurance policy on their "cargo" of £30 per slave and intended to recoup this expense. Legal scholar Andrew Lyall points out, "The fact that the [owners] had no concern for the bad publicity itself shows the

confidence that the slave interest had at the time."[47] The insurance
company refused to pay, and the case came to court and to the public
eye in 1783. Granville Sharp attended the trial and publicized the details.
He also unsuccessfully brought murder charges against the crew
(Captain Collingwood was dead when the murder trial occurred).[48]

News of the *Zong* incident reached Dr. Peter Peckard, an Anglican
minister who, in 1784, preached against slavery. He called slavery "a
crime, founded on a dreadful preeminence in wickedness" which would
"draw down upon us the heaviest judgment of Almighty God."[49] The
following year, as vice chancellor of Cambridge University, Peckard had
the role of choosing the topic of Cambridge's most prestigious essay
contest. Dr. Peckard's question for the essay was: "Is it lawful to make
slaves of others against their will?"[50]

The previous year's winner of the lower-ranking prize sought to do
what no other Cambridge student had ever done before—to win both
the lower- and higher-level prizes. A striking young man named
Thomas Clarkson committed himself to this task and won, despite
knowing nothing about the topic two months prior to submitting his
essay. After winning the prize in 1785, Clarkson immersed himself in
the antislavery campaign and quickly partnered with the leaders of this
cause—the Quakers.[51]

Clarkson and the Quakers decided to form an antislavery organization. On the afternoon of Tuesday, May 22, 1787, twelve men gathered
in a print shop and bookstore in London for their first meeting. The
group consisted of nine Quakers and three Anglicans: Thomas Clarkson,
Phillip Sansom, and their esteemed elder stateman and well-known
chairman Granville Sharp. They organized themselves over the next
month and decided to focus on one goal: the abolition of the slave trade.
They debated whether they should seek to eliminate slavery entirely and
emancipate all slaves or to focus on an intermediate goal of abolishing
the slave trade. They determined that eradicating slavery entirely was
too lofty of a goal, especially since it would require Parliament to
override the local lawmaking authority of their distant colonies. They

determined that if they could abolish the slave trade, "they were laying the axe at the very root."[52] Thus, in June 1787 they named their committee the Society for Effecting the Abolition of the Slave Trade.

After their fourth meeting, Clarkson began involving a young Parliamentarian named William Wilberforce in their cause.[53] In July the members began making lists of people to whom they should send their antislavery publications. Responses began arriving back to the committee the following month, with the second letter coming from John Wesley.[54] This marks the pivotal intersection between Wesley and the abolition society that sparked a flame that eventually led to the abolition of the British slave trade in 1807.

Wesley's letter to the committee begins, "A week or two ago I was favoured with a letter from Mr. Clarkson, informing me of his truly Christian design to procure, if possible, an Act of Parliament for the abolition of slavery in our plantations."[55] Thirteen years earlier, in his *Thoughts upon Slavery*, Wesley had advised against calling upon Parliament, but now Wesley changed his mind and supported the committee's efforts. Wesley further explains how Methodists in America had "already emancipated several hundred of the poor Negros, and are setting more and more at liberty every day. . . . This is making a little stand against this shocking abomination."

Notice that Wesley advocates for emancipating slaves—this is the first time in his life that he called for this. He had not called for emancipation decades earlier when he was in Georgia. He had not called for emancipation when he knew that his friend George Whitefield enslaved Black people at his orphanage in Georgia. He had not called for emancipation thirteen years earlier when he published *Thoughts upon Slavery*—in fact, in his abridgment, Wesley deleted Benezet's comments about emancipation. Prior to this letter, it was clear that Wesley was against the slave *trade*, but it was unclear if Wesley was against the *institution* of slavery. In 1787, however, Wesley came to the point where he publicly advocated for emancipation, which shows that he was also against the institution of slavery. This was a major change for Wesley.

While 1787 would mark a major turning point in Wesley's anti-slavery crusade, he had been increasing his energies in that direction for a few years. In 1783, Wesley published stories in his *Arminian Magazine* of the saga his previously enslaved friends Little Ephrain Robin John and Ancona Robin Robin John endured over a decade earlier. Later that same year, Wesley proclaimed in his sermon *The General Spread of the Gospel* his end-times expectations that his generation was experiencing "only the beginning of a far greater work—the dawn of 'the later day glory.'"[56] Wesley was increasingly optimistic about God's hand in the political and social issues of his day. Two years later, Wesley published a letter in the *Arminian Magazine* explaining how the author manumitted a slave.[57] Just prior to the formation of the committee in 1787, Wesley also published the letter Benezet wrote to Wesley in May 1774. Just a month before being contacted by Clarkson, Wesley explained in his sermon *Of Former Times* that "No 'former time' since the apostles left the earth has been 'better than the present.' . . . [God] is hastening to renew the whole race of mankind in righteousness and true holiness."[58]

By the time Clarkson and the committee reached out to Wesley, he was more than ready to assist their cause. Wesley wrote to the committee in August and promised to print and send *Thoughts upon Slavery* "to all my friends in Great Britain and Ireland, adding a few words in favour of your design, which I believe will have some weight with them."[59] Within three months, Wesley completed the task.[60] A week after Wesley wrote to the committee, he crafted his sermon *The Signs of the Times* in which he states, "'The times' which we have reason to believe are at hand . . . the time of 'the later day glory,'" which included, "living in uniform practice of justice, mercy, and truth."[61] Also in August, Wesley published a summary of Granville Sharp's 1772 Somerset case in the *Arminian Magazine*.

Wesley's flurry of antislavery activity that began in August 1787 continued into the next year, primarily through his quickest means of communication with the masses: the *Arminian Magazine*. In January, he published a letter on the slave trade by Thomas Walker, a Manchester merchant and chairman of their antislavery society who also had experience mobilizing petition drives that called on Parliament to address the issue.[62] In April and May, Wesley published the December 1787 resolutions of the Manchester Society for the Purpose of Effecting the Abolition of the Slave Trade in which they called on people to petition Parliament to address the slave trade.[63] In July and August, Wesley published "A Summary View of the Slave Trade," arguing for the abolition of the slave trade. In October and November, Wesley presented poetry written against slavery, which included the lines, "Thy followers only have effaced the shame, inscribed by slavery on the Christian name."[64] For all of 1788, Wesley used his powerful publishing capacities to advocate for the abolition of the slave trade. Other periodicals also highlighted the changing winds of interest in the slave trade. The popular monthly London publication the *Gentleman's Magazine* has no discussion of slavery or the slave trade in 1787, but in 1788 it included sixty-eight references to it.[65] January 1788 was also the month well-known minister and "Amazing Grace" hymn writer John Newton confessed his long-held secret concerning his previous involvement in the slave trade and announced his support for the abolition movement in his book *Thoughts upon the African Slave Trade*.

Wesley also began preaching against the slave trade. On January 28, 1788, the mayor of Bristol called together twenty people who formed the Bristol committee against the slave trade; they met and collected signatures petitioning against the trade at Guildhall which was less than half a mile from Wesley's Methodist New Room meeting house.[66] Within weeks, proslavery merchants in Bristol began organizing against the "present alarming crisis" of abolitionism.[67] On March 6, the Bristol Society of Merchant Venturers met and drafted a petition to Parliament. They argued, "That the trade to Africa constitutes a very important branch in the British commerce, annually employing at least two hundred ships in the different ports of this Kingdom, with valuable cargoes consisting in a great measure of the manufactures of this

Country."[68] These Bristol merchants feared that the antislavery movement would ruin their businesses.

At six thirty that evening, Wesley mounted the pulpit of the New Room, a ten-minute walk from where the Merchant Venturers had met earlier that day. It was well known what Wesley would be preaching about that night, since he had announced his sermon topic two days earlier. Wesley wrote, "The house from end to end was filled with high and low, rich and poor."[69] That is when something strange happened:

> About the middle of the discourse . . . a vehement noise arose, none could tell why, and shot like lightning through the whole congregation. . . . The people rushed upon each other with the utmost violence, the benches were broken in pieces, and nine-tenths of the congregation appeared to be struck with the same panic. In about six minutes, the storm ceased, almost as suddenly as it rose. And all being calm, I went on without inter-ruption. . . . It was the strangest incident of the kind I ever re-member and believe none can account for it without supposing some preternatural influence.[70]

Wesley implies that he believed the disturbance to be supernatural. A prominent Wesley scholar believes it was a powerful thunderstorm. It also could have been an attempt by slave-trading merchants to disrupt Wesley's campaign against slavery.

Wesley declared the following day a day of prayer and fasting, "that God would remember those poor outcasts of men and . . . make a way for them to escape and break their chains in sunder."[71]

In Wesley's final years, he continued his antislavery efforts primarily through letter writing. In 1790, Wesley wrote to Methodist minister and eventual executor of Wesley's will, Henry Moore, "I would do any-thing that is in my power toward the extirpation of that trade which is a scandal not only to Christianity, but humanity."[72] From his deathbed Wesley wrote his final letter in which he exhorted William Wilberforce in his efforts in Parliament to abolish the slave trade: "Go on, in the

name of God and in the power of his might, till even American slavery
(the vilest that ever saw the sun) shall vanish away before it."[73] With
this, Wesley's campaign against slavery ended, and shortly thereafter,
Wesley died.

At the age of sixty-eight, John Wesley read Anthony Benezet's letter.
This sparked a new, antislavery chapter in Wesley's life. Two years prior,
Wesley had proclaimed endless praises of his slaveholding friend and
frequent coworker George Whitefield. What would Wesley's legacy be
if he had died shortly after Whitefield? Wesley would certainly be remembered as the founder of Methodism, but he also would have been
known as a close associate and beneficiary of the slave trade.

But Wesley did not die in his late sixties. He lived nearly two more
decades, and he spent those years growing in his advocacy for enslaved
people and against the slave trade. Wesley listened to the often overlooked and frequently dismissed Quakers. He reconsidered his previously held beliefs about how God wanted Christians to engage political
and social causes. He used his relationships and publishing platform to
champion the cause of antislavery.

Wesley's legacy would continue after his death—yet not in the way
he might have hoped, as we will see.

PART 4

LEGACY

11

THREE LEGACIES

OUR STORIES DO NOT END when we die. John Wesley lived eighty-seven years. Within his lifetime both Jonathan Edwards and George Whitefield were born and died. Wesley's life bookends the core of our story. Yet all of our stories continue on with our family, friends, and others—we all have a legacy.

We will reflect on *our* legacies in the next chapter. In this chapter, we will take a look at the legacies Wesley, Edwards, and Whitefield left regarding slavery.

JONATHAN EDWARDS'S LEGACY

Although Edwards eventually disapproved of the slave *trade*, he still enslaved Africans and promoted slavery as an *institution*. He grew up in a family and community that believed enslaving other humans was culturally and biblically supported, and enslaved people served Edwards in his childhood and until the day he died in 1758. Surprisingly, his followers would extend and connect ideas in Edwards's own teaching to help them argue for abolition.

We trace the theological legacy of Jonathan Edwards through his followers known as the New Divinity or the Edwardseans. Two of the most prominent Edwardseans were Samuel Hopkins (1721–1803) and Jonathan's son Jonathan Edwards Jr.—often called Jonathan Edwards the Younger (1745–1801). Both of these men began their ministerial careers not only teaching proslavery beliefs, but also enslaving Africans—following their mentor, Jonathan. But for both of them, something eventually changed.

Samuel Hopkins intended to pursue a ministry path in the foot-steps of George Whitefield, but Hopkins promptly changed his path when he heard Jonathan Edwards preach. Smitten with Edwards, Hopkins went to live with him for further ministerial study and training. From December 1743 until April 1770, Hopkins put into practice what he learned from Edwards as pastor of a Congregational church in western Massachusetts. After Edwards's death, Hopkins ob-tained some of his mentor's unpublished works and put them into print—perhaps most importantly *A Dissertation Concerning the Nature of True Virtue*. This work articulated disinterested benevolence as the key ethical mandate to glorify God by seeking the ultimate good of another person without consideration about how it benefits or does not benefit yourself.

Hopkins's work on *True Virtue* in 1765 set the stage for a major change in his life. Until that time, Hopkins, like his mentor, had sup-ported slavery and enslaved a Black person.[1] But sometime before Hopkins moved to his next church in 1770, he freed his slave. We do not know the exact details of this change of mind, but we do know what happened next. His next pastorate brought him to First Congre-gational Church in Newport, Rhode Island—which was a major hub of the transatlantic slave trade. This was the same location where Jon-athan Edwards purchased Venus as his slave in 1731. Having recently freed his slave, Hopkins observed with great abhorrence the cruelty and injustice of the slave trade on a daily basis. This sparked his ad-vocacy for abolition.

Three years later, in 1773, Hopkins circulated a letter seeking to raise funds for two former slaves.[2] His community questioned Hopkins's ac-tions. His memoir states that "His church members, his best friends, his nearest neighbors, nearly all the respectable families of the town, were owners, and many of the most accomplished merchants on the island were importers of slaves."[3] From the time of his arrival in Newport he preached repeatedly against the slave trade, prompting some of his church members to leave.[4]

Hopkins amplified his antislavery work in 1776, when he published *A Dialogue Concerning the Slavery of the African*, which he dedicated to the Continental Congress. He sent copies to the Congress and many prominent citizens in all of the colonies. The introduction notes "more than half a million of persons in these colonies, who are under such a degree of oppression and tyranny as to be wholly deprived of all civil and personal liberty," and argues from, "not merely political reasons, but from a conviction of the unrighteousness and cruelty of that trade, and a regard to justice and benevolence."[5] The main theme of *True Virtue*—benevolence—forms a key part of Hopkins's reasoning. He explains in further detail, "If all who have slaves would act such a just, wise, and benevolent part towards them, and treat them in any measure as they would desire their own children . . . our slaves might all be set free."[6] That same year, Hopkins published a plea to common citizens in *An Address to the Owners of Negro Slaves in the American Colonies.*

Hopkins continued his abolitionist work for the rest of his life through his sermons, publications, financial collections, direct door-to-door pleading with slaveholders, and serving in roles within the New York Manumission Society and the Pennsylvania Society for the Manumission of Slaves.[7] One of the most fascinating moments of his life was when he challenged his fellow Edwardsean Joseph Bellamy to release his slave. Bellamy "defended the system with the usual arguments."[8] But, when Hopkins pressed Bellamy to release his slave, the following dialogue occurred.[9]

Bellamy considered the slave a most faithful and judicious servant; that in his management of the farm, he could be trusted with everything; and that he was so happy in his servitude, that he would, in the opinion of his master refuse his freedom, were it offered to him.

Hopkins: Will you consent to his liberation, if he really desires it?

Bellamy: Yes, I will.

Hopkins: Call him, and let us try.

The slave was then at work in the field. He came.

Hopkins: Have you a good master?

Enslaved Man: Yes.

Hopkins: Are you happy in your present condition? Would you be *more* happy if you were free?

Enslaved Man: O, yes, massa, me would be much more happy.

Bellamy: You have your desire; from this moment you are free.

Hopkins had come a long way from continuing his mentor Jonathan Edwards's slaveholding. Hopkins changed his mind and tactics to advance the cause of abolitionism as an expression of enjoying God by prioritizing the happiness of *all* of his neighbors.

As a child, Jonathan Edwards Jr.'s upbringing was quite different from his father's; the vast majority of Edwards Jr.'s friends in Stockbridge were Mohican Indians. Yet Jonathan Edwards Jr. grew up, like his father, in a slaveholding household—including during his time in Stockbridge. After Edwards graduated from the College of New Jersey, later known as Princeton, he went on to further his theological studies under Samuel Hopkins and Joseph Bellamy—who were both, at that time, advocates of slavery.

Edwards completed his theological training under Hopkins and Bellamy and obtained his license to preach. The following year, at the age of twenty-two, he twice delivered a sermon titled "Questions" in New Haven and Kingston, Rhode Island, beginning in May 1767. A year and a half later, White Haven Church in New Haven, Connecticut, hired him as their pastor. His delivery of the "Questions" sermon in different locations may have been efforts to secure a job as pastor, akin to an interview.

"Questions" presented biblical explanations for the moral permissibility of slavery while dismissing the problematic circumstances of the trade.[10] Edwards argued that God passively allows unpleasant things to happen to humans. "[God] winks at it [slavery]: [He] lets a people in great measure alone about it, and provides [what] shall be done if they do practise such things."[11] Edwards's phraseology is taken from the King James Version of Paul's speech in Athens as Paul looked at the temples and idols; Acts 17:30 reads, "And the times of this ignorance God winked at; but now commandeth all men every where to repent" (KJV). Historian John Ericson states that in 1767 Jonathan Edwards Jr. believed that God's stance on slavery was that slavery is "distasteful, but to be endured as human folly."[12] Further, Ericson argues that, at that time, Edwards had a more rigid view of slavery than his father.[13] One might hope that the younger Edwards might have adopted a stance moving toward antislavery due to his childhood experiences being a minority in his childhood home of Stockbridge, or to external influences in the era of the 1760s moving toward antislavery positions. The evidence shows that in 1767, Edwards was more committed than his father to defending slavery. But things were about to change.

Over the next six years, Edwards radically changed his view on slavery. While the exact influences are difficult to document, it seems that the American contradiction of fighting for liberty, or the common refrain of freedom from "slavery" to Britain, even as the American colonies enslaved Africans, was one factor in his change of mind. Another factor was reading and extending the concepts of his father's writings—similar to what Samuel Hopkins experienced when he published and reapplied the same writings in that era as described earlier.

In 1773, six years after preaching his proslavery sermons, Edwards delivered a sermon discussing African enslavement and sent anonymous antislavery letters the the *Connecticut Journal* and *New Haven Post-Boy*, which were published in October, November, and December.[14] In these publications Edwards argues for total abolition. Eighteen years later he delivered a sermon titled *Injustice and Impolicy of the Slave Trade, and the Slavery of the Africans* which mirrors the content of these letters. By then he had helped create the Connecticut Society for the

Promotion of Freedom and the Relief of Persons Unlawfully Holden in Bondage, which engaged in pamphleteering, lobbying, letter writing, and litigation for the abolitionist cause.[15]

In recent decades, scholars and pastors have revived a keen interest in the writings of Jonathan Edwards Sr. Many of these people eventually discover his proslavery beliefs and enslavement of several Africans. Response to these facts range from ignoring them to eliminating all of Edwards's writings from libraries. Samuel Hopkins and Jonathan Edwards Jr. neither ignored nor eliminated Edwards Sr. from their lives. What they did was admit his wrongs and seek to understand his beliefs better. In the process of understanding Edwards Sr. better, they were able to extend and construct powerful arguments against slavery.

GEORGE WHITEFIELD'S LEGACY

George Whitefield did not leave a family behind after his death. His wife had already died, and no children survived. Nor did he, like Wesley, leave a growing movement—apart from his influence on the few remaining Calvinistic Methodists. Whitefield's legacy lived on primarily in the people he preached to, among those he sparked into evangelistic ministry, and through his writings. His other legacy is his beloved Bethesda orphanage and his hoped-for but ill-fated college near Savannah, Georgia.

When Whitefield died, as we saw earlier, his estate included everything at Bethesda, including buildings, livestock, and slaves. Whitefield gave "that building, commonly called the orphan-house, at Bethesda . . . and likewise all other buildings, lands, negroes, books, furniture, and every other thing whatsoever" to the "Right Honourable Selina, Countess dowager of Huntingdon."[16] Lady Huntingdon controlled Whitefield's beloved Bethesda for the next twenty-one years.

Selina Hastings, the Countess of Huntingdon, was a member of the British aristocracy who came to embrace Whitefield's teaching in 1739. She became Whitefield's primary financial patron throughout his life and made him her personal chaplain. Whitefield designated in his will sums of money for friends, relatives, "his old London servants, poor widows at Tottenham Court chapel . . . the Tabernacle [London] poor," and White workers at Bethesda. George Whitefield, however, left nothing for the orphans or enslaved people under his care. While he could have, he made no mention of manumission; Whitefield's enslaved Africans were his property and transferred to the Countess of Huntingdon.[17] One biographer explained that her inheritance of Bethesda, "was to be her biggest problem, and her worst failure."[18]

James Habersham, the original manager of Bethesda and then successful Savannah merchant, enacted Whitefield's final directions to increase the number of slaves to around seventy in order to meet the financial needs of the property; Habersham did so immediately.[19] Tragedy struck on May 30, 1773, around eight at night when a fire broke out that consumed almost all the buildings on the property. Speculation of the origin of the fire ranged from lightning to arson.[20] James Habersham sent a letter to the countess, saying, "Bethesda College, with the very neat chapple adjoining it, was totally burnt down . . . The Institution has met with very many checks and disappointments, I may say to appearance sentences of Death, upon it, but this last is truly humiliating and a heavy stroke indeed."[21] Thus, within three years of his death, Whitefield's beloved Bethesda orphanage and hoped-for college had mostly burned to the ground. It was in complete chaos.

Habersham and two other Savannah men contributed five hundred pounds to help repair and rebuild the property.[22] In March 1776, British ships arrived at Tybee Island, near Bethesda. Over two hundred Black people made their way to the fleet, hoping to gain their freedom by joining the British. Several of these people included runaway slaves from Bethesda. Later, the manager of Bethesda asked the captain of the ship for the slaves to be returned. The captain declined the request.[23]

As the area slowly settled into American hands in the 1780s, Lady Huntingdon tried to reestablish Bethesda as a college by sending a schoolmaster in June 1788; less than two years later he had failed and returned to England. The following year, Selina died. Whitefield had entrusted Selina with his dreams for a legacy, hoping she would support the orphans and establish a college. Instead, she failed to establish a college, the halls were empty of orphans, and she lost control of the property to the new state of Georgia. Whitefield's legacy was nowhere to be found. Nearly fifty years would go by before the site was utilized again.

Today, the original site of Bethesda is now home to Bethesda Academy, a private boarding and day school for boys in grades six to twelve. It is "dedicated to the founding mission of George Whitefield, who emphasized a love of God, a love of learning and a strong work ethic."[24] The modern-day work at Bethesda might be closer to Whitefield's vision than any other time in its history.

JOHN WESLEY'S LEGACY

The legacy of John Wesley eclipsed those of Whitefield and Edwards because of the vast and powerful establishment of Methodism in Britain and America. Wesley left no wife or children to carry on his name, but when he died, Methodism continued.

Wesley's legacy regarding slavery is magnified through the growth and checkered history of early Methodists' varied approaches to slavery. Wesley adopted abolitionism only near the end of his life and built his arguments on natural law, not directly on biblical foundations. This background prepared his followers to adjust their approach to slavery over time because Methodists, like most evangelicals, prioritized evangelism above everything else.

Wesley originally sought for Methodists to remain in the Church of England. In England this was difficult, but during his life Wesley worked hard to maintain his ideal. In America, this goal was practically impossible upon the dawn of the American Revolution—the Church of England was hardly a fashionable choice in the new American republic. This is why, at the Christmas Conference in December 1784, eight years after the formal beginning of the American revolution, Methodists in America formed the Methodist Episcopal Church.

Meanwhile, after Wesley died in 1791, Methodists in Britain gathered a plan in 1795 for British Methodists to formally separate from the Church of England.[25] The membership of Methodists in Great Britain in 1800 was 96,078. This grew to 518,156 by 1850.[26] The early growth of Methodism in Britain was impressive, but their multiplication in America is almost difficult to believe. In 1800 American Methodists numbered 65,181; by 1850 this number had grown nearly twentyfold to 1,185,902 members; Methodism was the single largest denomination in America—over a third of all Americans were Methodist.[27] By 1900, there were over four million members.[28] Wesley's Methodism held the largest religious influence in the antebellum era of America; Wesley's approach to slavery influenced America's divided beliefs about slavery during this period.

Wesley, in his last recorded letter before he died, encouraged Wilberforce to continue his efforts to abolish the slave trade—which Wilberforce, a Church of England member, would help achieve in Britain sixteen years later. Modern Methodists will often celebrate anecdotes, such as Wesley's Wilberforce letter, as evidence of John Wesley's antislavery stance. Yet they fail to notice how late in life Wesley spoke up, how little his primary text on the subject (*Thoughts upon Slavery*) is referenced by non-Methodists, and the inconsistent stance on slavery among Methodists in the decades following Wesley's life.

Methodist historian Donald Mathews wrote, "Although Wesley never proposed a plan for getting rid of slavery, he did provide early Methodists with an incipient antislavery sentiment as well as the moral urgency to enforce it."[29] Yet, in Mathews's otherwise acclaimed work *Slavery and Methodism*, he writes, "In 1743 when [Wesley] wrote the General Rules [of Methodism], he had prohibited 'the buying or selling of bodies and souls of men, women, and children, with an intention to enslave them.'"[30] And yet Wesley wrote no such thing. The phrase Mathews claims Wesley wrote in 1743 is from a 1788 addition in the American edition of the *General Rules*, of which the editor of the critical edition states, "the history of its insertion [in 1788] remains a mystery."[31]

This sort of mistake is common among Methodist historians—they assume, for example, that the statements and teaching of American Methodists (of which Wesley was not one) in 1788 reflect what he stated and enforced in 1743. Wesleyan scholar Irv Brendlinger claimed that Wesley "was the first major religious leader, known worldwide, to take a clear stand against slavery."[32] But this overlooks the transatlantic fame Quaker religious leaders Benjamin Lay, Anthony Benezet, John Woolman, and others achieved well before John Wesley. Furthermore, several collections of early antislavery writings include a vast array of documents but do not include anything written by John Wesley.[33] Meanwhile scholars like Mathews are aware that early American Methodists needed to supplement Wesley's writings with non-Methodist publications. The strongest antislavery pamphlet early American Methodists used was not from Wesley or another Methodist; it was from a Presbyterian named David Rice.[34] Wesley's antislavery legacy, which certainly exists in his late writings, was a brief and shallow resource for the soon-to-be-meteoric growth of Methodists. This is most evident in America.

Early American Methodists held a strong antislavery stance. In 1780, Francis Asbury supervised the passage of an agreement against slavery at their spring conference. Their minutes record the following:

Question 16: Ought not this Conference to require those traveling preachers who hold slaves to give promises to set them free?
Answer: Yes.

Question 17: Does this Conference acknowledge that slavery is contrary to the laws of God, man, and nature, and hurtful to society; contrary to the dictates of conscience and pure religion, and doing that which we would not others should do to us and ours? Do we pass our disapprobation on all our friends who keep slaves, and advise their freedom?
Answer: Yes.[35]

Three years later, the Conference revisited the issue, stating:

Question 10: What shall be done with our local preachers who hold slaves contrary to the laws which authorize their freedom in any of the United States?

Answer: We will try them another year. In the meantime let every assistant deal faithfully and plainly with every one, and report to the next Conference. It may then be necessary to suspend them.[36]

The following year, in 1784, they continued their discussion, writing:

Question 12: What shall we do with our friends that will buy and sell slaves?

Answer: If they buy with no other design than to hold them as slaves, and have been previously warned, they shall be expelled, and permitted to sell on no consideration.

Question 13: What shall we do with our local preachers who will not emancipate their slaves in the states where the laws admit it?

Answer: Try those in Virginia another year, and suspend the preachers in Maryland, Delaware, Pennsylvania, and New-Jersey.[37]

Question 22: What shall be done with our travelling preachers that now are, or here after shall be, possessed of slaves, and refuse to manumit them where the law permits?

Answer: Employ them no more.[38]

In 1780, the American Methodists made an outright declaration against slavery, but in the span of just four years, the lack of adherence among their people is clearly a problem. The journals of Methodist minister Thomas Coke provide a window into what was happening. On March 30, 1785, Coke recorded talking to a Mr. Jarrat: "We now talked largely on the minutes concerning slavery: but he would not be persuaded. The secret is, he has twenty-four slaves of his own: but I am afraid, he will do infinite hurt by his opposition to our Rules."[39] Six weeks later, Coke recorded, "I lodged at the house of Captain Dillard, a most hospitable man, and as kind to his negroes as if they were White servants. It was quite pleasing to see them so decently and comfortably clothed. And yet I could not beat into the head of that poor man the evil of keeping them in slavery, although he has read Mr. Wesley's Thoughts on Slavery, (I think he said) three times over."[40] Exasperated by constant pushback and physical danger threatened upon him, three weeks later Coke wrote, "We thought it prudent to suspend the minute concerning slavery, on account of the great opposition that had been given it, our work being in too infantile a state to push things to extremity. However, we were agreeably informed that several of our friends in Maryland had already emancipated their slaves."[41] The minutes of the American Methodists that year stated,

> It is recommended to all our brethren to suspend the execution of the minute on slavery till the deliberations of a future Conference; and that an equal space of time be allowed all our members for consideration, when the minute shall be put in force." An additional note was added that stated, "We do hold in the deepest abhorrence the practice of slavery; and shall not cease to seek its destruction by all wise and prudent means.[42]

Coke departed America and returned in 1787. Upon his arrival, he learned that slaveholders not only threatened to have him arrested, but one slave owner threatened to kill him.[43] An early biographer of Coke wrote, "If Dr. Coke had continued his direct attack upon the slave trade, he must have abandoned the United States, and desisted from his great work, without breaking the fetters which the Africans wore."[44] With this, the grand antislavery declarations early American Methodists voiced began to fade into the background as Methodist ministers believed that the only way to accomplish their primary aim of evangelism was to accommodate both proslavery and antislavery views. Similar lack of unity and outright racism led to Richard Allen forming the African Methodist Episcopal Church in 1787, and in 1796 the African Methodist Episcopal Zion Church formed. Further division came in 1844 when the Methodist Episcopal Church, South began to break away to form their own conference over the issue of slavery.

Frederick Douglass's *Narrative* provides a chilling snapshot of his experience of Methodism in this era. Douglass wrote,

> In August 1832, my master attended a Methodist camp-meeting . . . and there experienced religion. I indulged a faint hope that his conversion would lead him to emancipate his slaves, and that, if he did not do this, it would, at any rate, make him more kind and humane. I was disappointed in both respects. . . . If it had any effect on his character, it made him more cruel and hateful in all his ways; for I believe him to have been a much worse man after his conversion than before. Prior to his conversion, he relied upon his own depravity to shield and sustain him in his savage barbarity; but after his conversion, he found religious sanction and support for his slaveholding cruelty. . . . I have seen him tie up a lame young woman, and whip her with a heavy cowskin upon her naked shoulders, causing the warm red blood to drip, and in justification of the bloody deed, he would quote this passage of Scripture—"He that knoweth his master's will, and doeth not, shall be beaten with many stripes."[45]

The account of Douglass's horrific experience in 1832 was not unlike what John and Charles Wesley had heard regarding slavery a century earlier in their experience in America. John Wesley would be horrified to know that Douglass's account was brought about by Methodists—and yet this is a part of the legacy Wesley left.

Remarkably, in the appendix of his *Narrative*, Douglass wrote, "What I said respecting and against religion, I mean strictly to apply to the *slaveholding religion*; for, between the Christianity of this land, and the Christianity of Christ, I recognize the widest possible difference."[46] This "difference" is evident in Douglass's *Narrative* when he praises the Black Methodist Christians who helped him, as well as his membership in the AME Zion church in Bedford.

Wesley, like every human, had no direct control over the thoughts and actions of other humans, and by the time of Douglass's experience Wesley had been dead for decades—yet the name of Wesley and Methodism are inseparable. I believe Wesley would be rolling over in his grave wondering if he could have done anything different while he was still alive to close the gap of the "widest possible difference" of the Christianity of America and the Christianity of Christ.

Wesley lived long enough, fortunately, to take an explicit antislavery stand. We will never know whether Edwards or Whitefield would have repented of their views and actions regarding slavery if they had lived into the abolitionist era of the Quakers and others who paved the way that Wesley was fortunate to live long enough to experience. While the Quakers were the catalyst for much of the late-eighteenth-century antislavery movement, they failed to live up to many of their own ideals— evidenced today by so few Black Quakers. A study of this issue from within the Quaker community found that eighteenth- and nineteenth-century Friends created this issue because "Many Friends did not fully accept people of African descent as 'fit' for membership in their society, or for that matter, to be their friends. . . . Quakers of European descent have been unable to separate themselves from the attitudes and behaviors of a wider culture based on false notions of differences between the races."[47] The official minutes of the Atlanta Quakers in 2000 urged their committees and groups to make a commitment to becoming a "fully diverse institution of human equality."[48]

The legacies of Wesley, Whitefield, and Edwards are all soiled by the stain of slavery. Whitefield's legacy is bleak, with only the recent efforts at Bethesda Academy as a bright spot. Edwards's immediate legacy perpetuated his beliefs and practices of enslaving others, but fortunately his heirs underwent a transformation—some of which was sparked by ideas within Edwards's own writings—and became abolitionists. Wesley's legacy regarding slavery might be the most complicated because it started off advocating for abolition but crumbled when many of his followers faced growing opposition and were not equipped by Wesley to respond with strong biblical and theological arguments to sustain their abolitionism.

We have examined an extensive history and could end here, but this history demands an evaluation of what we might learn from it. We can't fully understand the past, just as much as we can't fully understand ourselves today. I agree with historian Tzvetan Todorov, who writes, "The historical facts are well known and easy to look up. But facts don't come with their meanings attached, and it is the meaning that interests me."[49] We can, and should, reflect on the history that we have examined to see how it might influence our lives today.

12

OWNERSHIP TODAY

"**Tell your story to your fiancé**, all of it." This was a simple assignment I was given during premarital counseling.

My fiancé and I knew each other well—so well that we were engaged, had our wedding day circled on our calendars, and were looking forward to our marriage. We knew each other's stories better than anyone. Yet this assignment had a few twists. We were to plan two date nights. On the first one, I told my story, uninterrupted, from beginning to end, not skipping any important part—but also not needing to go into all the nitty-gritty details. When I was done, I answered any questions. Then we would pray together. On the second date, we flipped roles.

We laughed and cried; there were times when the silence hung thick in the air, and at other times we could have finished each other's sentences. After completing the assignment, we knew each other better and also felt a bit relieved to get a few heavy, embarrassing, and shameful things off our chests. Yet one moment months later crystalized the full weight of what we had done.

On our wedding day, we held hands, looked into each other's eyes and said, "I do." We told each other: I marry you—all of you. I *know* who I'm marrying and I accept *all of you*. I recognize what makes you who you are—warts and all.

You can't divide a human. You can't discard the parts you dislike and keep the parts you enjoy. I wasn't marrying just the parts of my wife that I especially liked. I was marrying all of her. And she was marrying all of me.

As a Christian, I am thankful that the Lord does this with me. "But God demonstrates his own love for us in this: While we were still sinners, Christ died for us" (Romans 5:8). Christ knows *all of me* and says yes to me.

Ownership, in this book, refers most clearly to the institution of slavery. The idea of ownership is also a challenge for White evangelicals to *own* the White evangelical legacy of slavery and invite all readers to learn from it to guide us in other areas of our lives.

When White evangelical Christians look back at our ancestors, we can't split individual people into separate parts. They are whole people—warts and all—just like you and me.

OWNING THE FAILURES OF OUR HEROES

There is freedom in owning our failures. Acknowledging failure frees us. We have nothing to hide; it is who we *are*. Scripture teaches, "Whoever conceals their sins does not prosper, but the one who confesses and renounces them finds mercy" (Proverbs 28:13). Many of us have tasted this freedom from personal experience.

Owning our *own* failures is one thing, but what about owning the failures of our ancestors and our heroes? Some of us might say, "I had nothing to do with Edwards, Whitefield, or Wesley. Those people lived hundreds of years ago. Why even bring them up? It's best to ignore them completely."

Consider for a moment Matthew's presentation of Jesus' genealogy. Matthew, as a Jewish man, went out of his way to own and highlight "individuals of unquestioned and questionable backgrounds" of his own heritage.[1] Women had no independent legal status and were not usually listed in genealogies, yet Matthew lists five women. He does *not* include the eminent and celebrated Old Testament women such as Sarah, Rebecca, or Leah. Matthew, instead, *includes* two prostitutes (Tamar and Rahab), a Gentile (Ruth), and a woman raped by David (Bathsheba). Jewish readers would have expected Matthew to be silent about all women, especially these women, but he highlighted them nonetheless. Joe Kapolyo's commentary about the purpose of Matthew's genealogy applies to why we must own the failures of our heroes: "Prostitutes and Gentiles are welcome, despised women are received with respect, both sinners and saints are drawn to him."[2] Our human heroes are both sinners and saints and must be remembered this way.

Evangelicals have our own genealogy that traces back to enslavers such as Whitefield and Edwards. We need not hide or ignore these facts. We need the courage and wisdom of the same God who inspired Matthew's strategic genealogical honesty. Many White evangelicals have a spiritual genealogy that traces back a generation to people like John Stott and Billy Graham, back another generation to Aimee Semple McPherson, D. L. Moody and Charles Spurgeon, then further back through people like Charles Finney, and originates with Edwards, Whitefield, and Wesley. If you take a close look at each of them, all of these evangelical Christians have flaws—all are both sinners and saints.

African American pastor Dr. Charlie Dates addressed Jonathan Edwards's slavery and how to navigate the failures of our heroes.[3] Dates explained that the general theological commitments of slaveholders can be trusted because "Scripture is replete with failed men who teach us much about how to walk with God." Dates argues that we can still learn from people who owned slaves. And yet the historical context of any individual, including Edwards's context, is not an excuse for slavery, nor any sin. Dates added that "interpreting Edwards in light of his slave ownership keeps evangelicals from hero worship," and that this is why "when we teach Edwards, we must tell the class upfront of his shortcomings." When Judgment Day comes, each of us should not congratulate ourselves for being better than Edwards because, in our modern wisdom and piety, we don't enslave people. The measuring stick for each of us is not Edwards; it is Christ.

How do we own the failures of our heroes? By standing in solidarity with our fellow fallen Christians, declaring that we too are sinners, saved by grace, proclaiming, "We shall have no other gods beside thee," while also learning from our mistakes.

When we recognize the failures of our heroes, our eyes have been opened and we cannot unsee what we've seen. We can no longer claim to be blind. Martin Luther King Jr. explained, "Slavery in America was perpetuated not merely by human badness, but also by human blindness. . . . The whole of slavery was largely perpetuated by sincere though spiritually ignorant persons."[4] The failures of our heroes can open our (perhaps sincere, yet blind) eyes.

Once we've seen, we cannot and should not forget or conceal the failures of our heroes. MLK explained that when we forgive our enemies, "certainly one can never forget, if it means erasing it totally from his mind."[5] We need not pretend that the person we remember was a perfect person; that is not true. We remember that our hero was a fallen human person; failure is the prerequisite for forgiveness.

The failures of our heroes lead many of us to pointing fingers at each other and creating enemies. The heroes themselves, such as Edwards, Whitefield, and Wesley, might become enemies. The fans and admirers of Edwards, Whitefield, and Wesley might become enemies. The critics and cancelers of Edwards, Whitefield, and Wesley might become enemies. Yet we are reminded that Jesus tells us to love our enemies (Luke 6:27-28). Loving our enemies includes holding people accountable and expecting change. Osheta Moore explains that loving our enemies also transforms "the way I think of enemies, from monsters to fellow wounded humans trying to make their way in a dangerous world."[6]

Owning the failures of our heroes requires us to acknowledge the wrong they've done, holding them fully accountable for their actions and any underlying false beliefs—they are without excuse. We must also learn from their mistakes—if our eyes have been opened to their failures, we can no longer claim to be blind to our own. We are called to love them as fellow fallen sinners in need of God's forgiveness—and if this is difficult, which is likely, we remember Jesus urges us to forgive others as we have been forgiven ourselves.

OWNING WHITE AMERICAN EVANGELICAL CHRISTIAN HISTORY

The evangelical legacy of slavery we've learned about through the lives of Edwards, Wesley, and Whitefield is a history that modern White evangelicals must own as ours. It's part of our genealogy.

For many of us this history might seem distant and unrelated to our lives. Others might feel it is unnecessary and unhelpful to shine a spotlight on the egregious actions of these men. But I think that unearthing and owning this legacy is instructive, healthy, and helpful for how we live our lives today.

Power. The history of Christianity is replete with misuses of power. We saw previously that early evangelicals inherited a belief that God structured society so that masters owned the human freedom of their slaves. Modern evangelicals no longer believe that God ordains humans enslaving other humans. Yet the evangelical focus on preaching and presenting the "offer" of the new birth must be acknowledged as a tempting concept ripe for the misuse of power by modern evangelicals.

It might seem like the evangelical emphasis on the unrestricted power of the Holy Spirit to regenerate souls through the new birth would flatten Christian power structures, but it didn't. Early evangelicals became naturally drawn to celebrities and those who seemed to have special access to manifest the transformative saving, regenerative, and transformational power of God. Evangelicals sadly became power brokers.

Christian celebrity, like power, has the potential to be used for good. George Whitefield was "the first transatlantic celebrity of any kind."[7] Evangelicals from their very beginning have tended to seek experiences channeled through talented church leaders who appear to have the power to deliver God's work in their lives. While modern evangelicals rightly reject slavery, we must own that we are especially prone and vulnerable to other abuses of power.

Racism. Racism came naturally to many early evangelicals in America as a manifestation of the power they wielded in their ministries.

While the institution of slavery did not originate racially, the color of one's skin provided a way to exercise power over other humans. As we saw earlier, the primary reason slavery was originally illegal in the colony of Georgia was in order to serve as a "no Black people" buffer in order to spot Black slaves from the British colonies fleeing southward for their freedom in the Spanish colony in modern-day Florida. It was only when the White colonists, including George Whitefield, decided they could not survive financially without slave labor that slavery was made legal in Georgia. We also recall that Jonathan Edwards never enslaved a White person; he and his wife enslaved Black people.

Early evangelical abolitionist movements, such as those by the Edwardseans and some Methodists, show that some White American evangelicals confronted overt racism. Yet by and large, modern Black Americans reject the label of *evangelical*.[8] This is despite the fact that modern American Black Protestants are in greater alignment with the theological principles of evangelicalism than are America's White Protestants.[9] In modern America, sadly, the easiest way to spot a self-acknowledged evangelical is by their skin color.

How can modern White American evangelicals own our history of racism and White ethnocentricity? By acknowledging it, repenting of it, and providing a posture of open arms to people of all races who have every right to navigate our open arms on their own terms and in their own timing.

Biblicism. One of the classic marks of evangelicalism is biblicism. The original core of this emphasis was a belief that all spiritual truth is found in the Bible.[10] Early evangelicals held an elevated devotion, respect, and belief that the Bible is inspired by God. In early America this belief met head-on with a strong spirit of independence. American evangelicals believed they had the right to use and interpret the Bible however they saw fit, lest they bite the hand—independence—that fed them their freedom.[11] When early White American evangelical tendencies toward power and racism met with this approach to the Bible, the theological and biblical crisis of the Civil War is unsurprising.[12]

Mark Noll has shown that a key hermeneutical approach and general success of the American proslavery position was that it was simple to understand and defend from the Bible. Many Americans found the nuanced biblical reasoning typically employed in the antislavery position less convincing, while those outside the United States found the antislavery position easier to accept.[13]

The White American evangelical commitment to self-evident biblicism contributed to the angst of American fundamentalism in the early twentieth century. Later, American evangelicals were the last Americans to hold on to the belief that segregation in schools and marriage was the clear teaching of the Bible. Legalized segregation lasted until *Brown v. Board of Education* in 1954; though, for example, segregation continued at Whitefield's Bethesda Home for Boys until 1989, and informal segregation continues among evangelical Christians in America.[14]

Modern White American evangelicals must own our history of justifying slavery and other egregious beliefs held under the banner of self-evident biblicism. We must learn to pause when we see our interpretation of the Bible as a simple "I'm right and you are wrong," "either-or" conclusion. This approach to the Bible supported the proslavery evangelicals who felt that that quoting "slaves, obey your earthly masters" (Ephesians 6:5, Colossians 3:22) proved their argument. Modern White American evangelicals need not reject our elevated priority of the Bible, but when we use the Bible we must embrace patience over urgency, openness over defensiveness, charity over power hoarding, community over independence, and humility over pride—for God opposes the proud but gives favor to the humble (1 Peter 5:5, James 4:6, Matthew 23:12, Proverbs 3:34). If the hermeneutic of evangelicals is a godly one, whatever interpretations we land on will be unmistakably full of love, joy, peace, patience, kindness, goodness, faithfulness, gentleness, and self-control (Galatians 5:22-23).

Evangelism. White American evangelicals must own that we've used evangelism—sharing the good news of Jesus Christ—as a blindfold for our sin in our thirst for power and as an excuse for blatant racism.

Evangelicals are overdriven by evangelism and "saving lives" while over-looking the "lived lives" of the people we encounter. We must remember that evangelicals have enslaved Black people under the guise of evangelism. We must remember that antislavery evangelicals have preached, "Slaves, obey your earthly masters" in order to evangelize enslaved people. We must remember that the Society for the Propagation of the Gospel branded the word *S-O-C-I-E-T-Y* on the Black people they evangelized even as they enslaved them.

Evangelism is not a trump card that nullifies the entire counsel of God. White American evangelicals must find a proper place for evangelism under the larger umbrella of loving God and neighbor.

OWNING YOUR INFLUENCES: THE SOCIETY YOU WERE BORN INTO

In the first part of this book, we examined the circumstances into which Wesley, Edwards, and Whitefield were born. Some of these details were simply factual: where they lived, what year they were born, etc. The more thought-provoking parts were the social, cultural, religious, and ideological environments in which they were raised and nurtured. When we take these into consideration and understand their upbringings, we can comprehend more easily why these men participated in slavery in the ways they did. Of course, these influences do not condone their participation in these activities. Yet we must acknowledge that these men had no choice where or when they were born, who their parents were, or what religion, or even type of Christianity, they were born into.

Careful Bible readers know that one of the most basic rules of understanding the Bible properly is to understand the original culture, influences, and circumstances of the author and recipient (if known) of each biblical book we study. This work allows us to understand and interpret better. As we seek to understand our own lives, we might not like what we find. Historian Susan Neiman writes, "Even those who subscribe to the doctrine of original sin in the abstract tend to ignore it when things get particular. . . . We want our ancestors to be honorable and honored."[15] Rather than expecting perfection, Christians above all other people should *expect* to find dishonorable things in our past.

We must not move on quickly from examining the circumstances these men were born into and those which *you* were born into, this is where the important work begins. In many ways, this might be some of the easiest personal work we can do, because we cannot accept blame or praise for the unchosen circumstances of our birth and upbringing. I would like you to consider, first, the circumstances of *your* birth and upbringing, and second, the circumstances of your most formative religious and character upbringing. For some people these will be identical. In other cases, like my own, they are not quite identical.

Below are some questions to consider about the formative influences in *your* life.

1. What was the geographical and socioeconomic setting of your birth and childhood?

2. Who were your friends in your younger years? Did they and their families have similar backgrounds as you?

3. Who were your primary religious influences in your younger years?

4. Was any specific type of Christian identity, emphasis, or belief set predominant among your religious influences?

5. How might your formative influences have shaped your view of other people and, in particular, your view of people who are unlike you racially, economically, religiously, geographically, and nationally?

6. If you were in your parents' and formative spiritual mentors' shoes, is there anything that you would have done differently to shape you?

OWNING YOUR PARTICIPATION: THE ACTIVITIES AND IDEOLOGIES YOU PERPETUATE

In the second part of this book, we learned how Wesley, Edwards, and Whitefield "passed forward" much of what they received from the people and circumstances of their formative years. What is in mind at this point is not a passive reception or circumstantial osmosis that we receive in our formative years. We considered, instead, their active participation, through their choices, in making decisions for which they are responsible. Perhaps we could call this reaching an "age of accountability." We must remember that while people are absolutely responsible for their actions, people also tend to mimic the actions which shaped their formative experiences. Well-worn habits and norms are difficult to reroute.

After a lifetime of driving in America, it took a lot of preparation, focus, and courage for me to drive on the other side of the road in the United Kingdom. When I returned to the United States, I quickly readjusted to the way I naturally understood roads to work. The most instinctual, and easiest, way to live life is to continue in the direction that you were formed.

Thus, while absolutely reprehensible, when we learn that Edwards bought slaves, we recognize that he was continuing a generational norm. What is more surprising is that his son, Jonathan Edwards Jr., eventually rejected slavery. We learned that despite Whitefield's ancestors not owning slaves, when he saw his chance to become the first enslaver in his family, he took it. Again, this should not surprise us because there is no evidence in his upbringing or background that taught him *not* to enslave people. Whitefield's family had prospered, in part, on the revenue that came from the Bristol slave trade economy. Thus we should not be surprised that, when provided the possibility to enslave another person, he embraced an opportunity, in keeping with his upbringing, to also make revenue through the institution of slavery. We would hope that Whitefield and others knew better than to accept the reprehensible beliefs and actions of his family, especially since many esteem Whitefield as a Christian hero. Yet, instead of knowing better, he failed to reconsider what he was taught to know. This is where Wesley is a more complicated figure, because he could be thought of as a Whitefield without the American experience of Whitefield. Would Whitefield have become an enslaver if he had stayed in England? My suspicion is no. Would Wesley have enslaved Black people if he, like Whitefield, had spent much of his adult life and ministry in America? My suspicion is yes.

This "what if" question is a dangerous one, but it serves a purpose for our own lives. I have had many "fork in the road" moments in my own life that make me wonder what would have happened if I had gone the other way. I wonder what I would have done otherwise.

Below are some questions to consider about *your* participation in the norms handed to *you*.

1. When did you become your own person in regard to your choices? What events, milestones, or reasons contributed to this?

2. What have you perpetuated from your formative years that you are proud of? What things surprised you?

3. Who are the most influential people in your life that you find yourself thinking, "I'm just like them?"

4. What was a decision that seemed natural to you but, upon further reflection, surprised you?

5. What attitudes toward race, culture, and economic and spiritual norms formed you that you passively or actively continued?

OWNING YOUR ACTIONS: THE CHANGES YOU MAKE THROUGHOUT YOUR LIFE

Near the end of Wesley's life, he spoke out against slavery. Sadly, the same cannot be said of Whitefield or Edwards, but it can be said of the followers of Edwards.

Change is not easy, especially in areas that are deeply established. When I lived in Spokane, Washington, I had a thirty-mile drive to work every day. Drivers put snow tires on their cars in the winter that created year-round grooves in the roads. In order to get out of the grooves in the road, I had to turn the wheel much harder than elsewhere. This problem increased in the winter, when the grooves gathered snow and ice. In those months, changing directions felt like a bobsled run that bobbled down the road while I hoped to make even the simplest of lane changes. The deeper the rut, the harder it is to change.

For eighteen hundred years, Christians were deep in the rut of supporting the institution of slavery. This book described people in the eighteenth century who attempted to gain momentum to change direction. While some progress was made throughout the nineteenth century, White Christians continued to slide back and forth with the ongoing repercussions from supporting the institution of slavery and how it was applied to Black people. Thankfully, very few Christians in the world today support the institution of slavery. This is not to say that the residual effects of the institution are no longer felt—they are. Yet micro changes led to macro changes whereby we can now see that Christians changed their beliefs about the institution of slavery.

We were all born into a specific set of circumstances, and we all perpetuate many of the beliefs and norms we received in our formative years. We are not, however, identical copies or shadows of our parents, mentors, and influences. We are unique and choose different paths from these people every day of our lives. Some of these differences are small, such as our favorite food or music genre, but others can be quite large, such as our religion, beliefs, dreams, and lifestyle choices. In addition to our unique identity, we continue to change throughout our lives.

Stop and think for a moment: are all of your beliefs, dreams, and lifestyle choices exactly the same as when you were half your age? Are you confident that if you were to live another thirty years you won't change in any way at all? I think all of us admit that we have changed over time and this change will continue in the future. I want to highlight two sources of change.

The first source of change is passive. These sources are those that are floating down the river you are already in. They are the ideas and influences that you hardly notice. These changes come from microscopic nudges in a slightly different direction; over a long period of time, you end up at a different destination.

The second kind of change is active. This change requires intentional effort. Edmondson and Brennan advise, "We are not primarily concerned with what we must *say* or *know*—though incredibly important—but what we must *do* and *stop doing* in order to see change."[16] Anyone who has been in a swift stream knows the effort it takes to change directions or guide yourself to the shore for safety. MLK explains, "Like life, racial understanding is not something that we find but something that we must create . . . the ability of Negroes and whites to work together, to understand each other, will not be found ready-made; it must be created by the fact of contact."[17]

John Wesley was floating down a swift stream of proslavery beliefs when others shouted out to him that he must change his course immediately. The courageous voices of enslaved people and their advocates trumpeted their pleas Wesley's way. While others ignored these voices, Wesley eventually listened and acted. More specifically, Wesley listened to people others overlooked and discredited. At the same time, Wesley had his own internal instincts in his theology that led him to believe more than ever that God was concerned about the improvement of the world *now*. Wesley's internal instinct met with external evidence that prompted him to action.

Below are some questions to consider about navigating change in *your* life:

1. What was one of the first major changes you chose to make in your life?

2. How are you different from who you were ten or twenty years ago? Which of your beliefs or attitudes changed?

3. What is something that you considered changing or adopting, but didn't?

4. What are the key sources, or voices, that have influenced significant changes in your life in the past?

5. Do you think one day in the future you will change some of the beliefs and attitudes that you hold right now? Which ones come to mind as possibilities?

6. Which unlikely voices (like the Quakers for Wesley) stir your heart and mind right now?

For much of my own Christian experience, I was taught to fear and resist changing my beliefs and actions. I was discipled to "contend for the faith that was once for all entrusted to God's holy people" (Jude 3). My teachers taught me that the best way forward was to deepen, and rarely question or push against, the foundation I was given. Yet my teachers confused the faith Jude speaks of with their own applications of the faith.

The absolute focal point and center of faith in its simplest form is "Jesus is Lord" (Romans 10:9, 1 Corinthians 12:3). To stray from this confession was, indeed, to depart from Christianity. Alongside that proclamation, Jesus taught us to pray repeatedly, "your kingdom come, your will be done, on earth as it is in heaven" (Matthew 6:10). Whenever we pray—which should be always—we ought to ask and desire for our earth to be more and more like heaven—now. Implied in the Lord's Prayer is that this is *not* true *now*. This implies that there is work to be done in new and creative ways in which we reflect God's Word and the moving of his Spirit. We should always be open to change because we are told to pray for this change.

I wish my mentors had taught me how to discern ways to make God-honoring changes in my life—changes that honor and proclaim my confession that "Jesus is Lord." Protestants ought to be leading the charge when it comes to challenging established Christian beliefs and practices—their origin arose, of course, out of protest, challenge, and willingness to change in response to the Word of God. To question the established norms of my Christian upbringing was something I feared to do out loud. Instead, I had to do it in private, through hushed personal conversations and quietly learning alternate views wherever I could find them. Most often, and even in most of my seminary experience, I had to guide myself if I wanted to consider a different perspective. Nearly all the Christians I was around tended to provide the best version of their view and the worst (or no) version of alternate views. It took me quite a while to realize that the church past and present has plenty of beliefs about which faithful Christians disagree, and that there are some things that Christians have come to realize they once believed wrongly—most notably (now), the institution of slavery.

Today, the internet and social media platforms provide an endless diversity of information and wide availability of a myriad of communities. Earlier in my life, investigating alternate beliefs rarely happened, and when it did, it was a slow and private process. Today, change happens fast, often too fast and with few wise guides to help us navigate the journey. We should remember that the tipping point of Wesley's change came when he came into contact with writings and accounts from far outside his spheres of influence; he listened to Quakers who reported and reflected on the accounts of enslaved Africans. Outsider information and reporting changed Wesley's actions and the course of his life and ministry.

What alternate voices along the shore of my stream should I listen to? How should I navigate my own internal questions and instincts about how to honor God? What are good, less good, and flat-out bad ways to process all of this? These answers require the precious and usually decades-acquired virtue of wisdom.

Over the years, I made changes about how I honor God in ways that depart from what I learned in my formative years. With all due respect to my formative influences, I changed how I balance my time and focus between ministry, family, and personal health. I changed who I choose to relate to—I have more friends and peers who are women and those who don't look like me or have the same beliefs as I do. I changed my views on the roles men and women undertake in the home, community, and church. Each of these changes came slowly and after much thought and reflection. Each of these changes represents a departure from what

I once believed and how I acted several decades ago. Alongside these changes are a myriad of beliefs and actions that I have *not* changed. I have, instead, retained and often strengthened many things I received in my formative years.

I cannot predict what specific changes I might adopt in the coming decades, but my earnest hope is that anything and everything about who I am will always proclaim that "Jesus is Lord" and contribute to seeing God bring heaven to earth to the best of my abilities.

OWNING YOUR LEGACY: THE STORIES AND INFLUENCE YOU LEAVE BEHIND

One of the major benefits from looking at the lives of Wesley, Edwards, and Whitefield is that because they lived hundreds of years ago, we can see how their lives influenced the lives of others. Many of us care deeply about the impact we make on those around us, yet we only see the tip of the iceberg. You *are* the living legacy of the family that raised you and your formative influences—living and dead. An in-depth biography about your parents and key mentors would likely discuss how they influenced you. This leads us to the question: what is *your* legacy?

Any level of self-awareness and humility allows us to concede that the legacy we leave is a mixed bag—the Bible and the entire great tradition of Christianity affirm that no human does everything right. The people we influence will need to reject and correct things we hand off to them—this process is inevitable. But wouldn't it be better, and wouldn't we want, to reject and correct those things earlier if we can spot them?

Imagine if Christianity's rejection of the institution of slavery occurred in the first century rather than the nineteenth century. Or imagine if this rejection came a generation before Wesley, Edwards, and Whitefield and they lived their lives and leveraged their enormous platforms to come to the aid of not only those in spiritual slavery to sin, but also those in actual slavery to humans?

Below are some questions to consider about *your* legacy:

1. What might younger people and future generations criticize about your life and beliefs? Do any of these opposing views have at least a grain of truth in them that you are willing to reconsider and weigh now?

2. How could you devote the rest of your life for God to use to bring heaven down to earth through the power of the Holy Spirit?

3. Where do the needs of the world intersect with your place in the world in a way you could participate in these redemptive tasks further?

4. How could you listen to and then lift up, support, and enable the next generation to further the work that needs to be done in the world?

5. What are you proud of and not proud of regarding your legacy as it stands right now? Are any changes needed now?

George Whitefield wrote, "I am content to wait till the day of judgment for the clearing up of my character: and after I am dead, I desire no other epitaph than this, 'Here lies G. W. What sort of a man he was, the great day will discover.'" Time has made many things clear about Whitefield's deeds, but the "great day" is still yet to come.

As we conclude, we apply MLK's words to Whitefield, the great evangelist and egregious enslaver: "An evil deed . . . never expresses all that he is. . . . The viciousness and evilness of his acts are not quite representative of all that he is. . . . We know that God's image is ineffably etched in his being."[18] MLK added, "We must not seek to defeat or humiliate the enemy but to win his friendship and understanding. . . . We love every man because God loves him."[19]

The basis of our hatred of the sin of slavery is because God hates slavery; meanwhile the basis for our love for our fellow sinners is because of God's love. Fellow White American evangelicals, may we own our past and let it shape how we own our lives and legacies; may we be rich in good deeds and reckon with our sins as we await the grace and love that await us on "the great day."

ACKNOWLEDGMENTS

I WOULD LIKE TO ACKNOWLEDGE THE RESEARCH, insight, and input I've received from the excellent scholarship and kind assistance of Chris Woznicki, Geordan Hammond, George Marsden, Ian Maddock, Jermaine J. Marshall, Joel Houston, John T. Lowe, Ken Minkema, Kyle Strobel, Mark Noll, Obbie Tyler Todd, Randy Maddox, Thomas Kidd, Tom Schwanda, VanJessica Gladney, and Vince Bacote.

My time in Savannah at the Bethesda Academy, hosted by President H. Michael Hughes, as well as at the Georgia Salzburger Society Museum and Library, hosted by the energetic and knowledgeable Assistant Curator Robert Peavy and others in the community, was incredibly helpful and full of hospitality.

I greatly benefited from correspondence and time spent in Bristol, England, with Amber Druce, curator of history, Bristol Culture & Creative Industries, Gary Best at John Wesley's New Room, and Mary Milton of the Bristol Archives. Additional time spent in Gloucester, England, with the staff of St Mary De Crypt Church, including Jessica Gordon, and correspondence with Paul Evans, senior archivist, Gloucestershire County Council, brought additional insights. The assistance of Joshua David Hall, assistant curator and genealogist, Stockbridge Library Museum & Archives, and Rick Wilcox of the Bidwell House Museum near Stockbridge, helped me time and time again.

Steven Purcell, Hannah Smith, Amy Crouch, and Grant Shellhouse of Laity Lodge provided me quiet space and top-notch hospitality during a particularly challenging portion of writing this book—thank you.

Professor Tom Greggs introduced me properly to the study of John Wesley and guided me with boundless scholarly and practical wisdom from the very beginning—including helping me navigate grim questions that became the catalysts for this book. My colleague Dr. Robin Thompson taught me much about the New Testament era understanding of slavery and provided a patient ear for my questions and comments while I worked on this project. My editor at InterVarsity Press and friend Ethan McCarthy believed in this project from day one and helped shape it to be so much better than what I could have done on my own. I am also incredibly thankful for Ted Olsen for his expert-eye and wisdom in the final stretch and for the entire team at InterVarsity Press. Of course, any errors that remain are my sole responsibility.

Thank you, also, to all the people who patiently listened to me process this difficult material as I explored it further—especially my wife, Erin, and our children, Caleb, Lilly, and Molly.

NOTES

1. WHY SLAVERY? SLAVERY HAS NOTHING TO DO WITH ME

[1]VanJessica Gladney, "A Bare and Open Truth: The Penn and Slavery Project and the Public," *Perspectives on History* (October 19, 2022), www.historians.org /research-and-publications/perspectives-on-history november-2022/a-bare -and-open-truth-the-penn-and-slavery-project-and-the-public.

[2]James Baldwin, "Unnameable Objects, Unspeakable Crimes," in *The White Problem in America* (Chicago: Johnson Publishing Company, Inc., 1966), 174.

[3]Douglas Wilson and Steve Wilkins, *Southern Slavery: As It Was* (Moscow, ID: Canon Press, 1996), 8.

[4]Wilson and Wilkins, 24.

[5]Wilson and Wilkins, 38.

[6]Douglas Wilson, "Not That Simple," *Blog & Mablog*, February 10, 2020, https:// dougwils.com/books-and-culture/s7-engaging-the-culture/not-that-simple-2.html.

[7]Cited by Rick Pidcock, "What Has John MacArthur Actually Said About Race, Slavery and the Curse of Ham?" *Baptist News*, June 20, 2022, https://baptistnews .com/article/what-has-john-macarthur-actually-said-about-race-slavery-and -the-curse-of-ham/.

[8]John MacArthur, "What Is Scripture's View of Slavery?" *Grace to You*, January 8, 2013, www.gty.org/library/bibleqnas-library/BQ010813/what-is-scriptures-view -of-slavery.

[9]MacArthur, "What Is Scripture's View of Slavery?"

[10]Esau McCaulley, *Reading While Black: African American Biblical Interpretation as an Exercise in Hope* (Downers Grove, IL: IVP Academic, 2020), 140.

[11]James Baldwin, *The Fire Next Time* (New York: Vintage, 1993), 81.

[12]Sean McGever, *Born Again: The Evangelical Theology of Conversion in John Wesley and George Whitefield* (Bellingham, WA: Lexham, 2020), 19.

[13]McGever, *Born Again*, 23.

[14]Jemar Tisby, *The Color of Compromise: The Truth about the American Church's Complicity in Racism* (Grand Rapids, MI: Zondervan, 2019), 22.

[15]Christina Barland Edmondson and Chad Brennan, *Faithful Antiracism: Moving Past Talk to Systemic Change* (Downers Grove, IL: InterVarsity Press, 2022), 64.

[16]National Public Radio, *Talk of the Nation*, February 11, 2009, www.npr.org /transcripts/100585048.

2. THREE MEN WHO WOULD CHANGE THE WORLD

[1]Mark A. Noll, *The Rise of Evangelicalism: The Age of Edwards, Whitefield, and the Wesleys* (Downers Grove, IL: InterVarsity Press, 2003).

[2]In this book, references to Wesley will be to John Wesley and not his brother Charles Wesley unless otherwise specified.

[3]For more on Wesley's and Whitefield's views on conversion and the new birth, see Sean McGever, *Born Again: The Evangelical Theology of Conversion in John Wesley and George Whitefield* (Bellingham, WA: Lexham Press, 2020) and Sean McGever, "The Theology of Conversion in John Wesley and George White-field," in *Wesley and Whitefield*, ed. Ian J. Maddock (Eugene, OR: Wipf & Stock Publishers, 2017).

[4]Thomas S. Kidd, *Who Is an Evangelical?: The History of a Movement in Crisis* (New Haven, CT: Yale University Press, 2019), 12; See also Noll, *The Rise of Evangelicalism* 53.

[5]Cited in Obbie Tyler Todd, *Southern Edwardseans: The Southern Baptist Legacy of Jonathan Edwards*, New Directions in Jonathan Edwards Studies 8 (Göttingen, Germany: Vandenhoeck & Ruprecht Gmbh & Co., 2022), 36.

[6]Timothy Larsen, "Defining and Locating Evangelicalism," in *The Cambridge Companion to Evangelical Theology*, eds. Daniel J. Treier and Timothy Larsen (Cambridge: Cambridge University Press, 2007), 5.

[7]Jeffrey W. Barbeau, *The Spirit of Methodism: From the Wesleys to a Global Communion* (Downers Grove, IL: IVP Academic, 2019), xv.

[8]Barbeau, 153.

[9]Stephen Tomkins, *John Wesley: A Biography* (Grand Rapids, MI: Eerdmans, 2003), 199.

[10]Todd M. Johnson and Gina A. Zurlo, *World Christian Encyclopedia*, 3rd ed. (Edinburgh: Edinburgh University Press, 2020), 6-8, 26.

[11]John Dunton, ed., *The Athenian Oracle: Being an Entire Collection of All the Valuable Questions and Answers*, vol. 1 (London: Andrew Bell, 1703), 545-48. There are many details surrounding this publication and account. The most simple is that the pages are out of order so those looking up this reference are

encouraged to begin looking after page 538 for the proper pages listed. The rest of the details require much more explanation that will be published elsewhere.

[12]Dunton, *Athenian Oracle*, 545.

[13]Advertisement, *The Tatler*, February 9, 1709, 2.

[14]Cited in David Dabydeen, *Hogarth's Blacks: Images of Blacks in Eighteenth Century English Art* (Manchester: Manchester University Press, 1987), 17.

[15]V. H. H. Green, *The Young Mr. Wesley: A Study of John Wesley and Oxford* (New York: St. Martin's Press, 1961), 309.

[16]Camille Wells Slights, "Slaves and Subjects in Othello," *Shakespeare Quarterly* 48, no. 4 (Winter 1997), 385.

[17]Act 4, Scene 2. Derek Hughes, ed., *Versions of Blackness: Key Texts on Slavery from the Seventeenth Century* (Cambridge: Cambridge University Press, 2007), 253.

[18]John Wesley, *The Complete English Dictionary Explaining Most of Those Hard Words, Which Are Found in the Best English Writers* (London: W. Strahan, 1753).

[19]John Wesley, *Journals and Diaries*, eds. W. Reginald Ward and Richard P. Heitzenrater, *The Bicentennial Edition of the Works of John Wesley*, vols. 18-24 (Nashville: Abingdon Press, 1988), 18:211.

[20]Wesley, 18:250.

[21]McGever, *Born Again*.

[22]Benjamin Franklin, *The Autobiography of Benjamin Franklin* (New York: P. F. Collier & Sons, 1909), 107-8.

[23]Thomas S. Kidd, *George Whitefield: America's Spiritual Founding Father* (New Haven, CT: Yale University Press, 2014), 260.

[24]Harry S. Stout, *The Divine Dramatist: George Whitefield and the Rise of Modern Evangelicalism* (Grand Rapids, MI: Eerdmans, 1991), xiii-ix.

[25]Madge Dresser, *Slavery Obscured: The Social History of the Slave Trade in an English Provincial Port* (London: Bloomsbury, 2016), 28.

[26]David Richardson, ed., *Bristol, Africa and the English-Century Slave Trade to Africa: Vol. 1 The Years of Expansion 1698–1729* (Gloucester, England: Alan Sutton Publishing, 1986), xv.

[27]J. H. Bettey, *Bristol Observed: Visitors' Impressions of the City from Domesday to The Blitz* (Bristol, England: Redcliffe Press, 1986), 66. Emphasis in the original.

[28]Cited in Bettey, 85.

[29]See "Trans-Atlantic Slave Trade—Database," *Slave Voyages*, www.slave voyages.org/voyage/database.

[30] Luke Tyerman, *The Life of the Reverend George Whitefield* (London: Hodder and Stoughton, 1876), 2:492.

[31] C. R. Hudleston, "George Whitefield's Ancestry," *Transactions of the Bristol and Gloucestershire Archaeological Society* 59 (1937): 235.

[32] Hudleston, 234-35.

[33] Arnold Dallimore, *George Whitefield: The Life and Times of the Great Evangelist of the Eighteenth-Century Revival,* vol. 1 (London: Banner of Truth Trust, 1970), 1:43.

[34] Boyd Stanley Schlenther, "Whitefield's Personal Life and Character," in *George Whitefield: Life, Context, and Legacy,* eds. David Ceri Jones and Geordan Hammond (Oxford: Oxford University Press, 2016), 12.

[35] Dallimore, *George Whitefield,* 1:50.

[36] For a fuller account of Whitefield's conversion, see McGever, *Born Again,* 119-33.

[37] Kidd, *George Whitefield,* 48.

[38] Tyerman, *The Life of the Reverend George Whitefield,* 1:2.

[39] Cited in Michael J. McClymond and Gerald R. McDermott, *The Theology of Jonathan Edwards* (Oxford: Oxford University Press, 2012), 637.

[40] John T. Lowe, "Jonathan Edwards," in *American Religious History: Belief and Society through Time,* ed. Gary Scott Smith (Santa Barbara, CA: ABC-CLIO, 2021), 150.

[41] John E. Smith, Harry S. Stout, and Kenneth P. Minkema, eds., *A Jonathan Edwards Reader* (New Haven, CT: Yale University Press, 2003), vii.

[42] Smith, Stout, and Minkema, vii.

[43] Mary Pierpont, Sarah's mother, had a slave whom Mary manumitted in her will. Jonathan and Sarah executed the will, and thus the manumission, a few weeks after Mary's death on November 25, 1740. As a point of clarification, the slave was owned by Sarah's mother (Mary), not Sarah's stepmother. Ken Minkema confirmed with me that a previous claim that the slave was owned by Sarah's stepmother was not accurate. This means that Sarah grew up with a slave serving her in her house. Kenneth P. Minkema, "Jonathan Edwards's Defense of Slavery," *Massachusetts Historical Review,* Race & Slavery, 4 (2002): 43; William Richard Cutter, ed., *New England Families, Genealogical and Memorial: A Record of the Achievements of Her People in the Making of Commonwealths and the Founding of a Nation,* vol. 3 (New York: Lewis Historical Publishing Company, 1913), 1158.

[44] Ansars may have had a wife named Phyllis, also a slave, who lived with them. The Edwards family may have had a maid named Mercy Brooks, though the evidence is inconclusive. Thank you to Ken Minkema and John Lowe for their

private correspondence with me clarifying these details. See also Kenneth P. Minkema, *The Edwardses: A Ministerial Family in Eighteenth-Century New England* (unpublished dissertation: University of Connecticut, 1988), 159; Minkema, "Jonathan Edwards's Defense of Slavery," 24.

[45]Antony Dugdale, J. J. Fueser, and J. Celso de Castro Alves, "Yale, Slavery, and Abolition" (The Amistad Committee, 2001), 3, www.yaleslavery.org; George M. Marsden, *Jonathan Edwards: A Life* (New Haven, CT: Yale University Press, 2003), 93.

[46]Dugdale, Fueser, and Alves, "Yale, Slavery, and Abolition," 12.

[47]Larry E. Tice, *Proslavery: A History of the Defense of Slavery in America 1701–1840* (Athens, GA: University of Georgia Press, 1987), 141-45.

[48]Edgar J. McManus, *A History of Negro Slavery in New York* (Syracuse, NY: Syracuse University Press, 1966), 26-27; Thelma Wills Foote, *Black and White Manhattan: The History of Racial Formation in Colonial New York City* (New York: Oxford University Press, 2004), 76-77, 132-33, 138, 141.

[49]Gerald R. McDermott, "Conclusion: Edwards's Relevance Today," in *Understanding Jonathan Edwards: An Introduction to America's Theologian*, ed. Gerald R. McDermott (Oxford: Oxford University Press, 2009), 201-17.

[50]McClymond and McDermott, *The Theology of Jonathan Edwards*, 643.

[51]John Piper, *Let the Nations Be Glad!: The Supremacy of God in Missions*, 3rd ed. (Grand Rapids, MI: Baker Academic, 2010), 227; Thank you to Obbie Tyler Todd for bringing these Piper references to my attention in our conversations and in his work: Todd, *Southern Edwardseans: The Southern Baptist Legacy of Jonathan Edwards*, 184-85.

[52]John Piper, *Desiring God* (Sisters, OR: Multnomah Publishers, 2003), 22.

[53]The exception being Sarah's paternal grandparents, John and Thankful Pierpont, who were born in England before coming to New England.

3. WHAT PRECEDED THEM

[1]David Brion Davis, *The Problem of Slavery in Western Culture* (New York: Oxford University Press, 1988), 31.

[2]David Brion Davis, *Inhuman Bondage: The Rise and Fall of Slavery in the New World* (Oxford: Oxford University Press, 2008), 30.

[3]James Walvin, *Short History of Slavery* (London: Penguin Books, 2007), 7.

[4]Daniel C. Snell, "Slavery in the Ancient Near East," in *The Cambridge World History of Slavery: Volume 1: The Ancient Mediterranean World*, ed. Keith Bradley and Paul Cartledge, (Cambridge: Cambridge University Press, 2011), 7-17; Gad Heuman, ed., *The Routledge History of Slavery* (London: Routledge, 2012), 7.

[5]Walvin, *Short History of Slavery*, 8-18.

[6]Jennifer A. Glancy, *Slavery as Moral Problem: In the Early Church and Today* (Minneapolis, MN: Fortress Press, 2011), 9.

[7]See Jennifer A. Glancy, *Slavery in Early Christianity* (Minneapolis, MN: Fortress Press, 2006); Glancy, *Slavery as Moral Problem*; John Anthony McGuckin, *The Path of Christianity: The First Thousand Years* (Downers Grove, IL: IVP Academic, 2017), 1056-89; Esau McCaulley, *Reading While Black: African American Biblical Interpretation as an Exercise in Hope* (Downers Grove, IL: IVP Academic, 2020), 137-63; Dale B. Martin, *Slavery as Salvation: The Metaphor of Slavery in Pauline Christianity* (Eugene, OR: Wipf & Stock, 2021); William J. Webb, *Slaves, Women & Homosexuals: Exploring the Hermeneutics of Cultural Analysis* (Downers Grove, IL: InterVarsity Press, 2001); Hector Avalos, *Slavery, Abolitionism, and the Ethics of Biblical Scholarship* (Sheffield, England: Sheffield Phoenix Press, 2013); Mark A. Noll, *The Civil War as a Theological Crisis* (Chapel Hill, NC: University of North Carolina Press, 2015).

[8]McGuckin, *The Path of Christianity*, 1060.

[9]McCaulley, *Reading While Black*, 151.

[10]Ignatius, "Epistle to Polycarp," in *The Ante-Nicene Fathers: Translations of the Writings of the Fathers Down to AD 325*, vol. 1 (Peabody, MA: Hendrickson Publishers, 1994), chap. 3.4 (ANF 1:94-95).

[11]Lactantius, "A Treatise on the Anger of God," in *The Ante-Nicene Fathers*, chap. 18 (ANF 7:275).

[12]McGuckin, *The Path of Christianity*, 1069.

[13]Kyle Harper, *Slavery in the Late Roman World, AD 275–425* (Cambridge: Cambridge University Press, 2011), 4, 348; Matthew Elia, "Ethics in the Afterlife of Slavery: Race, Augustinian Politics, and the Problem of the Christian Master," *Journal of the Society of Christian Ethics* 38, no. 2 (2018): 104.

[14]McGuckin, *The Path of Christianity*, 1070.

[15]McGuckin, *The Path of Christianity*, 1071; Glancy, *Slavery as Moral Problem*, 81-82. Glancy points out that killing a slave brought a lesser penalty than a woman who left her husband or committed adultery. The church thought adultery was worse than killing a slave.

[16]Davis, *Inhuman Bondage*, 34-35; Glancy, *Slavery as Moral Problem*, 97-100; McGuckin, *The Path of Christianity*, 1062.

[17]Homily 4 on Ecclesiastes, excerpted in McGuckin, *The Path of Christianity*, 1083-84.

[18]Davis, *The Problem of Slavery in Western Culture*, 34-40; Walvin, *Short History of Slavery*, 22-28; Moses I. Finley, *Ancient Slavery and Modern Ideology* (New York: Viking Press, 1980), 47.

[19]This section on Islam follows Walvin, *Short History of Slavery*, chap. 3; Martin A. Klein, "Islam and Antislavery," in *Encyclopedia of Antislavery and Abolition*, ed. Peter Hinks and John McKivigan, 2 vols. (Westport, CT: Greenwood Press, 2007), 375-79.

[20]Rudolf T. Ware III, "Slavery in Islamic Africa, 1400–1800," in *The Cambridge World History of Slavery, Volume 3, AD 1420–AD 1804* (Cambridge: Cambridge University Press, 2011), 47.

[21]Richard Hellie, "Russian Slavery and Serfdom, 1450–1804," in *The Cambridge World History of Slavery, Volume 3*, 275-95.

[22]Frances Gardiner Davenport, ed., *European Treaties Bearing on the History of the United States and Its Dependencies to 1648*, Papers of the Department of Historical Research (Washington, DC: Carnegie Institution of Washington, 1917), 23.

[23]Davenport, *European Treaties Bearing on the History of the United States*, 22.

[24]David Olusoga, *Black and British: A Forgotten History* (London: Picador, 2021), 50-51.

[25]Nick Hazlewood, *The Queen's Slave Trader: John Hawkyns, Elizabeth I, and the Trafficking in Human Souls* (New York: William Morrow, 2004), 179, 269.

[26]Rik Van Welie, "Slave Trading and Slavery in the Dutch Colonial Empire: A Global Comparison," *New West Indian Guide / Nieuwe West-Indische Gids* 82, no. 1/2 (2008): 57-58.

[27]African slaves appeared in North America prior to 1619, notably in Spanish Florida in the 1560s. Davis, *Inhuman Bondage*, 124.

[28]Betty Wood, *Slavery in Colonial America 1619–1776* (New York: Rowman & Littlefield Publishers, 2005), 2-3.

[29]Wood, *Slavery in Colonial America*, 8.

[30]Wood, *Slavery in Colonial America*, 11.

[31]The Body of Liberties can be found at https://history.hanover.edu/texts/masslib.html. I have adjusted the archaic spellings for easier reading.

[32]Olusoga, *Black and British*, 70.

[33]Walvin, *Short History of Slavery*, 52; J. David Hacker, "From '20. and Odd' to 10 Million: The Growth of the Slave Population in the United States," *Slavery & Abolition* 41, no. 4 (October 2020): 843.

[34]Jack P. Greene, "Colonial South Carolina and the Caribbean Connection," *The South Carolina Historical Magazine* 88, no. 4 (1987): 197.

[35]Wood, *Slavery in Colonial America*, 12.

[36]Wood, 79.

[37]Olusoga, *Black and British*, 73.

[38]Olusoga, 75.

4. WHAT THEY ASSUMED

[1] Matthew Henry, *Matthew Henry's Commentary on the Whole Bible: Complete and Unabridged in One Volume* (Peabody, MA: Hendrickson, 1994), 2256.

[2] Henry began publishing parts of his commentary in 1708 and added additional books in 1710. Henry died in 1714, after which, the complete edition of his commentary was published.

[3] Richard Baxter, *The Practical Works of the Reverend Richard Baxter* (London: James Duncan, 1830), 4:203-4.

[4] Baxter, 4:213.

[5] The six themes were gathered by examining the works and writings of many sources, including: *The Edwardian Homilies* (1547–1571), Richard Hooker (1554–1600), William Perkins (1558–1602), William Gouge (1575–1653), John Cotton (1584–1652), John Eliot (1604–1690), Richard Baxter (1615–1691), Stephen Charnock (1628–1680), John Owen (1616–1683), John Tillotson (1630–1694), Morgan Godwyn (1640–1686), Samuel Willard (1640–1707), Matthew Henry (1662–1714), Cotton Mather (1663–1728), and Thomas Boston (1676–1732).

[6] Church of England, *The Two Books of Homilies* (Oxford: Oxford University Press, 1859), 105.

[7] Church of England, *Two Books of Homilies*, 105.

[8] Mark Chapman, *Anglican Theology* (London: T&T Clark, 2012), 106.

[9] Richard Hooker, *The Works of That Learned and Judicious Divine, Mr. Richard Hooker*, ed. John Keble (Oxford: Clarendon Press, 1874), 3:344 (Ecclesiastical Laws 8.3.5).

[10] William Perkins, *The Works of William Perkins* (Grand Rapids, MI: Reformation Heritage Books, 2020), 10:187.

[11] William Gouge, *Of Domestical Duties*, ed. Greg Fox (Edinburgh, IA: Puritan Reprints, 2006), 428. The page reference is from the ebook. The print version of the ebook omits this section. Compare with the 1622 edition. William Gouge, *Of Domestical Duties* (London: John Haviland, 1622), 591.

[12] John Owen, *The Works of John Owen*, ed. William H. Goold (Edinburgh: T&T Clark, n.d.), 3:609-10.

[13] Wendy Warren, *New England Bound: Slavery and Colonization in Early America* (New York: Liveright, 2016), 229.

[14] Perkins, *The Works of William Perkins*, 2:237-38.

[15] Perkins, 4:139-40.

[16] Perkins, 10:187.

[17] Gouge, *Of Domestical Duties*, 428.

[18] Stephen Charnock, *The Complete Works of Stephen Charnock*, ed. James Nichols and James Nisbet (London: W. Robertson; G. Herbert, 1864), 2:161.

[19] Samuel Willard, *A Complete Body of Divinity* (Boston: Green and Kneeland, 1726), 614.

[20] Henry, *Matthew Henry's Commentary on the Whole Bible*, 637.

[21] Davis, *The Problem of Slavery in Western Culture*, 165.

[22] Perkins, *The Works of William Perkins*, 10:186.

[23] Perkins, 10:186.

[24] Perkins, 10:187.

[25] John Cotton, *An Abstract of The Lawes of New England* (London: R. Coules and W. Ley, 1641), 11-12.

[26] Daniel R. Coquillette, "Radical Lawmakers in Colonial Massachusetts: The 'Countenance of Authoritie' and the Lawes and Libertyes," *The New England Quarterly* 67, no. 2 (June 1994): 189-94.

[27] Baxter, *The Practical Works of the Reverend Richard Baxter*, 4:212-20.

[28] Baxter, 4:217.

[29] Baxter, 4:215-17.

[30] Baxter, 4:217.

[31] Baxter, 4:217.

[32] Willard, *A Complete Body of Divinity*, 614.

[33] Henry, *Matthew Henry's Commentary on the Whole Bible*, 127, 183.

[34] Church of England, *The Two Books of Homilies*, 510.

[35] Bray, Gerald, *A Fruitful Exhortation: A Guide to the Homilies* (London: Latimer Trust, 2014), 127.

[36] Church of England, *The Two Books of Homilies*, 574.

[37] Church of England, 551, 553.

[38] Hooker, *The Works of That Learned and Judicious Divine, Mr. Richard Hooker*, 3:606.

[39] Gouge, *Of Domestical Duties*, 481.

[40] Gouge, 427.

[41] Gouge, 431.

[42] Gouge, 468.

[43] Baxter, *The Practical Works of the Reverend Richard Baxter*, 4:91.

[44] Baxter, 4:204.

[45] Baxter also provided a guide for catechizing families. The questions include: "Q. 35. What is the duty of masters to their servants?" and "Q. 38. What is the duty of servants to their masters?" Baxter, 19:209-10.

[46] Baxter, 4:209.

[47]Willard, *A Complete Body of Divinity*, 616.

[48]Henry, *Matthew Henry's Commentary on the Whole Bible*, 183. Comments on Leviticus 25:39-55.

[49]Perkins, *The Works of William Perkins*, 2:237; Gouge, *Of Domestical Duties*, 430, 485; Willard, *A Complete Body of Divinity*, 616.

[50]Morgan Godwyn, *The Negro's and Indians Advocate, Suing for Their Admission to the Church, or, A Persuasive to the Instructing and Baptizing of the Negro's and Indians in Our Plantations* . . . (London: J. D., 1680), 14.

[51]Cotton Mather, *A Family Well-Ordered* (Boston: B. Green & J. Allen, 1699), esp. 66-71.

[52]Cotton Mather, *A Pastoral Letter to the English Captives, in Africa, from New-England* (Boston: B. Green & J. Allen, 1698).

[53]Mather, 15.

[54]Cotton Mather, *The Glory of Goodness* (Boston: T. Green, 1703).

[55]Randall Fowler, "Puritanism, Islam, and Race in Cotton Mather's *The Glory of Goodness*: An Exercise in Exceptionalism," *Rhetoric and Public Affairs* 21, no. 4 (Winter 2018): 594.

[56]Cotton Mather, *The Negro Christianized* (Boston: B. Green, 1706), 1.

[57]Mather, 15.

[58]Mather, 24.

[59]Cotton Mather, *Diary of Cotton Mather 1681–1708*, Massachusetts Historical Society Collections (Boston: Plimpton Press, 1911), 564-65.

[60]Mather, 579.

[61]Cotton Mather, *Diary of Cotton Mather 1709–1724*, Massachusetts Historical Society Collections (Boston: Plimpton Press, 1912), 363.

[62]Mather, 477.

[63]Church of England, *The Book of Common Prayer: The Texts of 1549, 1559, and 1662* (Oxford: Oxford University Press, 2011), 211.

[64]Davis, *The Problem of Slavery in Western Culture*, 203-4.

[65]Baxter, *The Practical Works of the Reverend Richard Baxter*, 4:213.

[66]Baxter, 4:217.

[67]Godwyn, *The Negro's and Indians Advocate*, ix.

[68]Godwyn, 107.

[69]Godwyn, 111.

[70]Godwyn, 142.

[71]Godwyn, 140. A 1667 law of the Virginia General Assembly stated that baptism of the enslaved did not affect their unfree status.

[72]Morgan Godwyn, *A Supplement to the Negro's and Indians Advocate* (London, 1681), 3.

[73]Mather, *The Negro Christianized*, 16.

[74]Mather, 16-17.

[75]Davis, *The Problem of Slavery in Western Culture*, 210.

5. WESLEY IN GEORGIA

[1]Allen D. Candler, ed., *The Colonial Records of the State of Georgia*, vol. 1 (Atlanta: The Franklin Printing and Publishing Company, 1904), 11.

[2]Candler, *The Colonial Records of the State of Georgia*, 1:1:50-52.

[3]Candler, 1:1:31-44.

[4]Candler, 1:1:44-49.

[5]Allen D. Candler, Wm. J. Northen, and Lucian Lamar Knight, eds., *The Colonial Records of the State of Georgia*, vol. 22 Part 1 (Atlanta: Chas. P. Byrd, 1913), 22:275-76.

[6]Candler, *The Colonial Records of the State of Georgia*, 1:1:51.

[7]Five years later, on January 16, 1740, a Captain Messey told the trustees, "Georgia is a fine Barrier for the Northern Provinces, and especially for Carolina; And is also a great security against the running away of Negroes from Carolina to Augustine [Florida], because every Negroe at his first appearance in Georgia must be immediately known to be a run away, since there are no Negroes in Georgia." Candler, 1:1:51, 361.

[8]Candler, 1:1:54.

[9]Edgar L. Pennington, "Dr. Thomas Bray's Associates and Their Work among the Negroes," *Proceedings of the American Antiquarian Society* 48 (1938): 316. Scott explains that the two groups operated "almost as one unified group." John Thomas Scott, *The Wesleys and the Anglican Mission to Georgia, 1735–1738: "So Glorious an Undertaking"* (Bethlehem, PA: Lehigh University Press, 2020), 10.

[10]For a detailed account, see Katharine Gerbner, *Christian Slavery: Conversion and Race in the Protestant Atlantic World* (Philadelphia: University of Pennsylvania Press, 2018), 91-137.

[11]David Brion Davis, *The Problem of Slavery in Western Culture* (New York: Oxford University Press, 1988), 220-21.

[12]Scott, *The Wesleys and the Anglican Mission to Georgia*, 21-23.

[13]John Wesley, *Letters*, ed. Frank Baker and Ted A. Campbell, *The Bicentennial Edition of the Works of John Wesley*, vol. 25-27 (Nashville: Abingdon Press, 1980), 25:436.

[14]Wesley, 25:439-41.

[15]John Wesley, *Journals and Diaries*, eds. W. Reginald Ward and Richard P. Heitzenrater, *The Bicentennial Edition of the Works of John Wesley*, vols. 18-24 (Nashville: Abingdon Press, 1988), 19:351.

[16]E. Merton Coulter and Albert B. Saye, *A List of the Early Settlers of Georgia* (Athens: University of Georgia Press, 2009), x; Luke Tyerman, *The Life and Times of the Reverend John Wesley* (London: Hodder and Stoughton, 1870), 1:142.

[17]Coulter and Saye, *A List of the Early Settlers of Georgia*, xi–xii.

[18]Coulter and Saye, 16.

[19]Coulter and Saye, 84.

[20]Scott, *The Wesleys and the Anglican Mission to Georgia*, 254.

[21]Russell R. Menard, "Slave Demography in the Lowcountry, 1670–1740: From Frontier Society to Plantation Regime," *The South Carolina Historical Magazine* 101, no. 3 (July 2000): 193.

[22]Wesley, *Journals and Diaries*, 18:169.

[23]Wesley, 18:506.

[24]Wesley, 18:170.

[25]Scott, *The Wesleys and the Anglican Mission to Georgia*, 142.

[26]Wesley, *Journals and Diaries*, 18:406.

[27]Charles Wesley and John Telford, *The Journal of the Reverend Charles Wesley, M.A.* (London: Robert Culley, 1909), 68-69.

[28]Wesley, *Journals and Diaries*, 18:410.

[29]Wesley, 18:448-51; Geordan Hammond, *John Wesley in America: Restoring Primitive Christianity* (Oxford: Oxford University Press, 2014), 149-50.

[30]Wesley, *Journals and Diaries*, 18:500; Hammond, *John Wesley in America*, 150.

[31]Wesley, *Journals and Diaries*, 18:180; 501.

[32]Wesley, 18:180.

[33]Wesley, 18:501-2.

[34]John Wesley, *The Works of John Wesley*, ed. Thomas Jackson, 3rd ed. (London: Methodist Reading Room, 1872), 11:75.

[35]Wesley, *Journals and Diaries*, 18:503.

[36]Wesley, 18:504.

6. WHITEFIELD IN GEORGIA

[1]John Wesley, *Letters*, ed. Frank Baker and Ted A. Campbell, *The Bicentennial Edition of the Works of John Wesley*, vol. 25-27 (Nashville: Abingdon Press, 1980), 25:471.

[2]Wesley, 25:472-73.

[3]George Whitefield, *A Further Account of God's Dealings with the Reverend Mr. George Whitefield* (London: W. Strahan, 1747), 11.

[4]Whitefield, 12.

[5]Allen D. Candler, *The Colonial Records of the State of Georgia: Original Papers, Correspondence, Trustees, General Oglethorpe and Others*, ed. Lucian Lamar Knight, vol. 21 (Atlanta: Chas. P. Byrd, 1910), 468.

[6]Charles Wesley, *The Early Journal of Charles Wesley* (London: Charles H. Kelly, 1909), 129.

[7]Wesley, 130.

[8]George Whitefield, *The Works of the Reverend George Whitefield*, ed. John Gillies (London: Printed for Edward and Charles Dilly, 1771), 3:466.

[9]Whitefield, 3:463.

[10]Letter from Whitefield to Benjamin Franklin on June 23, 1747. Cited in Peter Y. Choi, *George Whitefield: Evangelist for God and Empire* (Grand Rapids, MI: Eerdmans, 2018), 224; Whitefield, *The Works of the Reverend George Whitefield*, 3:484.

[11]George Whitefield, *A Continuation of the Reverend Mr. Whitefield's Journal, From His Arrival at London, to His Departure from Thence on His Way to Georgia* (London: Hutton, 1739), 4.

[12]Whitefield, *The Works of the Reverend George Whitefield*, 1:185; See also Peter Y. Choi, "Whitefield, Georgia, and the Quest for Bethesda College," in *George Whitefield: Life, Context, and Legacy*, ed. David Ceri Jones and Geordan Hammond (Oxford: Oxford University Press, 2016), 224-40.

[13]Frank Lambert, *James Habersham: Loyalty, Politics, and Commerce in Colonial Georgia* (Athens: University of Georgia Press, 2005), 46.

[14]Lambert, 46-47.

[15]Lambert, 47.

[16]Lambert, 50.

[17]Whitefield, *The Works of the Reverend George Whitefield*, 3:444.

[18]Whitefield, 3:435.

[19]Lambert, *James Habersham*, 54.

[20]John Gillies and Aaron C. Seymour, *Memoirs of the Life of the Reverend George Whitefield, A.M.* (Philadelphia: Simon Probasco, 1820), 34-35.

[21]Thomas S. Kidd, *George Whitefield: America's Spiritual Founding Father* (New Haven, CT: Yale University Press, 2014), 82.

[22]George Whitefield, *Fifth Journal: From His Embarking after the Embargo, to His Arrival at Savannah in Georgia* (London: James Hutton, 1740), 62-63.

[23]Whitefield, 74.

[24]Kidd, *George Whitefield*, 98.

[25]Whitefield, *Fifth Journal*, 82.

[26]Whitefield, *The Works of the Reverend George Whitefield*, 4:35-40.

[27]Katharine Gerbner, *Christian Slavery: Conversion and Race in the Protestant Atlantic World* (Philadelphia: University of Pennsylvania Press, 2018), 189.

[28]A. L. Oerter, *The Whitefield House on Ephrata Property at Nazareth, PA. 1740–1914* (Bethlehem, PA: Times Publishing Company, 1914), 8.

[29]George Whitefield, *Sixth Journal: After His Arriving at Georgia, to a Few Days after His Second Return Hither from Philadelphia* (London: James Hutton, 1741), 24.

[30]Tyerman, *The Life of the Reverend George Whitefield*, 1:380; George Whitefield, *Letters of George Whitefield, for the Period 1734–1742.* (Edinburgh; Carlisle, PA: Banner of Truth Trust, 1976), 507.

[31]Edward J. Cashin, *Beloved Bethesda: A History of George Whitefield's Home for Boys, 1740–2000* (Macon, GA: Mercer University Press, 2001), 50.

[32]Whitefield, *The Works of the Reverend George Whitefield*, 3:435.

[33]Colonial Records of Georgia cited in Choi, *George Whitefield*, 143.

[34]Whitefield, *The Works of the Reverend George Whitefield*, 3:449-50.

[35]Allen D. Candler, *The Colonial Records of the State of Georgia: Original Papers, Correspondence, Trustees, General Oglethorpe and Others*, ed. Lucian Lamar Knight, vol. 24 (Atlanta, GA: Chas. P. Byrd, 1915), 434-44.

[36]Whitefield, *The Works of the Reverend George Whitefield*, 2:90.

[37]Whitefield, 2:127.

[38]Whitefield, 2:208-9.

[39]Betty Wood, *Slavery in Colonial Georgia: 1730–1775* (Athens: University of Georgia Press, 1984), 82.

[40]Thank you to Thomas Kidd for sharing with me letters he retrieved from the Williams Evangelical Library in London that provide these details. See also Kidd, *George Whitefield*, 209.

[41]Whitefield, *The Works of the Reverend George Whitefield*, 2:404-5.

[42]Whitefield, 2:463.

[43]Whitefield, 2:471-72.

[44]Whitefield, 4:473-75.

7. EDWARDS IN MASSACHUSETTS

[1]James Russell Trumbull, *History of Northampton Massachusetts* (Northampton: Gazette Printing, 1902), 2:44.

[2]George M. Marsden, *Jonathan Edwards: A Life* (New Haven, CT: Yale University Press, 2003), 114.

[3]Perry Miller, "Solomon Stoddard, 1643-1729," *The Harvard Theological Review* 34, no. 4 (1941): 278.

[4]Perry adds, "except when he was making his annual visit to Boston." Miller, "Solomon Stoddard," 279.

[5]Peter C. Holloran, *Historical Dictionary of New England*, 2nd ed. (Lanham, MD: Rowman & Littlefield, 2017), 474.

[6]Trumbull, *History of Northampton Massachusetts*, 2:65-66. In 1700, Stoddard was the thirteenth-largest landowner (of 103) in his community. Patricia J. Tracy, *Jonathan Edwards, Pastor: Religion and Society in Eighteenth-Century Northampton* (Eugene, OR: Wipf and Stock, 2006), 46.

[7]Trumbull, *History of Northampton Massachusetts*, 2:48.

[8]Marsden, *Jonathan Edwards*, 114.

[9]Kevin Michael Sweeney, "River Gods and Related Minor Deities: The Williams Family and the Connecticut River Valley, 1637–1790" (unpublished dissertation: Yale University, 1986), 348.

[10]Trumbull, *History of Northampton Massachusetts*, 2:174, 177.

[11]Trumbull, 2:328.

[12]See Chapter 5.

[13]Richard Baxter, *A Treatise of Self-Denial* (London: Robert White, 1675), 174.

[14]Baxter, 175-76.

[15]Baxter, 179.

[16]Richard L. Bushman, *From Puritan to Yankee: Character and the Social Order in Connecticut, 1690–1765* (Cambridge, MA: Harvard University Press, 1967), 287.

[17]Tracy, *Jonathan Edwards, Pastor*, 45.

[18]John E. Smith, Harry S. Stout, and Kenneth P. Minkema, eds., *A Jonathan Edwards Reader* (New Haven, CT: Yale University Press, 2003), 177; Jonathan Edwards, *Letters and Personal Writings*, eds. George S. Claghorn and Harry S. Stout, vol. 16, The Works of Jonathan Edwards (New Haven; London: Yale University Press, 1998), 14.

[19]Kenneth P. Minkema, "Personal Writings," in *The Cambridge Companion to Jonathan Edwards*, Cambridge Companions to Religion (New York: Cambridge University Press, 2007), 55.

[20]Jonathan Edwards, *Sermons and Discourses, 1723–1729*, ed. Kenneth P. Minkema, vol. 14, The Works of Jonathan Edwards (New Haven; London: Yale University Press, 1997), 14:497.

[21]Marsden, *Jonathan Edwards*, 132.

[22]Edwards's salary in 1731 is often highlighted because of his purchase of Venus, as discussed in this chapter. Many references to his salary state that he was

making £200 a year when he purchased Venus, but a closer reading of Trumbull *History of Northampton* (2:50) appears to indicate that Edwards made £140 in 1731 and £200 in 1732. The chronological entries made by Ken Minkema at http://edwards.yale.edu/research/chronology support my reading that Edwards was making £140 a year when he purchased Venus, which accounts for over half of his annual salary.

[23]Kenneth P. Minkema, "Jonathan Edwards's Defense of Slavery," *Massachusetts Historical Review*, Race & Slavery, 4 (2002): 30.

[24]Smith, Stout, and Minkema, *A Jonathan Edwards Reader*, 296-97.

[25]Minkema, "Jonathan Edwards's Defense of Slavery," 28.

[26]My suspicion is that Venus was renamed Leah after becoming a Christian. I appreciate conversations with Edwards scholar and historian John Lowe regarding his research and insight on this topic.

[27]Minkema, "Jonathan Edwards's Defense of Slavery," 43.

[28]I appreciate a conversation I had with Mark Noll about the possibility that Edwards may have known about Judge Sewall's ca. 1700 tract "The Selling of Joseph." Heejoon Jeon argues that there is no evidence that Edwards knew of Sewall's tract but admits that the arguments are very similar. Heejoon Jeon, "Jonathan Edwards and the Anti-Slavery Movement," *Journal of Evangelical Theology Society* 63, no. 4 (December 2020): 779.

[29]Kenneth P. Minkema, "Jonathan Edwards on Slavery and the Slave Trade," *The William and Mary Quarterly* LIV, no. 4 (October 1997): 823-34; Edwards, *Letters and Personal Writings*, 16:71-76. There is evidence that the "Draft Slavery Letter" may have been known prior to Minkema's discovery. John Lowe may publish this information, if confirmed, in the future.

[30]Minkema, "Jonathan Edwards's Defense of Slavery," 32.

[31]Minkema, "Jonathan Edwards on Slavery and the Slave Trade," 825.

[32]Edwards, *Letters and Personal Writings*, 16:73.

[33]Edwards, 16:73.

[34]Minkema, "Jonathan Edwards's Defense of Slavery," 42.

[35]Edwards, *Letters and Personal Writings*, 16:149.

[36]Minkema, "Jonathan Edwards's Defense of Slavery," 36; Marsden, *Jonathan Edwards*, 301-2.

[37]Minkema, "Jonathan Edwards's Defense of Slavery," 43.

[38]Tracy, *Jonathan Edwards, Pastor*, 157.

[39]For more details on Edwards's dismissal in Northampton, see Marsden, *Jonathan Edwards*, 341-74.

40Rachel M. Wheeler, "Edwards as Missionary," in *The Cambridge Companion to Jonathan Edwards*, Cambridge Companions to Religion (New York: Cambridge University Press, 2007), 199.

41Michael J. McClymond and Gerald R. McDermott, *The Theology of Jonathan Edwards* (Oxford: Oxford University Press, 2012), 560.

42McClymond and McDermott, 36.

43Jonathan Edwards Jr., *Observations on the Language of the Muhhekaneew Indians* (New Haven, CT: Josiah Meigs, 1788), preface.

44Electa Fidelia Jones, *Stockbridge, Past and Present, or, Records of an Old Mission Station* (Springfield, MA: S. Bowles & Company, 1854), 238.

45I owe this insight to a personal conversation with Kyle Strobel, for which I am thankful.

46Marsden, *Jonathan Edwards*, 1.

47Mark A. Noll, *America's God: From Jonathan Edwards to Abraham Lincoln* (Oxford: Oxford University Press, 2004), 24.

48Jonathan Edwards, *Ethical Writings*, ed. Paul Ramsey, vol. 8, The Works of Jonathan Edwards (New Haven; London: Yale University Press, 1989), 437.

49I am indebted to Kyle Strobel for suggesting I explore this argument and several of the ideas that follow in this section.

50Jonathan Edwards, *Sermons and Discourses, 1734–1738*, ed. M. X. Lesser and Harry S. Stout, vol. 19, The Works of Jonathan Edwards (New Haven, CT: Yale University Press, 2001), 739.

51Edwards, 19:741.

52Jonathan Edwards, *Sermons and Discourses, 1743–1758*, ed. Wilson H. Kimnach, vol. 25, The Works of Jonathan Edwards (New Haven; London: Yale University Press, 2006), 143.

53Edwards, 8:563.

54Edwards, 8:568.

55Edwards, 8:569.

56Edwards, 8:8.

57Edwards, 8:550.

58Edwards, 8:540, 545.

59Edwards does discuss "disinterested general benevolence," but the term "disinterested benevolence" utilized by modern Edwards scholars tends to lean on how the idea was developed by his later followers. Edwards, 8:617.

60Thank you to Mark Noll for informing me of the original name of this town.

61Edwards, *Letters and Personal Writings*, 16:622.

[62]John Ferguson, *Memoir of the Life and Character of Reverend Samuel Hopkins, D.D.: Formerly Pastor of the First Congregational Church in Newport, Rhode Island. With an Appendix* (Boston: L.W. Kimball, 1830), 85.

[63]Esther Edwards Burr, *The Journal of Esther Edwards Burr, 1754–1757*, eds. Carol F. Karlsen and Laurie Crumpacker (New Haven, CT: Yale University Press, 1984), 90.

[64]Edwards, *Letters and Personal Writings*, 16:731; For more information on Harry and slaves in the Burr family see Burr, *The Journal of Esther Edwards Burr*, 27, 90, 99, 138, 206, 213, 264, 298.

[65]I deeply appreciate personal conversations with George Marsden and John T. Lowe regarding Edwards and race.

8. WESLEY'S THIRTY-SEVEN-YEAR SILENCE

[1]John Wesley, *Journals and Diaries*, eds. W. Reginald Ward and Richard P. Heitzenrater, The Bicentennial Edition of the Works of John Wesley, vols. 18-24 (Nashville: Abingdon Press, 1988), 18:207.

[2]Wesley, 18:208.

[3]John Wesley, *Journals and Diaries*, eds. W. Reginald Ward and Richard P. Heitzenrater, The Bicentennial Edition of the Works of John Wesley, vols. 18-24 (Nashville: Abingdon Press, 1988), 18:259-61.Thank you to Mark Noll for alerting me to Wesley's meeting with Zinzendorf in Marienborn.

[4]Katharine Gerbner, *Christian Slavery: Conversion and Race in the Protestant Atlantic World* (Philadelphia: University of Pennsylvania Press, 2018), 150.

[5]Gerbner, 160.

[6]Helen Richards, "Distant Garden: Moravian Missions and the Culture of Slavery in the Danish West Indies, 1732–1848," *Journal of Moravian History*, no. 2 (2007): 64; Oliver W. Furley, "Moravian Missionaries and Slaves in the West Indies," *Caribbean Studies* 5, no. 2 (1965): 4.

[7]Furley, "Moravian Missionaries and Slaves in the West Indies," 4.

[8]John Gillies and Aaron C. Seymour, *Memoirs of the Life of the Reverend George Whitefield, A.M.* (Philadelphia: Simon Probasco, 1820), 34.

[9]Todd's autobiography was also issued as a monograph; see Silas Todd, *The Life of Mr. Silas Todd* (London: G. Whitfield, 1796).

[10]Todd, 6-8.

[11]June 28, 1740: Wesley, *Journals and Diaries*, 19:425.

[12]Birgit Brander Rasmussen, "'Attended with Great Inconveniences': Slave Literacy and the 1740 South Carolina Negro Act," *PMLA* 125, no. 1 (2010): 201.

[13]Rasmussen, 202.

[14]For more background, see George William Pilcher, "Samuel Davies and the Instruction of Negroes in Virginia," *The Virginia Magazine of History and Biography* 74, no. 3 (1966): 293-300; Jeffrey H. Richards, "Samuel Davies and the Transatlantic Campaign for Slave Literacy in Virginia," *The Virginia Magazine of History and Biography* 111, no. 4 (2003): 333-78.

[15]Wesley, *Journals and Diaries*, 21:21-22.

[16]Samuel Davies, *The Duties of Christians to Propagate Their Religion Among the Heathens, Earnestly Recommended to the Masters of Negroe Slaves in Virginia: A Sermon Preached in Hanover, January 8, 1757* (London: J. Oliver, 1758), 30-31.

[17]Wesley, Journals and Diaries, 21:42-43.

[18]John Wesley, *Notes Upon the New Testament* (London: William Bowyer, 1755), 438.

[19]Wesley, 581.

[20]Wesley, 558.

[21]Frank Baker, "The Origins of Methodism in the West Indies: The Story of the Gilbert Family," *The London Quarterly & Holborn Review* 185 (1960): 15; Michael Jagessar, "Early Methodism in the Caribbean: Through the Imaginary Optics of Gilbert's Slave Women—Another Reading," *Black Theology* 5, no. 2 (July 1, 2007): 155, https://doi.org/10.1558/blth2007v5i2.153; Nathaniel Gilbert to John Wesley, July 22, 1765. *Arminian Magazine* 6 (1783): 329-31. Letters not found in the Bicentennial Edition of the Works of John Wesley were accessed at the website of The Wesley Works Editorial Project at https://wesley-works.org/john-wesleys-in-correspondence.

[22]David Watts, *The West Indies: Patterns of Development, Culture and Environmental Change Since 1492* (Cambridge: Cambridge University Press, 1990), 313.

[23]Baker, "The Origins of Methodism in the West Indies," 9.

[24]Wesley, *Journals and Diaries*, 21:134.

[25]Wesley, 21:172.

[26]Nathaniel Gilbert to John Wesley, July 22, 1765. *Arminian Magazine* 6 (1783): 329-31.

[27]Jagessar, "Early Methodism in the Caribbean," 159.

[28]Francis Gilbert to John Wesley, May 16, 1763. *Arminian Magazine* 5 (1782): 159-60; Francis Gilbert to John Wesley, June 18, 1763. *Arminian Magazine* 5 (1782): 384-86; Nathaniel Gilbert to John Wesley, September 18, 1764. *Arminian Magazine* 5 (1782): 605-7; Nathaniel Gilbert to John Wesley, July 22, 1765. *Arminian Magazine* 6 (1783): 329-31.

[29]Wesley, *Letters*, 27:420-22, 426-29.

[30]John Lenton, "The Attitudes Towards Black Methodists in America and the West Indies of Some of Wesley's Preachers, 1770–1810," *Wesley and Methodist Studies* 3 (2011): 98.

[31]Lenton, 99.

[32]Gillies and Seymour, *Memoirs of the Life of the Reverend George Whitefield, A.M.*, 226.

[33]John Wesley, *Sermons*, ed. Albert C. Outler, The Bicentennial Edition of the Works of John Wesley, vol. 1-4 (Nashville: Abingdon Press, 1984), 2:330-47.

[34]Wesley, 2:340.

[35]George Whitefield, *The Works of the Reverend George Whitefield*, ed. John Gillies (London: Printed for Edward and Charles Dilly, 1771), 2:127.

[36]Irv A. Brendlinger, *To Be Silent . . . Would Be Criminal: The Antislavery Influence and Writings of Anthony Benezet*, Pietist and Wesleyan Studies 20 (Lanham, MD: Scarecrow Press, 2007), 50.

[37]Whitefield, *The Works of the Reverend George Whitefield*, 2:404-5.

[38]Wesley, *Letters*, 28:287-88.

[39]Whitefield, *The Works of the Reverend George Whitefield*, 3:496-97.

[40]While the name "Gearge" looks similar to the name "George," the original inventory lists the name as "Gearge." With so few enslaved people being named in the history of slavery, I retained this unusual name without "correcting" it, with the hope that this enslaved person had a chance to use their voice to retain how they wanted their name to be presented.

[41]Estate Records, Georgia Archives RG 49-1-1, https://vault.georgiaarchives.org /digital/collection/corp/id/3222/rec/1. The estate was inventoried on January 1, 1771, by Edwin Langworthy, Robert Bolton, and William Moore.

[42]Wesley, *Letters*, 28:287-88.

[43]John Wesley, *The Methodist Societies History, Nature, and Design*, ed. Rupert E. Davies, The Bicentennial Edition of the Works of John Wesley (Nashville: Abingdon Press, 1989), 9:398.

[44]John Wesley, *The Letters of John Wesley*, ed. John Telford (London: Epworth Press, 1931), 8:17. This letter will appear in vol. 30 of the Bicentennial Edition of the Works of John Wesley.

9. UNLIKELY VOICES

[1]Manisha Sinha, *The Slave's Cause: A History of Abolition* (New Haven, CT: Yale University Press, 2016), 1-2.

[2]Toni Morrison, *Beloved* (New York: Vintage, 2004), 225.

[3]Leonard S. Kenworthy, *Quakerism: A Study Guide on the Religious Society of Friends* (Kennett Square, PA: Quaker Publications, 1991), 17.

[4]Sinha, *The Slave's Cause*, 13.

[5]Quoted in Brycchan Carey and Geoffrey Plank, eds., *Quakers and Abolition* (Urbana, IL: University of Illinois Press, 2014), 2.

[6]Jennifer Rycenga, "Quakers and Antislavery," in *Encyclopedia of Antislavery and Abolition*, eds. Peter Hinks and John McKivigan (Westport, CT: Greenwood Press, 2007), 2:549.

[7]See Brycchan Carey, *From Peace to Freedom: Quaker Rhetoric and the Birth of American Antislavery, 1657–1761* (New Haven, CT: Yale University Press, 2012), 86-95.

[8]Jean R. Soderlund, *Quakers and Slavery: A Divided Spirit* (Princeton, NJ: Princeton University Press, 2014), 15-17; Marcus Rediker, *The Fearless Benjamin Lay: The Quaker Dwarf Who Became the First Revolutionary Abolitionist* (Boston: Beacon Press, 2017), 1-2.

[9]Rediker, *The Fearless Benjamin Lay*, 73-76.

[10]The full title for Lay's publication illustrates his intensity and criticisms (and yes, what follows is just the title of his book): "All slave-keepers that keep the innocent in bondage, apostates pretending to lay claim to the pure & holy Christian religion; of what congregation so ever; but especially in their ministers, by whose example the filthy leprosy and apostacy is spread far and near; it is a notorious sin, which many of the true Friends of Christ, and his pure truth, called Quakers, has been for many years, and still are concern'd to write and bear testimony against; as a practice so gross & hurtful to religion, and destructive to government, beyond what words can set forth, or can be declared of by men or angels, and yet lived in by ministers and magistrates in America. The leaders of the people cause them to err. / Written for a general service, by him that truly and sincerely desires the present and eternal welfare and happiness of all mankind, all the world over, of all colours, and nations, as his own soul."

[11]Rediker, *The Fearless Benjamin Lay*, 137.

[12]Soderlund, *Quakers and Slavery*, 27.

[13]Robert Barclay, *Views of Christian Doctrine Held by the Religious Society of Friends Being Passages Taken from Barclay's Apology* (Philadelphia: Friends' Book-Store, 1882), 35-36.

[14]Jonathan Edwards, *Sermons and Discourses, 1734–1738*, ed. M. X. Lesser and Harry S. Stout, vol. 19, The Works of Jonathan Edwards (New Haven, CT: Yale University Press, 2001), 19:124, see also 138.

[15]Joel R. Beeke and Mark Jones, *A Puritan Theology: Doctrine for Life* (Grand Rapids, MI: Reformation Heritage Books, 2012), 429-40; Hugh Barbour, *The*

Quakers in Puritan England (New Haven, CT: Yale University Press, 1964); Caleb Arnold Wall, *The Puritans Versus the Quakers: A Review of the Persecutions of the Early Quakers and Baptists in Massachusetts* (Worcester, MA: Press of D. Seagrave, 1888).

[16]George Whitefield, *Third Journal: His Arrival at London to His Departure from Thence on His Way to Georgia* (London: James Hutton, 1739), 59.

[17]Whitefield recorded baptizing Quakers. For example, see Whitefield, 96.

[18]John Wesley, *The Methodist Societies, The Minutes of the Conference*, ed. Henry D. Rack, The Bicentennial Edition of the Works of John Wesley, vol. 10 (Nashville: Abingdon Press, 2011), 10:122.

[19]John Wesley, *The Appeals to Men of Reason and Religion and Certain Related Open Letters*, ed. Gerald Cragg, The Bicentennial Edition of the Works of John Wesley, vol. 11 (Nashville: Abingdon Press, 1989), 11:254.

[20]Maurice Jackson, *Let This Voice Be Heard: Anthony Benezet, Father of Atlantic Abolitionism* (Philadelphia: University of Pennsylvania Press, 2009), 21-22.

[21]Anthony Benezet, *The Complete Antislavery Writings of Anthony Benezet 1754–1783: An Annotated Critical Edition*, ed. David L. Crosby (Baton Rouge, LA: Louisiana State University Press, 2013), 84.

[22]Benezet, 91-93.

[23]Prince Hoare, *Memoirs of Granville Sharp* (London: Henry Colburn and Co., 1820), 97.

[24]Andrew Lyall, *Granville Sharp's Cases on Slavery* (London: Hart, 2017), 42-46, 91-100; Adam Hochschild, *Bury the Chains: The British Struggle to Abolish Slavery* (London: Pan Macmillan, 2006), 41-46.

[25]Hoare, *Memoirs of Granville Sharp*, 97; E. P. Lascelles, *Granville Sharp and the Freedom of Slaves in England* (New York: Negro Universities Press, 1969), 139.

[26]Hoare, *Memoirs of Granville Sharp*, 97.

[27]Hoare, 98.

[28]Hoare, 98.

[29]Benezet, *The Complete Antislavery Writings of Anthony Benezet 1754–1783*, 113.

[30]Benezet, 119.

[31]Benezet, 181-83.

10. WESLEY SPEAKS ABOUT SLAVERY

[1]John Wesley, *Journals and Diaries*, eds. W. Reginald Ward and Richard P. Heitzenrater, The Bicentennial Edition of the Works of John Wesley, vols. 18-24 (Nashville: Abingdon Press, 1988), 22:307.

[2]John Wesley, *The Methodist Societies History, Nature, and Design*, ed. Rupert E. Davies, The Bicentennial Edition of the Works of John Wesley, vol. 9 (Nashville: Abingdon Press, 1989), 9:490-91.

[3]George S. Brookes, *Friend Anthony Benezet* (London: Oxford University Press, 1937), 418.

[4]Brookes, 308, 319.

[5]John Wesley, *The Works of John Wesley*, ed. Thomas Jackson, 3rd ed. (London: Methodist Reading Room, 1872), 11:14.

[6]Wesley, 11:24.

[7]Wesley, 11:34.

[8]Wesley, 11:36.

[9]Wesley, 11:37-38. The phrase "child of man" is used in the original.

[10]Wesley, 11:46.

[11]Wesley, 11:46.

[12]Wesley, 11:53.

[13]Brookes, *Friend Anthony Benezet*, 291. The exact legal ramifications of the Somerset case are not entirely clear. The judgment was generally understood to declare that all slaves in England were free, but this has been debated by legal scholars and historians. Andrew Lyall, *Granville Sharp's Cases on Slavery* (London: Hart, 2017), 56.

[14]Cited in Irv A. Brendlinger, *To Be Silent . . . Would Be Criminal: The Antislavery Influence and Writings of Anthony Benezet*, Pietist and Wesleyan Studies 20 (Lanham, MD: Scarecrow Press, 2007), 22-23.

[15]Wesley, *Letters*, 29:12-13, 167-68. Also see Randy Sparks, *Two Princes of Calabar: An Eighteenth-Century Atlantic Odyssey* (Cambridge, MA: Harvard University Press, 2009).

[16]Randy L. Maddox, "Salvation as Flourishing for the Whole Creation: A Wesleyan Trajectory," in *Wesleyan Perspectives on Human Flourishing*, eds. Dean G. Smith and Rob A. Fringer (Eugene, OR: Pickwick Publications, 2021), 18. I am indebted to conversations with Professor Randy Maddox for helping me see how Wesley's eschatology influenced his political and social concerns late in his life.

[17]John Wesley, *Explanatory Notes upon the Old Testament* (Bristol, England: William Pine, 1765), 3:2110.

[18]Maddox, "Salvation as Flourishing for the Whole Creation," 18. Emphasis in the original. See also Randy L. Maddox, "Millennial Hopes in the Wesley Family: Samuel Wesley Sr.'s Bequest," *Wesleyan Theological Journal* 55, no. 1 (Spring 2020): 202-3.

[19]Wesley, *The Works of John Wesley*, 11:53.

[20]Wesley, 11:54.

[21]Frank Baker, "The Origins, Character, and Influence of John Wesley's Thoughts Upon Slavery," *Methodist History* 22 (1984): 83.

[22]Wesley, *The Works of John Wesley*, 11:70.

[23]Wesley, 11:70.

[24]For examples of the complexity and history of this task, see Mark A. Noll, *The Civil War as a Theological Crisis* (Chapel Hill, NC: University of North Carolina Press, 2015); Mark A. Noll, *America's Book: The Rise and Decline of a Bible Civilization, 1794–1911* (New York: Oxford University Press, 2022), chaps. 10-11, 20-21.

[25]Wesley, *The Works of John Wesley*, 11:70.

[26]Wesley, 11:70.

[27]George Whitefield, *The Works of the Reverend George Whitefield*, ed. John Gillies (London: Printed for Edward and Charles Dilly, 1771), 2:404.

[28]Wesley, *The Works of John Wesley*, 11:74.

[29]Wesley, 11:75.

[30]Wesley, 11:77.

[31]Wesley, 11:79.

[32]Wesley, 11:70.

[33]Anthony Benezet, *The Complete Antislavery Writings of Anthony Benezet 1754–1783: An Annotated Critical Edition*, ed. David L. Crosby (Baton Rouge, LA: Louisiana State University Press, 2013), 151, 156, 158, 161, 182-83.

[34]It is not surprising that Wesley did not retain Warburton's sermon in his abridged account; Wesley and Warburton had been theological adversaries for decades. Additionally, Warburton's sermon extract that Benezet includes is not a particularly strong work against slavery. The sermon is primarily against financial greed. The history of publication for the Society for the Propagation of the Gospel presents a somber analysis of the sermon's substance. Noel Titus, "Concurrence without Compliance: SPG and the Barbadian Plantations, 1710–1834," in *Three Centuries of Mission: The United Society for the Propagation of the Gospel 1701–2000*, ed. Daniel O'Connor (London: Continuum, 2000), 251.

[35]Brookes, *Friend Anthony Benezet*, 85.

[36]Benezet, *The Complete Antislavery Writings of Anthony Benezet 1754–1783*, 197.

[37]Benezet, 207.

[38]Wesley, *The Works of John Wesley*, 11:71

[39]Wesley, *The Works of John Wesley*, 11:81, 89.

[40]John Wesley, *Sermons*, ed. Albert C. Outler, The Bicentennial Edition of the Works of John Wesley, vol. 1-4 (Nashville: Abingdon Press, 1984), 3:569.

[41]Wesley, *The Works of John Wesley*, 11:81.

[42]Wesley, 11:125.

[43]Wesley, 11:109.

[44]Wesley, *Journals and Diaries*, 23:46.

[45]Wesley, *The Works of John Wesley*, 11:145.

[46]See "Trans-Atlantic Slave Trade – Database," *Slave Voyages*, www.slavevoyages .org/voyage/database.

[47]Lyall, *Granville Sharp's Cases on Slavery*, 71.

[48]David Olusoga, *Black and British: A Forgotten History* (London: Picador, 2021), 204-5; Lyall, *Granville Sharp's Cases on Slavery*, 70-88; 239-374.

[49]Thomas Clarkson, *History of the Rise, Progress, and Accomplishment of the Abolition of the African Slave Trade by the British Parliament* (Philadelphia: James P. Parke, 1808), 1:166.

[50]Clarkson, 1:167.

[51]Adam Hochschild, *Bury the Chains: The British Struggle to Abolish Slavery* (London: Pan Macmillan, 2006), 87-94.

[52]Clarkson, *History of the Rise, Progress, and Accomplishment of the Abolition of the African Slave Trade by the British Parliament*, 1:230.

[53]Clarkson, 1:234.

[54]Clarkson, 1:356.

[55]Letter from John Wesley to the Committee for the Abolition of the Slave Trade, August 18, 1787. Published in *The Christian Advocate* 79 (Oct. 8, 1931), 2; Prof. Randy Maddox shared this letter with me; it will appear in vol. 30 of the Bicentennial Edition of the Works of John Wesley.

[56]Wesley, *Sermons*, 2:493.

[57]*Arminian Magazine*, vol. 8 (London: J. Paramore, 1785), 646.

[58]Wesley, *Sermons*, 3:453.

[59]Wesley letter to the Committee, August 18, 1787.

[60]Wesley, *The Letters of John Wesley*, 8:23.

[61]Wesley, *Sermons*, 2:525, 531.

[62]*Arminian Magazine*, vol. 8 (London: New Chapel, City Road, 1788), 263-64; Hochschild, *Bury the Chains*, 120-21.

[63]*Arminian Magazine*, 1788, 8:208.

[64]*Arminian Magazine*, 8:515.

[65]Hochschild, *Bury the Chains*, 129.

[66]Peter Marshall, *The Anti-Slave Trade Movement in Bristol* (Gloucester, England: University of Bristol, 1968), 6.

[67]Letter from wealthy Bristol merchant involved in the slave trade, John Pinney to William Coker on February 9, 1788. Cited in Marshall, 7.

[68]W. E. Minchinton, ed., *Politics and the Port of Bristol in the Eighteenth Century: The Petitions of the Society of Merchant Venturers 1698–1803* (Bristol, England: Bristol Record Society, 1963), 161.

[69]Wesley, *Journals and Diaries*, 24:70.

[70]Wesley, 24:70.

[71]Wesley, 24:70.

[72]Wesley, *The Letters of John Wesley*, 8:207.

[73]Wesley, 8:265.

11. THREE LEGACIES

[1]Samuel Hopkins, *The Works of Samuel Hopkins* (Boston: Doctrinal Tract and Book Society, 1852), 1:114.

[2]John Ericson, "When God Ceased Winking: Jonathan Edwards the Younger's Evolution on the Problem of Slavery," *Connecticut History Review* 57, no. 1 (2018): 24.

[3]Hopkins, *The Works of Samuel Hopkins*, 1:115.

[4]Hopkins, 1:116.

[5]Hopkins, 2:549.

[6]Hopkins, 2:582.

[7]Hopkins, 1:118.

[8]Hopkins, 1:118.

[9]Hopkins, 1:118.

[10]Ericson, "When God Ceased Winking," 16.

[11]Cited in Ericson, 18.

[12]Ericson, 18.

[13]Ericson, 21.

[14]Ericson, 27; Robert L. Ferm, *Jonathan Edwards the Younger, 1745–1801: A Colonial Pastor* (Grand Rapids, MI: Eerdmans, 1976), 94; Jonathan Edwards Jr., "The Injustice and Impolicy of the Slave Trade, and of the Slavery of the Africans," in *Early American Abolitionists: A Collection of Anti-Slavery Writings*, ed. Sarah Gamertsfelder (New York: The Gilder Lehrman Institute of American History, 2007), 137.

[15]Minkema, Kenneth P., and Harry S. Stout. "The Edwardsean Tradition and the Antislavery Debate, 1740–1865." *The Journal of American History* 92, no. 1 (June 2005): 57.

[16]John Gillies and Aaron C. Seymour, *Memoirs of the Life of the Reverend George Whitefield, A.M.* (Philadelphia: Simon Probasco, 1820), 302.

[17]Gillies and Seymour, 305.

[18]Edwin Welch, *Spiritual Pilgrim: A Reassessment of the Life of the Countess of Huntingdon* (Cardiff: University of Wales Press, 2014), 135.

[19]Edward J. Cashin, *Beloved Bethesda: A History of George Whitefield's Home for Boys, 1740–2000* (Macon, GA: Mercer University Press, 2001), 100.

[20]John R. Tyson, "Lady Huntingdon, Religion, and Race," *Methodist History* 50, no. 1 (October 2011): 35.

[21]Frank Lambert, *James Habersham: Loyalty, Politics, and Commerce in Colonial Georgia* (Athens: University of Georgia Press, 2005), 131.

[22]Cashin, *Beloved Bethesda*, 110-11.

[23]Cashin, 124.

[24]"FAQs and Facts," Bethesda Academy, www.bethesdaacademy.org /about-us/faqs-facts/.

[25]Richard P. Heitzenrater, *Wesley and the People Called Methodists* (Nashville: Abingdon Press, 2013), 353.

[26]David Hempton, *Methodism: Empire of the Spirit* (New Haven, CT: Yale University Press, 2005), 214.

[27]Roger Finke and Rodney Stark, *The Churching of America, 1776–2005: Winners and Losers in Our Religious Economy* (New Brunswick, NJ: Rutgers University Press, 2005), 57.

[28]Hempton, *Methodism: Empire of the Spirit*, 212.

[29]Donald G. Mathews, *Slavery and Methodism; a Chapter in American Morality, 1780–1845* (Princeton, NJ: Princeton University Press, 1965), 6.

[30]Mathews, 5-6.

[31]John Wesley, *The Methodist Societies History, Nature, and Design*, ed. Rupert E. Davies, The Bicentennial Edition of the Works of John Wesley, vol. 9 (Nashville: Abingdon Press, 1989), 70n11.

[32]Irv A. Brendlinger, *Social Justice Through the Eyes of Wesley: John Wesley's Theological Challenge to Slavery* (Ontario, Canada: Joshua Press, 2006), 12.

[33]James G. Basker, ed., *Early American Abolitionists: A Collection of Anti-Slavery Writings 1760–1820* (New York: The Gilder Lehrman Institute of American History, 2007); Roger Bruns, ed., *Am I Not a Man and a Brother: The Antislavery Crusade of Revolutionary America 1688–1788* (New York: Chelsea House Publishers, 1977); Christopher Cameron, ed., *The Abolitionist Movement: Documents Decoded* (Oxford: ABC-CLIO, 2014).

[34]Mathews, *Slavery and Methodism*, 14-15.

[35]Methodist Episcopal Church, *Minutes of the Annual Conferences of the Methodist Episcopal Church* (New York: T. Mason and G. Lane, 1840), 1:12.

[36]Methodist Episcopal Church, 1:18.

[37]Methodist Episcopal Church, 1:20.

[38]Methodist Episcopal Church, 1:21.

[39]Thomas Coke, *Extracts of the Journals of the Late Reverend Thomas Coke* (Dublin: Methodist Book Room, 1816), 61.

[40]Coke, 69.

[41]Coke, 74.

[42]Methodist Episcopal Church, *Minutes of the Annual Conferences of the Methodist Episcopal Church*, 1:24.

[43]Samuel Drew, *The Life of the Reverend Thomas Coke* (London: T. Cordeux, 1817), 180-81.

[44]Drew, *Life of Thomas Coke*, 183-84.

[45]Frederick Douglass, *The Narrative of the Life of Frederick Douglass, An American Slave, Written by Himself*, eds. William L. Andrews and William S. McFeely, Second Norton Critical Edition (New York: W. W. Norton & Company, 2017), 42-43. The Scripture cited is a light paraphrase of Luke 12:47 KJV.

[46]Douglass, 70. Emphasis in the original.

[47]Donna McDaniel and Vanessa D. Julye, *Fit for Freedom, Not for Friendship: Quakers, African Americans, and the Myth of Racial Justice* (Philadelphia: Quaker Press of Friends General Conference, 2009), 207; see also Cheryl Janifer LaRoche, *Free Black Communities and the Underground Railroad: The Geography of Resistance* (Urbana: University of Illinois Press, 2013).

[48]McDaniel and Julye, *Fit for Freedom, Not for Friendship*, 374.

[49]Tzvetan Todorov, *Hope and Memory: Lessons from the Twentieth Century* (Princeton, NJ: Princeton University Press, 2003), 1.

12. OWNERSHIP TODAY

[1]Matthew's list includes nine names in the same span where Luke's gospel lists eighteen; this illustrates Matthew's intentional choices regarding whom to include. Brian K. Blount, ed., *True to Our Native Land: An African American New Testament Commentary* (Minneapolis, MN: Fortress Press, 2007), 87; Tokunboh Adeyemo, ed., *Africa Bible Commentary: A One-Volume Commentary Written by 70 African Scholars* (Grand Rapids, MI: Zondervan, 2006), 1134.

[2]Adeyemo, *Africa Bible Commentary*, 1134.

[3]Dates's comments were in response to Thabiti Anyabwile's lecture at the Henry Center on the topic "Jonathan Edwards and Racism." The video can be viewed at www.youtube.com/watch?v=le2RwKU9yrc.

[4]Martin Luther King Jr., *Strength to Love* (Minneapolis, MN: Fortress Press, 2010), 37-38.

[5]King, 45.

[6]Osheta Moore, *Dear White Peacemakers* (Harrisonburg, VA: Herald Press, 2021), 31-32.

[7]Thomas S. Kidd, *George Whitefield: America's Spiritual Founding Father* (New Haven, CT: Yale University Press, 2014), 260.

[8]Jemar Tisby, "Are Black Christians Evangelicals?" in *Evangelicals: Who They Have Been, Are Now, and Could Be* (Grand Rapids, MI: Eerdmans, 2019), 267.

[9]Mark A. Noll, "Introduction: One Word but Three Crises," in *Evangelicals: Who They Have Been, Are Now, and Could Be* (Grand Rapids, MI: Eerdmans, 2019), 8.

[10]David W. Bebbington, *Evangelicalism in Modern Britain: A History from the 1730s to the 1980s* (London: Routledge, 2004), 12.

[11]See my review of Mark Noll's *America's Book: The Rise and Decline of a Bible Civilization, 1794–1911,* available at www.christianitytoday.com/ct/2023/july -web-only/mark-noll-america-book-bible-independence-civil-war.html.

[12]Mark A. Noll, *The Civil War as a Theological Crisis* (Chapel Hill, NC: University of North Carolina Press, 2015)

[13]Noll, 115-21; Mark A. Noll, *America's Book: The Rise and Decline of a Bible Civilization, 1794–1911* (New York: Oxford University Press, 2022), chaps. 10-11, 19-21.

[14]Edward J. Cashin, *Beloved Bethesda: A History of George Whitefield's Home for Boys, 1740–2000* (Macon, GA: Mercer University Press, 2001), 245-46; J. Russell Hawkins, T*he Bible Told Them So: How Southern Evangelicals Fought to Preserve White Supremacy* (New York: Oxford University Press, 2021).

[15]Susan Neiman, *Learning from the Germans: Race and the Memory of Evil* (New York: Picador, 2019), 23.

[16]Christina Barland Edmondson and Chad Brennan, *Faithful Antiracism: Moving Past Talk to Systemic Change* (Downers Grove, IL: InterVarsity Press, 2022), 7.

[17]Martin Luther King Jr., *The Radical King*, ed. Cornel West (Boston: Beacon Press, 2016), 185.

[18]King, *Strength to Love*, 45-46.

[19]King, 46.

INDEX

Like this book?
Scan the code to discover more content like this!

Get on IVP's email list to receive special offers, exclusive book news, and thoughtful content from your favorite authors on topics you care about.